THE FUTURE OF SHOPPING

The Future of Shopping

Traditional Patterns and Net Effects

Julian E. Markham
FSVA, NDD

First published 1998 by
MACMILLAN PRESS LTD
Houndmills, Basingstoke, Hampshire RG21 6XS
and London
Companies and representatives
throughout the world

ISBN 0–333–73180–8

A catalogue record for this book is available
from the British Library.

10 9 8 7 6 5 4 3 2 1
07 06 05 04 03 02 01 00 99 98

Copy-edited and typeset by Povey–Edmondson
Tavistock and Rochdale, England

Printed in Great Britain by
Antony Rowe Ltd
Chippenham, Wiltshire

Contents

List of Plates   vii

Preface   ix

Introduction   1

PART I   THE SHOPPING EXPERIENCE

1   Little New in the Shopping Centre and Retail World   5

2   The Personal Experience of Shopping   11

3   It's Not Enough to do it Well, Do It New   15

4   The World Wide Web, the Internet, Cyberspace and
    Retail Locations   22

5   Is There a Substitute for the Real Thing? Information
    Appliances   30

PART II   THE SHOPPING LOCATION

6   Traditional Shopping: From Bazaars to Shopping
    Centres   41

7   From Merchants to the Modern Consumer Boom:
    Effects on Towns   49

8   Out-of-Town and Town Centres   62

9   Town Centre Economies and Planners' Attitudes   78

PART III   LIVING WITH TECHNOLOGY

10 Technology: 'Haves' and 'Have-Nots'   95

11 Is Shopping a Chore? Being Digital and Big Brother   110

12 Giving the Customers What They Want   118

13 Computer Literacy   143

PART IV   THE FUTURE OF ELECTRONIC SHOPPING

14 Power Centres, Online, TV and Catalogues   161

15 Shopping on the Net and Security   172

16 Convenience, Comparison and the Retail Results   188

17 Price, Convenience, Electronic Retailing and the Internet
    Store   195

PART V   FUTURE TRENDS

18 The US Shopping Centre Experience and UK Trends   209

19 A View of the Future?   220

Bibliography and Acknowledgements   230

List of Plates

1   Isfahan, fabric bazaar
2   Passage de l'Opéra, Paris
3   A floating market, Bangkok
4   Southdale Plaza
5   Horton Plaza, San Diego
6   Universal City Walk, Los Angeles
7   The Plaza at King of Prussia, Pennsylvania
8   Peapod online grocery shopping and delivery service
9   Tesco product selector
10 BarclaySquare shopping mall
11 Social use areas (Universal City Walk)
12 Canal City Hakata, Fukuoka, Kyushu, Japan
13 Orchard Park Mall. Kelowna, BC, Canada
14 St Louis Union Station, St Louis, Missouri

Preface

My reasons for embarking on a book about shopping in the future stemmed from my intense interest in the subject. This has been something which I have had during over thirty years in the estates profession and which has been encouraged by my close study of the success of the American shopping centre industry. The American centres have been a guiding light to every European over the years, not only because of their size and design, but also because of the management principles which have been applied by knowledgable landlords and active aggressive retailers. As time has passed, so Europeans have caught up to the extent that centres are often indistinguishable from their American counterparts, and sometimes surpass them. This has been greatly due to the efforts of those who have been involved in the promotion of education through research and meetings of National Councils of Shopping Centres formed with the objective of disseminating more quality information. I am proud to have been involved in this process, through my own membership of the International Council of Shopping Centres since 1969 and as a founder member of the British Council of Shopping Centres since 1984.

My approach has, however, always been based on the fact that I am a surveyor and developer. My opinions are strictly based on the development and management effects and trends of shopping centre development. This is always predicated on the fact that the shopper is the most important element. Therefore, when I wanted to look forward to the likely effects of the newest innovation of electronic shopping on traditional shopping, it was important that I did not over-extend my belief into thinking that I am an expert in computers or software. My objective was to consider as much relevant published information by experts, or reports recorded in newspapers, magazines and periodicals, and consider the effects and trends which these might indicate.

The problem has always been that some of the information obtained during the writing of the book might be superseded by the date of publication. Secondly, some of the reported facts and events have proved to be difficult directly to attribute based on the writer's style, although I have tried to be sure that the references are authentic or based on reasonable foundations. Unfortunately, there is nothing I could do to overcome this fact because technology is moving so rapidly. However, I think that the conclusions I have reached would not materially differ, because I have needed to use a broad-brush approach to trends, historical facts and my own experience. Experience of casting my mind forward on many assumed effects within the large matrix of considerations when undertaking a shopping centre development, probably not due to open for trade for many years ahead, is an important and well-tuned tool necessary for success.

This book is not intended to be a textbook, although I hope it provides information which will be a useful guide. It is, rather, an opinion and overview of the likely effects, which may sometimes be contentious but are nevertheless sincerely expressed, which I think will indicate what will be the future of shopping and the net effects on it.

My thanks and appreciation are given to the many people who think I have the experience and knowledge of the shopping centre industry to proffer an opinion and who have encouraged me to put my thoughts on paper. I particularly want to thank my son, Steven, for his invaluable advice and contribution.

JULIAN E. MARKHAM

Introduction

When I had the idea of writing this book I felt that I had the experience necessary to take a view of shopping from a real estate professional's standpoint. As a qualified valuer and surveyor, and with more than thirty years' experience of developing, promoting and managing shopping centres and individual shops in Britain and several Continental European Countries, as well as long experience of shopping centres in the United States of America, I would be able to draw on a great deal of knowledge. My experience and technical knowledge of computers, software, and specifically the new rapid advances in technology including the Internet, was restricted to my personal use of my computer. Much more was needed. As a result, I asked my son, Steven Markham, if he would assist me. Steven has spent his entire adult education and working life in gaining an invaluable knowledge of software and computers. In addition, he formed a specialist software retail company which operated several central London branches and has also been the Retail Director of a young, expanding and very successful fashion group. He has been able to offer a unique contribution to the technical research with the benefit of a retail perspective. As such, much of the opinion which I have obtained is based on a broader base than my own experience and assumptions. It is, I hope, more valuable because it takes account not only of my own developer's optimism – a factor which has had to be carefully recognised in gaining an objective view – but Steven's more biased leaning toward technology being the answer to the future. The fact that such a cautious conclusion of opinion of the effects of technology on the established retail habit has been reached serves as a more balanced stance than any opinion I may have reached without his research. It also becomes an even judgement without the interests of commercial gain, as often exposed in claims by online shopping promoters.

The opinions given in this book are clearly my own, but Steven's invaluable contribution by providing me with so much research data which has influenced those opinions, is acknowledged with love and thanks for his tireless efforts.

Part I
The Shopping Experience

1 Little New in the Shopping Centre and Retail World

I have always been interested, and often intrigued, by the way all matter of things evolve and revolve. Probably due to an earlier sensitivity to a change of professional direction, from the arts to valuation and property development, I had the urge to look at the reasoning behind many decisions and positions. This developed through a strong appetite for specific knowledge of my newly adopted professional path, and then to a more generalised desire to add other commercial acumen. Most probably as a result I have always tried to look forward and gauge the probable effects of a move, trend or decision. Obviously this has not always been possible or successful, but it does, I think, explain how and why I have been so interested in changes in fashion, style and usage, whether they concern property or other matters, which can have a profound effect on property. In particular, shopping centres rely on their popularity among their patrons, and those shoppers have a conception of current fashion and style which must not be offended to the extent that they object to visiting those shops. The shops themselves must be modern and, as well as offering up-to-date and well-presented merchandise, attune their environments to the shoppers' sensibilities.

These comments may be considered rather self-evident and have no need to be said yet again. However, the evidence tends to contradict the assumption that we are often conscious of the effects of previous experiences. Let me expand with a few examples of how the past is forgotten when a supposedly new idea is announced and how the future should, as a consequence, be subject to question and intelligent logic.

This book will attempt to make a case that there is little new in the shopping centre and retail world, but merely a different, updated or technological way of presenting and producing it. It asks whether such new ways alter the public's perception or its habitual use of a system which has come into common usage. As a really basic fact, one could conclude that most discoveries were real things awaiting man's ingenuity to find them. They existed, but we simply did not know it. Inventions, on the other hand, need man to use thought, skill, production and application. Nevertheless, inventions are often as a result of earlier work and updated refinement by the use of more modern methods and technology to meet new requirements and fashions. The aeroplane was invented and flew for many years with power from the internal combustion engine before Sir Frank Whittle invented the jet engine, to do the same thing with greater power and speed. On the argument that the engine, not the plane, was the item invented, it was still based on the original concept and operation of an engine which, although in a different form, was used to power the machine. The advantages of the new invention over the old is something which is usually claimed at its disclosure, but the real value is usually not seen and objectively assessed until some time after it has been in use. The jet engine allowed planes to fly faster, get travellers to their destination sooner and improved military competitiveness. The invention of the pneumatic tyre was to make the wheel more efficient and comfortable, but it was an improvement to the wheel and might not be considered a totally new concept. Naturally, I have ignored the improvements to the structural design and the use of new or different materials needed to accommodate the consequential effects of such added power and stress.

More pertinent as an example for the defined purpose of this book, the computer holds a special position in the consideration of inventions and could be argued to be so dramatically revolutionary to all normal operations, commercially, industrially and socially, that the 'refinement' explanation will not hold water. Yet the abacus has been used for centuries, has led to the mechanical then electronic adding machine and to the calculator. The quill led to the fountain pen and the typewriter, and the index card to the mechanical punched card sorter. The crystal set became the wireless with valves and then to the transistorised radio set. The earliest computer was a brilliant auto-mechanical contraption of wheels and cogs which ground out the permutations at a pace restricted by its parts, then updated by the introduction of a massive collection of bulbs enabling it to collate huge amounts of information, originally driven by the wartime need to decipher codes faster. The evolution of these massive cabinets taking up large rooms, through the mainframes using tape reels, to the personal computers we have today, became possible because of the skill of those brilliant men who invented the silicon chip. Yet my premise is still true that today's personal computer is a refinement of what went before, albeit on a scale fed by the self-perpetuating acceleration of technological progress.

The same can be said for fashion. We do not need to repeat stories of how styles have been seen many times, nor the way hemlines of women's skirts have gone up and down. I live in expectation that I may be able to wear my old 'kipper' ties with others in high fashion in the future. Such comments apply equally to property, with early arcades being replicated in modern times as speciality arcades or shopping routes between two streets, and open shopping centres being reintroduced by what the Americans call the "demalling effect of removing roofs from enclosed centres. Of course, all of these re-introductions carry a subtle design change to accord with modern times and thinking, but the basic concept of the use and requirement remains much the same.

We cannot count the number of times we have all heard someone say 'I thought of that years ago.' The fact is that we did not do anything about fulfilling ambitions for the idea, either because we did not think it would work or were unable to carry it out. In any event, timing is an essential element in any idea or product and it is necessary to have the right conditions present for revolution. It is on the basis of this premise, plus my assumption of the return cycle of fashion, opportunity and social acceptance, that I think the recent promotion of online shopping, or more broadly stated, electronic commerce, must be viewed. We have had mail order, catalogue and television shopping for a very long time and those businesses have been moving into the modern age by use of more sophisticated methods of publicity, promotion and sales. The availability of the fax, modem and personal computer have added a dimension for electronic shopping which is a natural extension of the shopping evolution. When we look at the present stage of development of electronic shopping, and online shopping via the Internet in parti-cular, we should be aware that this could be a style which has been introduced as a 'revolution about to change habits in a fundamental way, but which could equally be called a variation which only adds choice and convenience to what we already have in place. That status quo could be a situation which is so historically ingrained in the shoppers' psyche and forms such a leisure and habitual activity that such, a comparatively, small variant will have little effect on the whole process of traditional shopping. We should also think about the way all newly introduced 'improvements' have been claimed to be a major advantage over the old and established use: such claims can really be objectively assessed only after they have proved themselves with time.

The fact is that I have always had a questioning mind. Not as a destructive trait but in a constructive manner in order to see whether new methods, technology or trends might improve the opportunities open to us in the future. Of course, it is useful, perhaps essential, to also gauge whether such new items might pose a threat to the existing way of doing things and consider how to change ourselves and the way we do things. My attitude of question and debate has given me a reputation for being somewhat contentious on occasion. I do not see anything wrong in this, but do find it odd and worrying when the perceived 'audacity' of refusal to accept without any question claims by commercial interests that computer shopping will end traditional shopping as we know it, leads to calling me a 'flat earther'. I hope you will see that this is unjustified.

About 120 years ago, there was the greatest communications revolution ever seen – it was called the telephone.

Some forty years ago when I was a student, I worked for a local grocer's during my holidays. Each week customers would telephone and relay their orders which we wrote down. Then we packed the goods into cardboard boxes and placed them on the front of a bicycle which I dutifully cycled delivering the boxes to the customer. My employer delivered other items in a small van. Personal deliveries then ceased with a few exceptions. Personal shopping continued and grew. The offers and attractions increased. Forty years later, when those customers are more mobile and most have access to cars, it is being suggested that tele-shopping, the Internet and the various variants, up to virtual reality, is the way forward.

We should deduce from this that no matter how sophisticated the management system, it is finally dependent on the individual in the supply chain, but more importantly the individual with the demand – that is, the customer. Even at the grocer's the customer giving the order was usually someone who visited the shop, knew the produce and had purchased it before. They had used and experienced the actual goods and were aware of the offers. They had seen it, touched it, used it. Most of the goods were staple, that is to say not impulse purchases. In today's market the exotically stuffed olives or newly seasoned kettle crisps are items which the customers will take from the shelf on impulse but may not remember on a remote order.

Neither would they be likely to buy a belt, handbag, hat, shoes or scarf from a fashion store, to accessorise a dress, without a good sales assistant being present. That is the point of a well trained sales person. And you can shop with a friend from another house or with the family – you can't do that with tele shopping. You can't all shop for different types of things at the same time at home, but you can share the enjoyment at a shop of discovery with someone looking for something they want. You can share the pleasure of browsing and handling items which you may want in the future and discovering it, in three dimensions, with your partner. One of the greatest problems for retailers bearing the overheads of a centre may be the cost of personal service and advice which will then be used by unprincipled consumers to make the choice and order by telephone at the cheapest price. The retailer wants to maximise sales by suggesting additional items the customer may not be considering and by good salesmanship achieve added value. In short, remote shopping such as tele-shopping or virtual reality lacks an essential ingredient. There is no see, touch, feel or smell experience. There may not be any second opinion, either from a companion or a salesperson. The customer wants to feel the melon to see if it is ripe, look at the steak to see if it's fat or lean. They want to see the colour and texture with their own eyes and sensations rather than the colour shown on a monitor where the colour control may be too high or low. They almost always need another opinion on how they look, how a garment compliments them or how it fits. The retailer wants to use selling techniques to entice the customer to feel and buy something that would otherwise be overlooked. Over the years supermarkets have spent fortunes in developing psychologies to make shoppers buy more. From the early days of music which was slow during off peak times, to make the shopper dwell, to faster at busy times to get the customer through the store, on to scattering coffee grounds on the floors to enrich the appetite. Stacking principles to get the best effects, for example, with staples out of ready grasp and sight but expensive or exotic at eye height, and with the early lessons that shoppers are afraid to take a can from a perfect stack in case they spill them all. That is why cans are in a jumble. Sweets are located at checkouts for the parents to quieten fractious children. The aroma of freshly baked bread in supermarkets is not an accident. I would like you to keep that simple statement in mind as we look at why and how retailers and shoppers see whether the traditional shopping patterns will be changed in the future. We must ask ourselves whether it will ultimately be the shopper's voluntary choice of a personal experience, as originally supposed in my opening paragraphs, or a choice influenced by the retailers' 'spin doctors', the 'smell of freshly baked bread', or finally a 'graphic representation and listing over The Internet'?

2 The Personal Experience of Shopping

Clothing and shoe shoppers are the most promiscuous of Britain's consumers, according to a report issued at the end of June 1996 by Harris International Marketing. Shoppers travel further, with an average of four and a half miles, and visit more shops each trip (more than five) when looking for clothes than any other shopping category. Harris says this is an indictment of retailers' merchandising and service skills, which gives clothing and shoe shops only one chance in five of making a sale. Maybe it could also be concluded that the desire of shoppers for these articles is so great that five shops feel they can be profitable by offering competing yet comparison choice. However, this shows that shoppers for the more personal choice items, their own clothes and comfortable well fitting and fashionable footwear, are more than willing to shop personally even if more inconvenient.

Retailing is simply about giving the customer what she or he wants. Merchandising, advertising and promotion influences the customer to reach the decision and choice. The pleasure of most shoppers is to have the purchase there and then. Part of the pleasure of a new purchase is to take it home, or use it, dwelling on the possession of a new asset. This 'want' changes over time, and indeed has changed dramatically over the past ten–twenty years. We should ask whether the customer knows what she or he wants. It is pretty certain that most developers, and more particularly investors, have not known what the customer wanted, and also did not care as long as the rent cheques were received from the tenant each year. In recent times, though, there has been a huge increase in awareness and implementation of active management. Centre Managers for shopping centres, active promotion and a general acceptance that enabling the right environment to be created for retailers to maximise their sales, is recognised as being beneficial for all concerned. It is now universally seen that the form of shopping centres certainly derives from shoppers' needs and their perception of the experience. The conception of shopping centres is more scientific, influenced by greater

11

market studies of demographics. Many questions have to be answered on specific proposals, but the fundamental over-riding preferences of shoppers are still simple items, although the answers are far from simple. Does the shopper visit one centre rather than another because the environment is nicer, with better palm trees, parking and food courts, or because it has a more appropriate selection of shops and merchandise? Or is it merely because it is more convenient or cheaper? Do shoppers simply fall into only a few categories? In other words, is it a matter of convenience and price, or price alone, or a leisure experience? Obviously these categories have sub-divisions but are also intra-active.

MasterCard International sponsored a consumer survey conducted by Yankelovich Partners to discover why consumers are increasingly deciding to shop from home. They surveyed 502 shoppers who include traditional shoppers, TV shoppers and computer shoppers. The results are interesting. Seventy-five per cent of all respondents said that they were no longer secure shopping in malls. Stories about theft, gang presence and physical assault in parking areas were commonplace. Yet some of my friends in America say that the malls are the only places where they do feel safe. Retailers are more and more conscious of service charges in malls and have to keep an eye on those costs which add to their overheads, while having to compete with other retailers on price. It is accepted that service charges are a burning issue. Landlords are pressed for service to maintain the allure of a centre and, unfortunately, the provision of security is one of the highest, if not the highest, budgeted item in the yearly service charge. The retailers object to the high costs and it is usual for some compromise to be reached as a result. The irony is that many retailers employ their own security guards at their stores at higher direct cost to them. The provision of Closed Circuit Television (CCTV) has not appeared to be a final deterrent to crime so far, and is often ignored by offenders. The good news is that the quality of CCTV is improving rapidly and the problems of poor pictures and video evidence, which has made identification difficult in the past, is being more evidentially reliable. There still remains a paradox, because CCTV is used most effectively as an early warning system which can be successful only if additional static security personnel are available to monitor the screens and other mobile security guards are available to react to prevent potential incidents. Thus the cost is increased, not reduced, as a result of more sophisticated precautions. In general, whatever the economic effects, the public is more concerned today with crime and violence and recognition of the effects on trade cannot be relegated solely to the landlord or the trader.

Sixty-two per cent claimed that they had left a shop because there had been no salesperson available to help them with a purchase – even, in some cases, when they already had the article and had abandoned it. Especially in the case of impulse purchases, this is extremely counter-productive for a retailer, because it allows the customer additional time to ponder the purchase and have a change of mind. When retailers are relying, more and more, on impulse and service on the argument that online shopping can be used for predetermined product purchases, poor service is adding to the potential competitive problems. Furthermore, the customer becomes frustrated and irritated.

Most consumers felt that sales assistants were not sufficiently knowledgeable about the products on sale. This is not surprising in view of the thousands of products which may be on offer in the average large store. However, such units are usually departmentalised and assistants should have a good general knowledge within the defined area. The conclusion drawn by some commentators is that home shopping television presenters are better educated in the single product being promoted than a shop assistant can be in hundreds. Even if this is true, it is a simple problem to overcome by training of sales staff by a retailer to ensure that the general background knowledge of a specialised sector, and frequently the long experience of the virtues of many of the products, is utilised properly. I think it is doubtful to say that an actor who is trained to speak lines about a product, and who has no other knowledge, can be better placed in this respect. It must be attitude, commitment, training and a sense of welcoming service which should overcome the problems.

Over half the respondents in the survey said they would be willing to pay a little more for products if they could be bought faster. In our time-poor society consumers often have to shop for items which are relatively uninteresting and repetitive. If this takes longer than necessary it adds to the 'chore' factor disproportionately.

As might be expected in view of the source of the survey sponsorship, by a credit card company, the final question is: 'Why not try home shopping?' In view of the customers' apparent dissatisfaction, as claimed, with traditional retail stores, forecasters have predicted that as many as 40 per cent of all shoppers will try home shopping in the next two years. 15 per cent may become home shopping regulars. These estimates are surprisingly high, not because of the basic assumption on which they are based, but because the figures of computer ownership and use by female shoppers appear to be much lower than supporting anything like the percentages predicted. But, in any event, the promised boom in home shopping is not considered likely over the next ten years unless and until shopping mediums become interactive. This is because – and this is the telling conclusion – people would rather actively shop than sit at home watching a television.

Price alone as an attraction is unlikely to provide an enjoyable experience. Price can be associated with enjoyable shopping, but enjoyable shopping should also include convenience and, perhaps more importantly, entertainment. And we should remember that leisure time is increasing not decreasing. Longer holiday periods in jobs have become the norm. Flexitime and outworking have grown. Earlier retirement gives more time for the 'greying' population who have money to spend and enjoy. Anyone remotely connected to the shopping centre industry knows the heightened attention entertainment has received over the past few years. 'Entertainment' can have several meanings. To some, the multiplex cinemas and food courts, to others, the experience when shopping in stores that originated in the entertainment industry, such as Disney or Warner Brothers shops. Others may think of the shopping experience when visiting other innovative groups, such as Leading Edge. For most families there is simple pleasure in a few hours' window shopping, special purchases, a meal and a day out. Under normal trading conditions it might not show, but after two recessions in ten years, customers are increasingly discriminating and sales staff have to use positive sales techniques. If such discrimination is evident, and the need for personal attention is so important, the question is how an impersonal screen, or even a discount store with no expert sales help, can satisfy these needs.

3 It's Not Enough to do it Well, do it New

For most retailers, the early 1990s showed the smallest sales gains in thirty years. The decline has caused reassessments of the retail environment strategies and has obscured the more basic set of changes which have been happening for a longer period. For example, in the middle of the turmoil, there have been a number of successes as well as failures.

One of the most important changes is summed up in the term 'value marketing'. This is indeed a major change, as can be seen from the prospects of car sales, clothing, office furniture, homes or hardware. There is a powerful tendency to move away from luxury items and toward more practical, less costly alternatives which are perceived to do the job just as well. The manufacturers at the higher end of the market have all faced significant difficulties. Mercedes, Saks Fifth Avenue, Ralph Lauren and IBM are examples of this. On the other hand, companies in America such as Wal-Mart, Lexus, The Gap and Gateway 2000, which have developed strategies to meet the needs of consumers in the middle range, have prospered.

As the move toward consumer needs, and not only their desires, continues, the most effective means of marketing and distribution also changes correspondingly. Sales were targeted by the stimulation of 'image and trappings of luxury' through advertising, merchandising and packaging; now practices are emphasising value and solid information as the basis on which to make a decision to purchase. The spectacular performance of Wal-Mart in new formats and strategies of mass merchandising are being followed by almost all parts of retailing. Discount stores in America are currently a $110 billion industry, the national base of 450 Club stores is predicted to grow to 950, and the number of Deep Discounters to grow from 900 to 18 000, with discounters likely to increase from 4400 to 7000, according to an estimate from McKinsey & Co. The projection, according to some industry sources, is that within ten years a typical city of 1 million people will have five or six warehouse stores, 10–11 deep discount stores and 26–28 mass merchant stores.

15

Marketing strategies have had many new drivers in the past 100 years. Today, it's no longer enough to do it well, you also need to do it new. The realities of today's rapidly changing and extremely competitive markets are challenging all parts of traditional market wisdom and practise. These changes are each having their effect on the strategies of producers through advertising and marketing media and the mechanisms of the retail system itself.

The entire economy is being influenced by innovation and the introduction of 'something new'. The current situation may be illustrated by looking at the evolution of the competitive requirements of business success over the past century, when a simple industrial economy has been transformed into the more complex, quickly changing intelligent economy which now exists.

At the outset of the industrial era from 1900 to 1930, success depended on the ability to produce greater volume with use of new techniques and mass production. From 1930 to 1950, volume production was easy but resulted in pricing pressures with success dependent on managing costs. With volume and costs on a level keel, from 1950 to 1970, quality and reliability was required. Then service became paramount with the shift to a customer-driven market place between 1970 and 1985. In the period 1985 to 1992 the market was not getting easier, having provided the accepted facts. Thus, speed to market and meeting customer needs became the key to achieving a growth in market share. Since about 1992, there has been a New Age innovation in progress. The key words have been defined as, Surprise, Delight, Surpass.

Today, the prerequisite for success has moved beyond being a low-cost producer, having TQM (Total Quality Management), customer obsession, and JIT (Just-In-Time) procedures which are found in all successful organisations. They are not considered options for success but essentials. The new factor needed to succeed today is the introduction of true innovation, which not only dramatically impacts existing operations, but actually surprises and delights customers by surpassing their expectations. Once innovations are introduced in the system they trigger the need for other innovations at other points. The economy is now in a continuous process of innovation and frantic efforts to advertise brands in order to earn customer loyalty are of substantially lessening value.

With cost control procedures in place, new fast inventory replenishment systems operational and stores at every sales generator, retailers are finding it difficult to find ways to make their offer different from their competitors. They are also struggling to increase their thin profit margins. One way for retailers to achieve this is to get exclusive products from their suppliers. More and more retailers want to avoid selling the same items as their direct competitors; their objective is to create a total design concept that makes them different from those competitors, ranging from store layout, to signage, to different products. They want to promote a message of being distinctive, not more of the same.

This is resulting in the appearance of relationships between retailers and suppliers that are much less personal and promotion-orientated than in the past. Companies are shifting their attention, from the mechanics of the sales process to the integrity and quality of the product.

Clearly new products and retailing concepts must offer function with a creative, competitive, angle. Product innovation is not the same as new products. The latter may too often be mere updates of existing ones, or show small design changes or improvements of performance. The real innovations become the leading standards. For example:

- Nike reinvented footwear with the change of sports shoes from the mundane to high fashion and the idea that all footwear should be comfortable. The entire industry changed and Nike became a global brand.
- Sony used creative applications of technology to old product lines with the Walkman as a classic example.
- 3M has introduced Scotch Tape and Post-It Pads, disposable paint brushes and continues to serve and delight its customers.
- Nintendo has led the world into new hand-held, interactive, video-based computers and with Sega, and Sony Playstation video games are in a third of the homes with children in the industrialised world.
- Kodak is thinking ahead with its 'disposable' cameras. Its new disk camera does not require film at all. This has been adopted by a number of manufacturers to the extent that digital cameras are becoming commonplace.

In the past, when shoppers were not as aware as they are today, selling fantasy obtained shoppers who were loyal 'dreamers' about the brand message and who were associating with the image portrayed. Now, consumer awareness has increased with more intelligent and sophisticated needs to which sellers have to appeal.

Few things typify the economy and traditional views of products, customer behaviour and markets than the concept of 'brands'. Corporate strategies and industries revolved around brand competition and within the huge advertising and marketing industry the role of the brand in the minds of consumers was the driving force. However, recent events are calling into question these basic concepts. The decision of Philip Morris to reduce the price of Marlboro cigarettes to combat the increase in sales by competitors supplying non-brand cigarettes by discounters is a good example. At the same time there are big increases in the sales of private labels and the indications that some manufacturers will discontinue some brands.

The conclusions on this are far from easy because there are conflicting reports from consumer surveys about brand loyalty. In some areas it is falling, but in others it is rising. The major manufacturers are hoping that the established loyalties will continue, but they are increasing their advertising, with *Advertising Age* in America reporting that the top 200 brands increased expenditure in 1992 by 8.7 per cent, to $11.7 billion. At the same time the same major manufacturers continued to allocate higher proportions of their overall budgets away from advertising to promotion, where more than $30 billion was spent.

It is interesting that the Marlboro decision has caused such a stir. It should be remembered that it is over thirty years since the initial success was caused by the last industry packaging innovation, the flip top box. For over seventy-five years, the essence of American economy was exemplified by the image of major brands. Just the names of these brands have been seen to have values in billions. Marlboro, Cadillac, Texaco, Budweiser, Nestlé, Rolls Royce, Mercedes Benz, Rolex, IBM, etc. all carried a message and image far beyond the actual product, becoming icons of luxury or excellence.

The Marlboro Man is the perfect example of how the power of advertising and creative use of the media were able to project an image which captured the minds and hearts of consumers. This, of course, was during an age when consumers were much less informed than they are today. Now, after a period when the feeling of abundance has waned, the increasing changes in the perceived value of those brands have brought their effectiveness almost to a stop. The ability to manufacture a product with decent quality is no longer such a competitive asset. This has become easy and retailers have been assailed with as much product as they want. In order to respond, manufacturers have tried to produce the next 'power brand' to keep their output going at the same rate, but the explosion of new products has been, for the most part, items which do not offer anything new at all.

According to Bill Gorman's *New Product News*, there were 16760 new product introductions in 1992 in America, an increase of some 20 per cent over 1991 and over twice the number of new products introduced five years earlier. Taking account of the levels of sophistication in the consumer research market, advertising and promotion, this could be taken to indicate real success. This was not the case, with failures of 80 per cent during the 1990s, up from 70 per cent during the 1960s, 1970s and 1980s. Today, consumers have become smarter about the actual value and benefits of the options available, and cannot be attracted merely through clever advertising.

This information seems a strange topic for me to include in a subject concerned with home shopping. The reason is that so much of the present hype centres on the amazing range of products which will be available through the Internet. Once again, I come to the conclusion that it is an unlikely scenario to believe that someone producing or marketing a niche product which has not been followed up by major retailers as a strong sales product will succeed. The ability of the merchant to set up a Home page at very small cost, even working from home, does not provide confidence that the offer will be a success. If a failure, that merchant will be unlikely to continue and the customer will be left with nothing but an 'empty shop' next time. And that raises the question about continuity – for parts, service or replacement, for example. If the rate of failures experienced by major businesses, with all the help of the consumer behaviour, survey, marketing promotion and advertising industries, is in line with the figures given here, and the products are much of the same, what hope can the majority of Home Shopping 'amateur' providers have to succeed?

But if what you buy is important, so is where you buy it. The concept of the 'Category Killer' was invented by Toys "Я" Us, as it assured the best and largest selection of toys at the lowest possible price. L. L. Bean demonstrated that good customer service and loyalty can be built and maintained at long distance, through the mail and over the phone, with solid reliable products and excellent attention to its customers. IKEA brought convenience and value added to design to the home furnishing market. Pioneering the ready-to-assemble concept IKEA grew from a reported 4289 million Dutch Guilders in 1986 to 10214 million Dutch Guilders in 1996.

I am not so stupid that I want to ignore possible effects of technology on our core business. The actual history of the phenomenally successful, then dramatically difficult, situation arising from problems of distribution at the Home Shopping Channel in the United States should not make any of us complacent.

Whatever the future in specific and real terms, it is presently an inescapable fact that there are estimated to be about 40 million Internet users at the present time. Further users are joining at a startling rate. In February 1996 it was estimated that 17 million American adults, or 1 in 11, have used the Web – double the most accepted previous estimate of Internet use. Since the United States must be considered the largest user market, this might cause some scepticism about the 40 million figure cited elsewhere. As for Britain itself, the RIPE European Hostcount which produces statistics for the European region, reported 5 122 501 Hosts at the end of September 1997. In mid–1997, Find/SVP thought that the question of how many people are on the Net will continue to be asked until 1999, when we will ask the question 'Why? We do not ask how many use the telephone'. They say that the number of people on the Net varies widely depending on the way 'Internet use' is defined. Given these conflicting factors, Tim Miller of Find/SVP [survey, April 1997] Emerging Technology Research Group, presented what he described as as 'Credible first quarter [1997] estimates' which include: 40–45 million total US adult users; 30–35 million used Web or another application besides e-mail in the previous three months; 25 million weekly Web users. The latest forecasts of the 1997 American Internet User Survey from Find/SVP are 31.3 million US adult users; and 55 million Americans poised to become Internet users.

There is the back-up data from a survey conducted by IntelliQuest in November and December 1996, and the presentation by Find/SVP and the 6th Graphics, Visualisation & Usability Centre survey in October 1996. These all showed a range of total US numbers from 40–47 million. More interesting is the finding that the number of US women on the Net is estimated to be between 41 per cent and 45 per cent. One survey has 45 per cent of those surfing the Web as being over forty years old and on education levels 56 per cent of respondents had completed college or had an advanced degree. The Net is still primarily used by the affluent, with only 18 per cent earning less than $25 000 a year. IntelliQuest had 73 per cent of users on the Net pursuing hobbies, 63 per cent getting information for work and 50 per cent planning trips. Cyberspace clearly still has a long way to go.

The number of World Wide Web users in Britain online increased by over 100 per cent during the six-month period between June and December 1996, according to NOP Research Group's most recent Internet UserStudy. Over a quarter of a million people are shopping online each month. In addition, the number of current users who said they would consider shopping online during the next six months increased by 69 per cent over the same period. Of those making purchases during the previous four weeks, three out of five spent less than £50, whilst one in seven spent more than £500. The findings claim to suggest that online shopping transactions totalling in excess of £1 billion will take place during 1997, given current levels of expenditure.

This number has obviously continued to grow significantly but whatever the exact numbers it would be silly to ignore the possible impact of such a massive audience on shopping habits in the future. The question, debated in greater detail elsewhere in this book, is how much of an impact these shoppers will have on traditional shopping centres as we presently know them. For example, will the main threat be aimed at other similar areas of purchase such as direct mail, catalogue shopping, power centres and discount retailers, or spill over into personal selection by visit? Will, as another hypothesis suggests, shoppers' habits be changed to any degree, making personal visits to the shopping centre either more selective or less frequent? It is argued by those who are promoting their electronic services that although the new services do not represent much by volume or value, they nevertheless feel that by the turn of the century, these services will have transformed the market of telecommunication operators and the traditional retailers.

4 The World Wide Web, The Internet, Cyberspace and Retail Locations

We should, at this early point, try to define the terms 'electronic commerce'. 'Internet shopping', 'online shopping', 'non-store retailing', 'virtual shopping' and 'cyber-shopping' are terms frequently used today in the retail and shopping centre industries. Generally, the usual discussion evolves around shopping which takes place on the Internet, including the World Wide Web, often called simply the Web. Television networks as an addition to systems which allow orders through fax links also fall within the realms of electronic commerce, but shopping on the Internet probably, more than any other, symbolises the concept.

Even today, and despite the amount of publicity given to the matter, many people who have come across the terms 'Internet' and the 'Web' are unsure of what they are. The Internet began as a governmental and military communications network in the early 1970s. It was then used by academics at research institutes as a tool which linked computers for the sharing of data and research information. The Internet has now come into use by many computer-users as a medium for communications, entertainment, research and the purchase of products and services.

The World Wide Web is a subset of the Internet that, unlike other Internet options like e-mail, provides sophisticated graphics, digitised pictures and audio and visual files, all with the ease of point and click access. It is on the Web that many retailers have set up 'home pages' which give a visual display and point and click options to scroll through listings, graphical representations of merchandise and pre-set payment forms.

People who have never used the Internet may be unclear how to approach cyber-shopping. Firstly, a fairly modern computer equipped with a modem line is needed. A computer that runs Windows[1] or

---

1. Windows is the software system produced by Microsoft Corporation. 'Windows' is the Registered Trademark of Microsoft.

Macintosh software is a common set up which allows for easy access to the Internet and the Web. Users must then subscribe to an Internet provider such as CompuServe, America Online (AOL), Prodigy, Demon or similar, and then load that company's basic access software onto their computer. The user is then ready to travel the information superhighway on their computer.

A user who knows the address of a retailer can enter it in the computer and travel directly to that retailer's home page. If the address is not known, or even the name of the retailers, the user can use one of several available 'search engine' options. These search engines are subprograms that find Internet addresses by matching search criteria specified by the user. The user will typically prompt the screen which has several pre-set search categories, such as hobbies, recreation and shopping. If shopping is selected, a list of store types will be displayed and the search can then be narrowed by selecting a particular store type. The available stores are located in several countries. When the particular store is found, the cyber-shopper is presented with the store's home page and from there point and click options allow search of merchandise categories, view of merchandise and the selection of payment options. An order can be made by typing the name, address and major credit card information into an order template and clicking on a 'send order' icon. In some cases the store will then send an e-mail message to confirm the order.

'Home shopping is not a threat to retailers, but can run alongside their existing business.' So said Bryan Mayoh, Managing Director of Littlewoods Home Shopping, at the Verdict Research Retail Conference at the beginning of October 1996. He said, 'Customers like to go shopping so home shopping will never take over from the high street.' Although he qualified his opinion by also stating that the challenge facing retailers would be to cater for customers both on the high street and in the home, this is a significant statement from the head of one of the leading catalogue and mail order companies in Britain.

Mayoh thinks that 'significant costs are associated with building up a presence' and that retailers already benefit from the support and reassurance their high street visibility gives to customers. He believed that retailers should be aware of the many disadvantages as well as the advantages. Without a powerful brand name people were less willing to pay up front for goods and there were high costs arising from returned goods. This is a direct comment on the problems highlighted elsewhere regarding the ease with which any trader can operate on the Internet and the risk shoppers may take in ordering goods and paying in advance without the security of redress for non-delivery or faulty items. Mayoh also highlighted the necessity of having a separate warehousing system for delivery to individual people, rather than bulk systems to branch stores. Most importantly, he predicted a continuing future for catalogues despite the arrival of electronic shopping methods, feeling that despite interactive television, catalogues would remain the means of communicating with customers. Again, this is an important feature of the general argument that interactive home shopping is not a cut and dried alternative, even to mail order. On that basis, the argument for it to replace traditional high street or shopping centre visits is even more contentious.

Another seemingly sound argument, based on projected, but at this stage questionable, logic, has been put forward as a strong warning to property people, and which might, if correct, upset one of the most prevailing and fundamental guides to best investment principles. It has been claimed that Cyberspace strikes at the heart of commercial real estate by radically diminishing the value of location. The logic behind this statement is that information technology is allowing workers to operate externally from the office or shop and, in any event, will need less space as a result. In effect, if staff need not be located centrally, the location is less important for the company. Until now location has been the over-riding gauge of investment valuation because it underwrites the security of finding another tenant in the case of vacancy more easily than an outlying, secondary or unfashionable place. 'Location, location, location' have always been quoted as the three most important investment criteria. In addition to the impact on office space, the idea is that electronic retailing will remove much of the pedestrian traffic, mean fewer shops, allow shoppers to shop from home, and generally reduce the locational value of the retail premises which may be represented only by an Internet page.

James Young, in his article 'The Information Age and the Potential Effects on the Commercial Real Estate Market', in 1995, thought that current trends portended a growing surplus of commercial space. He wonders whether a prolonged period of excess space will lead to lower rents and values. Gloom and doom is portrayed by suggestions that corporate raiders will use technology to radically reduce real estate costs by dumping space, substituting software for staff and actively moving employees out of the office to tele-work. In this scenario, landlords and lenders will lose their immunity from the machinations of take-overs.

The argument consequently follows that commercial landlords, tenants and lenders need to have strategies to protect their investments. They will need to change their views about risk, returns and security of assets when looking at investment opportunities in the Information Age. So far, I have repeated the argument in principle. Since it is a line which we should expect – and, indeed, is based on a logical assessment of the effects of technology in an ideal progression of the growth of the use of technology – we should see how the argument is supported. Then, perhaps, we can look at the likely human response and the likely real response of property owners.

Most of the space required for office work is becoming unnecessary through the substitution of software to increase employee productivity, and by moving tasks outside the office electronically. 'Tele-work', 'outworking' and other terms describe the result of fewer people doing more work in less space. Only recently has this become practicable through the use of personal computers, lightweight portables, modems, the Internet and close integration of tools to allow companies to accept tele-work as a means to increase productivity, cut costs and sustain employee morale.

It has been a given until now that retail space depends on location. Well located shops generate higher sales and therefore support the payment of higher rent. By removing the activity of buying something from the place it is sold by means of online services, retailers are given greater flexibility to provide better service to their customers with fewer locations. Since malls and shopping centres are the locations for retailers, this would mean a growing mismatch of space and the value of that space. The rate of retail space oversupply would be dependent on the customers' use of online shopping services which replace those units. In turn, the customers' acceptance is geared to the number and variety of retailers offering competitive services and goods. There must be an incentive for shoppers to go online and make the break from their customary habit of visiting the shops. However, it is admitted that store sales will not be harmed unduly unless there is a wholesale move to Cyberspace. The critical question is asked: Can traditional retail, online and catalogue sales all be successful side-by-side, or will online shopping destroy shop sales?

In the light of such a gloomy prediction, how can property men answer the danger of a destruction of location and market values? As a simple developer I have a more pragmatic attitude to the scaremongering and offer a few comments and examples in an effort to show that this is just what I have called it – scaremongering.

Overall, the premise is based, yet again, on the idea of Utopia, which is referred to later in some detail. If only, I often think, computer people and promoters of electronic futures would discipline themselves to live in the real world of normal people, with human responses and psychologies, they would be able to judge possible effects in this world instead of appearing, at times, to be on another planet. Logical conclusions of the type advanced here allow no deviation from the idealistic path for either human nature or basic economics.

Taking the simplest example, there is no recognition that the providers of the software, hardware and services for the expanding electronic market will have to operate from some space of acceptable standards to perform their own operations in an economic, efficient and centralised way. In other words, commercial space is, and will continue to be, required in growing amounts simply for those producers. In fact, think of the massive amount of office and manufacturing and distribution space currently occupied by computer companies and their satellite industries. In many cases this space was not occupied by others before they existed. It cannot be feasible that such producers and providers will be able to use tele-working to provide the same standard of service. And, on their own admission, the provision of such services is going to expand tremendously in the future. If location is unimportant how did Silicon Valley in California become a centre for the software industry or the Thames Valley in England the headquarters for the British manufacturers such as Digital Research and others?

A report from Healey and Baker issued in June 1996, after research company RSL interviewed 650 office workers, found that only 8 per cent of office workers work from home more than once a week and only 17 per cent said that they would like to work from home on a regular basis. The values which workers declared most important, in order, were the car park then air conditioning. A non-smoking policy was fifth in order of importance, followed by having shops nearby. This report would seem to support contentions that the use of the computer as an aid to outworking is not highly favoured by office workers. Furthermore, the most important requirement after features of the building and work conditions is the presence of shops. This is clearly at odds with the suggestion that workers will forego the simple everyday pleasures of visits to the shops by replacing it with use of online shopping either in the home or in the office. Obviously the deduction cannot be conclusive, based on such a small survey and one report, but it is indicative of the fact that the claims made by many providers of online services are equally inconclusive and remain at variance with people's present desires.

And let us examine some of the other statements shown above. Corporate take-over raiders will reduce the value of real estate by dumping property? Surely it is an economic fallacy to think that a take-over of capital assets will be contemplated on the basis that such assets will realise substantially less on disposal. Yet the dumping argument must mean that the values are being depressed by this action. If such a strategy was to be undertaken the successful acquirer of a company would be depreciating its own future assets in the process. This would undermine the capital value from within and might cause severe difficulties in funding the bid, or even making the bid price unacceptably low to the vendor.

It was also claimed that less space is becoming necessary due to software and resultant outworking. This may be true in some cases but I clearly remember when decentralisation was the vogue in the late 1960s and 1970s. Administrative office work was moved out of central expensive locations, leaving only executive offices in the prestige positions. The outcome was that managers needed to be in contact with both their administrative staff and their executives, and therefore needed offices in both locations. This doubling of space led to almost as much space in the central location, in many instances, plus the additional space which was decentralised. Whilst this example shows that many good and logical ideas tend to be thwarted by human practice, it is not the same as the present ease with which communications can be achieved between different areas. But the real experience of installing computers and computer suites in central offices with the intent of following the dream of the paperless office has shown that greater amounts of space have been needed, not less. Banks, for example, are taking bigger and bigger office buildings and people using computers every day can vouch for the reams of printouts and hard copy references which are stacked in offices and archives. These paper mountains were not with us prior to the introduction of computers. We had typed copies and photocopies in reasonable amounts but nothing approaching the present size.

Some time ago I was in the office of the Estates Director of a major supermarket group. In answer to my question about a certain store and the trading success, he went to a large pile of computer printouts stacked on the floor in a corner. He extracted the report for the previous week which showed all stores with trading returns by department and item. He confirmed that every director and manager was circulated with such a report each Monday. He also said that little of it was read but it was a useful tool if ever needed. So much for information technology! Now this information can be distributed by Intranet or e-mail but the reality is that a large number of directors cannot handle the systems efficiently. Recently I suggested to a top lawyer that instead of sending me a hard copy of a long document in draft by courier or over the fax, where it tied up the fax machine for a very long time, the file should be e-mailed. I would then have it and be able to make amendments and e-mail it back. The result was that it took almost two days because he had to ask for advice from his firm's IT department. In the meantime the document was faxed to me, not once but twice!

I was interested and somewhat amused recently to be told a story about the renting of warehouse space for use by executives to park their cars and work on laptop computers with mobile telephone connections. Apparently these executives are supposed to be working from home but they find it difficult to do so in the home environment both because of the constant interruptions and demands of their wives and families, callers and domestic responsibilities, and the lack of a discipline found in the office. Lack of personal contact with other fellow workers was also cited. Getting away and finding a quiet place to work, by driving their car to a drab warehouse, is one answer to the problem. In fact, it is a substitution of one space for another while losing the advantages of being in the central nerve centre of their main interest.

Retail locations will be destroyed by a wholesale changeover to online services? The estimates of trading volume promulgated by the most die-hard promoters of online shopping indicate that by the year 2020 only 15 per cent of *total* retail sales will be achieved. Although this is a staggering amount it must be compared to the present volume in America today of over $3 trillion. That, I believe, shows that even if the type of Armageddon scenario is realised, and I do not think that is likely, the amount of traditional retail space required will still be substantial. If there is a fallout of space it is likely to be felt in secondary locations and tend to reinforce the premium value of the best areas. Therefore, if valuation principles are consistent, values of the best space, such as high streets and the better malls, should increase not decrease. Cyberspace could, on my scenario, benefit property.

5 Is There a Substitute for the Real Thing? Information Appliances

At the British Council of Shopping Centres' Annual Conference in Edinburgh in 1991 there was a panel discussion on the future of shopping. When questions were invited, I put forward the view that the panel had not addressed the question at all. They had spoken of the form of centre design, leases and so on. I said that in an era when one could experience flying a 747 from an armchair, it must be possible to use virtual reality to experience visits to a shopping centre – in fact any shopping centre in the world! It was worthy of consideration – and still is – because of the obvious impact it could have on the industry. At that time, I was being somewhat contentious, using a general assumption that the advance of technology had to be seen as a means of retail development in the future. As it was meant as an argumentative question I did not raise the extreme difficulties of authoring such an expensive program. I had no definite ideas or knowledge, but the point of an expert brainstorming discussion group was to indicate where we might go. To my mind, this did not mean better design for lighting or entrance floor mats: we must borrow the introduction to Star Trek™ and consider if it is possible to go where no man has gone before! Naturally, I have given the matter a huge amount of thought since then. Above all I have been impressed by three facts: firstly, the software program development for normal simulations such as planes or racing cars is very expensive and lengthy to produce. The market for those simulations, with a few exceptions, is small and volatile and the computer literacy is generally focused on games playing coordination or business applications without the need for a wide-ranging intellectual capacity. It is likely, therefore, that the time lag required to update current merchandise listings or visuals, either on CD-ROM or online is likely to be too long for efficient updates. Relatively fast updates of listings or photographs can be achieved but will require very efficient coordinated marketing efforts. Good and successful retailers merchandise their shops to make the greatest impact and achieve the greatest sales.

The latest fashion item and accessories, the best selling lines, tend to be in the forefront, with slower selling lines moved to less prominent positions. The customer wants to see the newest, latest, offer and be seduced by it. The standard of shop window displays, high quality of design and fittings internally, shop displays and personal customer service are high investments made by retailers to engender sales. One must wonder if this can be achieved on a computer program.

According to *Shopping Centers Today*, in a special report on Value Retailing, several discount retailers are calling for reorganisation protection in the United States. A handful more are on the verge of bankruptcy. Jamesway, Caldor and Bradlees have all filed for Chapter 11[1] in the recent past. It would appear that convenience and price is not necessarily the over-riding reason to shop.

Second, it is a strange paradox that the growth and popularity of video rentals and improvements in VCR and television has been reflected in record attendance at cinemas. The British Video Association announced at its annual awards ceremony in October 1996 that there was an increased level of video rentals for the first time since 1989. Rentals in September showed an increase of 6 per cent year-on-year rise, giving the highest volume of rentals for any month for the previous five years and retail sales of videos increased by 4 per cent. Yet cinema chains are continuing to develop multiplex and multi-screen cinemas at an unabated pace. In December 1996 a report issued by the Central Office of Statistics in Britain showed that the number of people going to the cinema was up by 23.7 per cent to more than 30 million, and that they spent £93 million at the box office.

There are other examples to support this continuing desire for a personal experience. Televising live soccer on terrestrial and satellite television including Premier, First Division and Italian Serie A games has been reflected in steady increases in attendance at live matches. Live screening of major Rugby Union internationals, complete with close up action and replays, still sees 73 000 capacity at Twickenham and a big unsatisfied demand for tickets. At the lower level, the televising of Rugby Union club games has also coincided with

---

1. Chapter 11 is roughly the equivalent of an administrative order allowing the company to continue trade while insolvent and providing protection against winding up action by its creditors.

increased attendances. One must logically conclude that the public interest is whetted by the technological appetisers and, as Coca Cola would say, there is no real substitute for the real thing.

As a result of this heightened interest, better facilities have been possible, with increased investment by clubs in top class players and better sound systems, etc. at cinemas: the public becomes more attracted. So the spiral continues. It would be reasonable to think that tele-shopping would act in a similar way. Would the advertising effect of merchandising into the home increase the attendance at the actual shop? Indeed, as argued later, are many retailers following this line by using the Internet as a marketing tool? The deal made between the Premier League and BSkyB from 1997–8 guarantees each Premier Club a staggering multi-million pound income per season with a still major amount for two seasons for any relegated club. This income has enabled clubs to invest in better players and facilities. It therefore follows that a strong and attractive league is in the best interests of Sky because their programmes will be correspondingly more attractive. It also follows that online shopping providers would be best served by featuring strong traders who are well known with recognised brands. If Sky has shown such extraordinary success by supporting the live event it seems logical that online providers should follow this course. On that presumption, retailers will not disappear but will, instead, look forward to more custom as their attractions are advertised to Internet browsers. To put the argument simply, television, video and online are supports to the main activity providing ancillary services, including advertising and awareness.

Thirdly, in the short term, I have become more sceptical with regard to my previous feeling that computer literacy would become the norm among our young people. I am now less convinced that the recent results of standards among eleven year olds in Britain, and the results of computer literacy surveys in America, encourages the belief that sophisticated programs will be usable to the extent needed by the relevant targeted portion of the general public to justify the investment in home or virtual reality shopping of a very comprehensive nature. The development of pictograms or voice recognition systems in the future will probably alter that opinion, but it is likely to be a number of years before reaching that stage. We must certainly await the expected installation of integrated home information centres incorporating telephone, fax, computer and cable before seeing if the system will provide easily-used and cheap methods of access. A MORI survey published in October 1996 stated that forecasts of

Britain going totally online for work as well as play are confirmed as way off the mark. The poll discovered that 75 per cent of respondents did not know how to get onto the Internet, let alone how to use it once there, and that 43 per cent of the population does not use mobile phones, computers, electronic organisers or pagers.

Some moves have already begun through the introduction of Personal Computer Hegemony.[1] This clearly is not the same objective as an easy integrated communications system of the future but it does indicate the thinking among leading companies. It is another form of design to satisfy an increasing number of perceived needs without having to leave our armchairs. The question it raises is whether we stick to using computers for application of our skills, or do we integrate computing into the mainstream of appliance technology?

Intel, Compaq and CompUSA have a proposal for something called Intercast. This is a scheme which will permit the watching of television on a Pentium computer and receive related Web pages from the Internet at the same time. Intercast™ technology offers an easy way to get more out of television programmes you watch. Accessed through a PC, it combines the interactivity of a computer, the rich programming of broadcast and cable television and the world wide resources of the Internet. Philips and Sony are introducing WebTV, which is said to be a high resolution, high speed Internet 'experience'. In effect, it is a Black Box which is placed between the television and telephone inputs. A card slot in the box will allow it to be upgraded with new design plans. There will also be a port in the box so that credit cards can be inserted to make purchases over the Web. WebTV boxes made by Sony and Philips have, however, fallen foul of the US restrictions on the export of cryptographic equipment. Because the browser software in the boxes uses industrial strength routines, the whole thing is considered a weapon. This question is dealt with in more detail later in the book.[2]

Intel, Compaq and CompUSA sell computers and computer devices and Philips and Sony sell electronic appliances. It is not likely that any of them will provide objective assessments of the future advantages and disadvantages because they have their own

---

1. Personal Computer Hegemony – Hegemony means Leadership (Greek *hegomonia*, from *agro*, to lead). Its general meaning is authority or influence, and I assume the use of the word in this context indicates Personal Computer leadership.
2. See p. 178.

agendas to make profits from selling their own goods. There is an opinion that the movement to use the PC to replace everything we use such as televisions, radios, tape recorders, VCRs and answering machines is a way of reinventing the wheel in order primarily to solidify the computer producers' market share. That opinion thinks that it would be preferable to see the computer integrated into existing appliance technology, as it has been for years. This has been a successful approach because computers still cannot operate as efficiently or as cost effectively as many appliances, such as televisions and VCRs.

The message that simplification of use will be essential in the future is certainly getting through. Computer illiteracy and generally low standards of education, added to lack of funds among the poorer sector to purchase sophisticated means of accessing offers, means that a large market awaits gadgets which are as easy to use as the telephone. I reflect that even this simple statement is now being confused by the amazing amount of sophistication on quite ordinary telephone handsets. Memory recall, redial, hands free, diverting, conferencing, etc. makes some telephones difficult for non-technical folk and rank alongside programming of video recorders. The real and simple fact is that everything seems to be getting more difficult rather than simpler to use and one must presume that even a 'simple appliance' to be introduced will also be updated and developed in the future years, thereby presenting new problems to be addressed.

It is reasonably clear that many of the brightest brains concerned with software, hardware and computer science are working hard to discover methods whereby huge amounts of information can be transferred as easily as using a common kitchen appliance. Not only are major corporations tackling this problem, but small innovative firms are trying to come up with the solution. On the premise that the future is likely to be based on electronic gadgets that are as simple to use as the TV, everyone is racing to be first. New products ranging from wristwatch data phones to smaller personal computers are being developed as prototypes.

Appliances which can be used as easily as the telephone are seen as a way to allow the mass of people who are not presently wired into the Information Age. Although the personal computer may have already brought a large sector into Cyberspace, due to its high cost and complexity it relates mainly to the younger, better-educated and higher segment of the population. Therefore, the general opinion is that PCs in their present form are less likely to result in a mass market online. Laurence J. Ellison, President of Oracle Corporation, says 'The world is in need of computers that are easier to use and less expensive.' Oracle is just one of many trying to predict what such computers will be like. In their case, it is presently a stripped down version with the bare essentials for cruising the Web. Everyone is looking at the large market who have yet to enter Cyberspace, which is about 60 per cent of US customers and about 90 per cent of households around the world.

At this time nobody really knows what content will encourage the millions to switch from channel surfing to Web surfing. It is recognised, however, that the figures are so vast that huge amounts of money are being invested in designing information appliances around the world. International Data Corporation predicts that in the next three years the market will simply explode. By the year 2000, some 22 per cent of all Internet access devices, about 22 million units, will be machines other than PCs. It took the world PC industry a decade to reach that level of shipments.

There are predictions of what is the ideal information appliance. These are hedged by saying that they will be many different types. Ideas include simple variations of what we have today, such as slimmed down home computers adapted as Net cruisers, Web-surfing TVs, smart phones and Net-connected game players. Some ideas are wildly futuristic, such as that of Tim Berners-Lee, creator of the World Wide Web, who says it might even be inside a cereal box: 'My kids could rummage around for the free gift, take out a tube, unroll it to something flat, flexible and magnetic, stick it to the refrigerator, and start navigating the Web. From the Kellogg's home site to the wild blue yonder', he says. The point is that these appliances will be everywhere. 'You don't treat it as something special', says Berners-Lee.

It is generally agreed that the PC will survive because it has such a huge momentum with a market said to be approaching 70 million units per year, and also because it has proved to be very adaptable. 'The PC is the TV for the Internet', says Duncan Davidson, a Consultant with Gemini McKenna High Tech Strategies. Greg E. Blonder, Director of Customer-Expectations Research at AT&T Labs adds, 'Four years from now, five years from now, the PC will still be the information appliance.'

As in any evolution scenario the PC is adapting to meet the rising competition. Clearly the major consumer electrics companies have certain advantages over PC manufacturers because they have brand names that are used in every home, together with a marketing philosophy which focuses on how consumers want to use their products. That is an approach that PC manufacturers are only just starting to understand. 'We don't need breakthroughs in software or technology,' says Stan Shih, Chairman of Acer Inc., 'we need breakthroughs in business philosophy.' Acer, the electronics giant of Taiwan, is planning to move from computers into consumer electronics and plans to introduce a $500 Internet PC for sale in emerging markets such as China.

This recognition of the need for a new approach is also supported by William 'Bill' Gates III of Microsoft. In April 1996, they initiated Simply Interactive PC as a standard for a more consumer-orientated Wintel computer that includes a format for linking those PCs to a variety of consumer-electronic items. Gates says, 'We still have a long way to go to make the PC an appliance.' To assess how long, we can look at a recent poll by MIT when they asked people what invention they couldn't live without. The top answer was the automobile at 63 per cent while only 8 per cent cited the PC, which tied with the blow-dryer and was just below the microwave oven.

There is also a viewpoint that neither PC manufacturers nor consumer-electronic giants will be the future leaders in information appliances. The new market offers great opportunities for new entrepreneurial companies. As an example, some of the first information appliances to hit the market will be those designed by Diba Inc., started up by Farzad Dibachi, who was head of Oracle's new-media group. Diba has ideas for some 30 devices, each being a single-purpose item such as Diba Mail being a phone and e-mail combination.

Whatever the form of the future information appliance it is the software which will make it succeed or fail. Looking at the present systems, Web browsers have hidden the complexity of computers so that scanning the Internet is relatively easy, but improvements in software are still needed. The appreciation for the need for better software technology is acutely felt when one is side-tracked or overwhelmed on the Net – when, for example, a few words entered into a search engine answers with 26 983 possible matches. As a further result, software developers everywhere are working on ways to make the job easier for everyone, providing a user-friendly approach before the world's consumers rush to the Net. What is needed is an information appliance which is as easy as popping bread into the toaster to produce toast, and of course producing it at the right colour and definitely not burnt.

Whatever the final result, a startling report of a survey by Dataquest was announced in December 1996. It said that 93 per cent of American households do not intend ever to buy one of the various devices that enable access to the Web on domestic TV. This is obviously bad news for a product category that is supposed to appeal to the two-thirds of American households that do not own personal computers.

Part II
The Shopping Location

6 Traditional Shopping: From Bazaars to Shopping Centres

A review of the likely effects of technology on shopping would be fairly useless without a comparative review of traditional shopping as we know it. We should look at the historical background first, to see why and how the present shopping hierarchy has evolved and whether the basis for its undoubted success is likely to be undermined by new ideas. Then, perhaps, we should consider the present shopping developments – why they have taken their present form, their successes, and their failures. Then we should look at the future trends which are shaping new developments. Retailers' strategies are paramount, insofar as they echo the needs of the consumer.

These reviews will then need to be seen against the many facets of the present and future of electronic shopping developments, in order to gain a perspective on the effects, good or bad, of on-line shopping, and give a time frame of possible changes. I am pleased, if not a little self-satisfied, to remember that I raised the subject of the possibilities of computer information being endless in a paper I gave in February 1984. I said

> The new information era is going to happen. The whole structure of our families, single persons, work and leisure habits, will undergo a new outlook. How we change to meet this challenge will provide new opportunities. If we grab the opportunity and innovate, the next ten years holds amazing potential.

As I said earlier, I again raised the subject, more directly, during the British Council of Shopping Centres' Annual Conference in 1991. For these reasons alone, I feel that I have approached this task of seeking a reasoned and objective review of the effects of on-line shopping with some forethought and not as a protective knee-jerk reaction to the sudden realisation of a new phenomenon.

Shopping development has, until now, been concentrated on the primary need to locate as conveniently as possible to the shopping public estimated to be within it's conurbation. I say 'until now', because the concept of online shopping offers the prospect that geographical boundaries cease to exist and that, consequently, location will become unimportant. However, it is a fact that historically location has been ingrained in the shopping process. Retailing started with market stalls being set up at the cross-roads, hamlets and fords of Medieval towns, or as bazaars in Eastern town centres (see Plate 1). These were places where people would either congregate as the hub of the community, or pass on their travels to and from places of residence or migration. The stalls traded in livestock and supporting necessities of everyday life. These focal points have tended to become our protected national heritages during the succeeding centuries.

Throughout Europe, Asia and Africa, great markets and fairs were held as a combination of shopping and other attractions. In Britain, the Romans formalised the system which was already well established before their arrival. The term 'Fair', attached to markets or fairs, came from the Roman word 'feria'. But the name for the market comes from the Anglo-Saxon word 'chepping' or 'chipping', which became the modern-day 'shopping'. Towns such as Chipping Norton, in Oxfordshire, England, are evidence of the origins of markets in such places.

In the thirteenth and fourteenth centuries the boundaries of the great fairs were subject to Royal Charters and local laws, and the clergy imposed regulations over the conduct of traders and their customers. Some fairs originated from Christian festivals and celebrated local events, such as the feast day of the local parish saint.

As seen, the earliest shopping centres were located in places which were the areas where people congregated. These were town and community centres because residents either lived in the immediate locality, or travelled to the centre of the town to transact commerce, or attend gatherings for social purposes. The towns grew as more space was required to house the residents, or commercial services and merchants to serve the growing populations. Civic and community amenities were established so that the town hall, libraries, art galleries, theatres, parks and other public needs were supplied. The spirit of the community hub increased. People knew that their social and commercial needs could be fulfilled within the town centre. As commerce broadened its geographical interface, visitors from other areas and other towns visited and spawned a quasi-tourist influx. Shops and merchandise changed to include articles which were unique to the area and became an industry for strangers who would advertise the qualities and products of the town to yet more people, who were introduced to its delights.

The development of the shop should be understood against the background of the differentiation of retail trade. This started with the closed society of the Guilds, which did not permit advertising, competition, or increased rates of exchange. It has developed until today, with capitalist marketing methods, promotion of demand and fast turnover of goods. As we have seen, this massive change, even over such a long time, was made possible by the improved transport systems, mass production methods, and mobility of consumers and commodities. The social changes, which have paralleled the changes in architecture and distribution, created the expanded bourgeois public which seeks the goods sold in these shops.

In the Middle Ages there were three social groups involved in retail trade. There was the hawker, who was a travelling retail dealer carrying his goods in a basket on his back. Even quite recently I remember signs above doorways saying 'No Hawkers'. The hawker dealt with anyone he could find and in small quantities. There was the shopkeeper, who was a settled retail dealer. He traded usually in cloth, spices, drugs, metal and iron wares. His business was located in a booth, being an open shop. The location and extent of his business was decreed by the Guilds and his supplies were provided from merchants and wholesalers. Thirdly, there was the handworker or artisan. He also often had his own shop in front of his workshop. He worked on commission or kept articles in stock and was part of a strictly regulated association. Specialisation began in retail with the end of the Middle Ages. The retail market had four main specialisations – grocery, dry goods, ironmongery and second hand goods.

About the middle of the eighteenth century a new type of shop evolved from this broad spectrum of retail business. This was referred to as the 'consumption goods' business. There were three different types. The fashion business developed out of the shop of the mercer concerned with the silk trade. It sold not only the material, but anything belonging to a fashionable outfit. Second, the interior decorating business from the shop of the tapestry maker. It grew to a large supply business able to furnish an apartment or salon with a range of goods including mirrors, candelabras, sofas, carpets, paintings and etchings. Thirdly, the luxury item business providing costly and superfluous objects, exotic curiosities, knick-knacks, and gifts. Its clientele consisted of browsers and people of leisure. Is it not curious that the terms are so similar to those used today on the Internet?

The three types of shops contained the basic ingredients of the future department store, catering to a mixed public from courtly society, wealthy nobility, and the nouveaux riches of the bourgeoisie. Their customers were not yet a mass market as we know it today, but it was an extensive section of the privileged class that wanted to be treated differently. These customers had the wish to be treated as they ordered and had reasonably unlimited credit to do that. Customer service, the decor of the shop and the enticement of the customer became a science for these shops. The large supply required high inventories, large investment and grand premises. To meet the demands of its customers, shops had to employ many staff and errand boys.

Common to these shops was the trade in luxury goods. The rise of the luxury business had a deep and lasting effect on the retail trade. During the early stages of capitalism, the wholesale trade had some branches which were capitalist without being involved with the luxury trade, but there seems to be no single capital retail dealership before the nineteenth century, which did not deal in luxury goods. In the period around 1700, it can be seen that the demand for luxury items, and the need or desire of the retailer to meet it, were connected to the increased tendency toward an extravagant lifestyle among the wealthy. These were the decades when the attempts to meet the demands of the wealthy for luxury items took the trader out of the artisans' role and radically advanced the development of capitalism.

A good example of the effects can be seen from a look at the Passage de l'Opéra in Paris in 1826, (see Plate 2). One could find fashion goods, luxury items, culinary delicacies, paintings and furniture side by side. It is, in effect, a department store, but still consists of individual shops. It is similar to a department store, because you can still buy a large variety of goods without leaving the building. Also the arcade offered other amusements and attractions and, therefore, became a social centre. Around 1800 other forms of development emerged, such as the bazaar and later the department store itself. The reason for the trend toward reorganisation was industrialisation, which gave mass production of identical merchandise, uniform pricing, great capital demand, rapid turnover, reduction of stock and a less personalised customer. Over-production caused competition, reduction of prices and faster turnover, which in turn caused expansion of the shopping area, increased supply and more sophisticated advertising.

If we take the development to its ultimate, as accomplished by about the end of the nineteenth century, the final stages of development of the retail trade into capitalist big business had mail order treating customers as a file card. Thus the final degree of general customer anonymity was reached.

The original state of the shop was a formless arrangement in which goods were spread out on the floor. To this day, such customs can be seen in similar form (see Plate 3). The next stage saw a market structure including carts, trading stands with a table and protective covering, movable stands, sturdy booths with locks, and finally rows of shops divided according to the groupings of artisans. As seen, the steps taken toward a marketing system was institutionalised by Guilds, class structure and urban authorities. The predecessor of the shop was the booth with two large wooden chests and two flaps which open up, one serving as a protective eave. The trader and the customer stood opposite one another in the normal manner of market vending. The space is leased, but evolves over time to allow the trader to have sufficient tenure or ownership to construct a building in place of the fixed booth. This became a series of rooms such as a storage room, shop and apartment. Nevertheless, the shop still retained the basic form of an open box which could be closed by a wooden flap.

Then provision was made for entry into the shop by taking the table inside the shop and shifting the site of trade to the interior. However, this gave the problem that the merchandise could not be directly seen by the customer passing by. Advertising, in the form of written names and signage, was used to attract the attention of the passing trade. The open shop was closed and the flap became the door and shop window. The invention of cast glass by the Frenchman, Lucas de Neheon, in 1688, made it possible to manufacturer larger, and more importantly, clear, glass plates which gave a better view into the shop. Although such glass was originally used for the production of mirrors, one of the main luxury items of the eighteenth century, mass production reduced the high price and made such glass available to people other than courtly circles.

The first glass windows appeared at the beginning of the eighteenth century, generally confined to the luxury goods businesses. It was not until the middle of that century, however, that shops with windows which offered a view of the inside and of the goods on display, were widespread. About 1850 the panes produced were large enough to give fewer divisions and permit just one sheet. In the nineteenth century the area of glass window became a feature, with the entrance being set back to provide greater display areas. The presentation of the goods became 'window dressings' which were the responsibility of a special decorator.

This evolution was aided by rapid extensions and improvements in roads and other means of communication. In effect, over relatively a quite short space of time, the developments and attractions of commercial success were transmitted to other towns which followed suit. As we know, this continued until the present day, when road, rail and air brings all towns and cities in easy reach of the traveller. This is an interesting comparison with the claims of the Internet promoters, that the Net has no quality of space, bringing its offer to your home, wherever it actually is geographically. It may be true that there is no need to endure the tedium of travel, but many find the travel and change of scenery a stimulation in itself, and clearly would be opponents of the 'sit at home and watch the screen' syndrome. Even travel offers the opportunity of shopping, such as at airports or stations (see Plate 14). Indeed the phenomenal success of airport shopping has shown that millions of business and tourist travellers continue to have the urge to shop personally, either for last-minute necessities or for other goods when they have the time to browse. Passengers, and those who are at airports for other reasons, seem to use their waiting time to good effect. Sales figures of shop units at airports are truly amazing and there are numerous examples of sales per square foot far exceeding levels usually seen in the high street. As a result more space is being planned at almost every airport for shopping centres around the travel lounges and concourses and base rents plus percentage rents based on turnover are rocketing due to the demand by retailers wishing to take advantage of this captive market. The lesson must be that people like to shop when they have time, or it is convenient. Apparently they do not ignore the opportunity to shop on the basis that they would rather use electronic or home shopping, even though they must carry their purchases as additional baggage on a plane or train, instead of the convenience of having it delivered to their home.

Shopping development, indeed all forms of retail and trading expression, must be seen in the context of an ever-changing environment of the town, region, country, continent, and in today's speed of communication, the world. This acceptance by professional developers has overcome their former stubborn refusal to accept that they are in the merchandising business, just as much as their retail tenants.

The essential success which any trader achieves enables him or her to make a profit and pay the rent. This stems from a successful shopping centre, welcoming the shoppers and catering for their needs and aspirations. Developers are obviously foremost, in the business of bricks and mortar, but this activity is merely the means of constructing the end product and investment value, which gives the tangible expression of the planning form to house the trading entity.

For many years both retailers and landlords have voiced the opinion that there is a partnership between them. This has, more often than not, been a hope rather than a reality. That there is a normal distrust between them is a reflection of the lease terms and negotiations, including often strong arguments and stances on the rent to be paid, the specific clauses in the lease setting out the use to which the shop may be put and the merchandise types which can be sold. Retailers feel that they are making a major capital investment in their unit and that they must be permitted to conduct their business without undue interference. As a result, they resent a landlord telling them what they may or may not be allowed to do. The landlord looks to safeguard his investment and wants to ascertain that the management principles applied maintain the quality of the property and the overall cohesion of the entire entity. Here lie the main bones of contention, for the retailer will resent rules and regulations which curtail his free hand at doing whatever may be thought necessary to be successful for his own shop, while the landlord has a dual perspective of allowing and encouraging the best trading results overall for a numerous collection of retailers. If, for example, a trader wants to deliver goods to his shop by trucking over a public mall during trading hours because he needs them, he is less interested in the effects on a neighbouring trader caused by his action than the landlord. It is interesting, however, to note how many times a retailer wants such freedom yet complains when another retailer ignores the same rules, causing the same type of disruption to him. The fact is that, particularly in managed shopping centres, the trading results of those where all traders observe rules which are for good of all tend to perform the best.

Nothing serves to illustrate the fact that landlords and retailers will continue to have different outlooks than the results of a panel at a shopping centre management conference I attended a few years ago. The topic of the discussion was 'What retailers really hate about shop leases'. One of the main 'hates' was that standard British leases have a clause which allows only upward rental escalations at the periodic reviews during the lease term. Why shouldn't rents go down as well as up if the rental value has declined? There was considerable feeling expressed on this argument, with the overall sentiment that landlords were grossly unfair. At question time, I pointed out that all of the retailers represented on the panel had large property portfolios and frequently leased shops which they no longer wished to occupy to other retailers. Did they have clauses in the lease agreements they agreed with their tenants which had rent reviews either upward or downward? There was an embarrassed silence, but finally it was conceded that in all cases they were upward only. They were thinking as landlords when they were in that position, contrary to their most strongly expressed views when they were thinking as retailers.

But wait, you may say. In America there is more of a partnership because retailers understand the need to cooperate fully for the ongoing success of a shopping entity and owners help their tenants because their rental income is based on a percentage of sales. There has certainly been a great deal of truth in that statement in the past, but landlords granted shorter leases and had the opportunity to get rid of poorly performing or non-complying tenants without restrictions of statutory regulations. Recently, however, there has been a lot of evidence that the close relationship between owners and traders has degenerated and that 'them and us' attitudes have surfaced.

7   From Merchants to the Modern Consumer Boom: Effects on Towns

The original merchants in the markets were wholesalers and they provided the goods in smaller quantities to the retailers. In fact, the word 'retail' means the sale of commodities or goods in small quantities, and is based upon the old English and French root, 'tailor' which had the original meaning of 'to cut [into small pieces]'. Nowadays, goods sold in retail trade are convenience, essential or durable goods. The description of convenience goods is applied to the criteria of price, value and style etc, essentially by function, and durables by reference to their longevity. Convenience goods are used for everyday essentials and necessities, such as food. In the United Kingdom the definition is restricted mainly to foodstuffs, while in the United States it usually includes other items such as liquor and hardware, chemists' supplies and some services such as dry cleaning. Comparison goods, on the other hand, are usually chosen with a view to price, quality, measure and suitability. Clothing and home decor items would be examples, and are part of a list which normally comprises durables and semi-durables.

The consumer boom, revolving around the motor car, exploded in America but overtook Europe even more quickly. A new attraction of a bourgeois life emerged, aided by governments seeking growth in their economies.

In a talk I gave in 1973, I referred to a study by Bell and Kahn which defined the emergence of a 'post-industrial society' in the next thirty years, in which time and space would no longer be a problem in communications. What prescience they had. By the year 2000, they said, the United States should be a post-industrial society with a *per capita* income of $7500 per annum. In 1994, still six years short of the millennium, the per capita income was *$22 047, rising to $23 208 in 1995 and $24 269 in 1996.* The income of the United Kingdom in 1994 *per capita* was $15 961 or about £10 900. Bell and Khan predicted that there would be only four work days of seven hours per day and the year would be 39 work weeks and 13 weeks of holidays. With weekends and holidays this would amount to only 147 working days and 218 days of leisure per year. All forecast within a single generation. No wonder that David Reisman acerbically commented 'leisure may become what workers recover from at work'. These projections, considered so fantastic at the time, are not so difficult to accept now. Even then, these factors should have had a most important bearing on retailing patterns, and the buildings required to meet them.

The view of the future predicted that populations would continue to achieve spectacular increases in income and changes in lifestyles. And so it came to pass. As people improved their standards of living, each one wanted their own house, garden, car, second car, second home. Roads had to expand, crossing and recrossing urban areas which already showed incredible land shortage. Thus, the most spectacular change in Europe, as in America, was the relentless spread of the suburb. Between many cities such as between Frankfurt and Mainz, or between The Hague and Rotterdam, it is difficult to see where one ends and the other begins. The density of the European countries can be illustrated by the example of the United Kingdom at 239 people per square kilometre in 1994 compared to 27 in America in 1995. This is an important fact to remember when thinking about transport, car ownership and regional shopping centre catchments and competition. The Randstadt in Holland is an almost continuous suburb and the Channel Tunnel has the potential to extend the pressures of South East England eastwards to the Rhine and Ruhr, giving planners tremendous, if not insoluble, problems as the suburbs spread still further.

During this period of vast and rapid expansion, the suburbs of nearly all cities appear almost the same with similar houses and cars, and local supermarkets selling the same Coca Cola, Persil and universal brand names. Above all, then, the suburbs with their conformity and populations, following firstly the American styles, then a more universal standard of product and lifestyle, illustrate the invasion of consumer durables which has, over the past twenty-odd years changed living habits.

Despite these factors and the general sameness resulting from the influence of consumer durables and more universal design applications, many regions retain an individual character which keeps making it difficult to be confident of an overall standardisation in the post-industrial society. In their living patterns, greatly influenced by national traits, there is still a big difference between, say, Paris or Hong Kong with their frantic intensity, and Amsterdam with its more relaxed and measured atmosphere similar to London.

Some people feel that the tourist industry aids and abets a false impression and a false facade to the centre of cities. It is felt that the Reeperbahn in Hamburg, Montmârtre in Paris or Rembrandtsplein in Amsterdam show more the character of foreign visitors than the local atmosphere, which is otherwise shown in the history and national architectural styles. In my opinion, it is not correct to base an opinion on tourist areas obviously catering for a specific target need and confined to a relatively small sector of the city, and pretend that the city itself no longer has an individual character, but is comparable with anywhere else. This failure to recognise individuality lends weight to the argument that electronic shopping can be anonymous in the same way, yet just as effective. Proper regard should be given to the attraction of a city, or a place in that city, for people to respond emotionally. If this is seen and accepted, the faceless shopping experience of online visits can be assessed and compared in a balanced way.

Throughout Europe, with some notable exceptions, the same mixture of new developments, mixed with obsolescent antiquated buildings, can be seen, combined with traffic congestion. The European intellect does not easily allow its tradition and history to disappear, but the pressures of traffic and demand for modernisation poses a tremendous problem for the planners. I suggested, in 1973, that the answer was not the creation of out-of-town centres, at the expense of the very hub of the community, as seen in America. Unfortunately, out-of-town development was allowed, and in some cases encouraged. Many such schemes were supported on the grounds that major space units, and bulk shopping in particular, should not be allowed in town centres, where they would add to traffic generation or destroy existing townscapes. At last the issue of more enlightened planning guidelines, albeit over twenty years later, have taken account of the effects wrought on our towns. The economic effects of major centres in Britain such as Lakeside, Thurrock, on the neighbouring old established town of Grays, the early effects of Metrocentre on Newcastle, and Meadowhall on Sheffield, or more recently of CentrO on Oberhausen in Germany, are examples. Even given that the massive regional centres are successful in their own right, and in some cases the cities or towns have finally redressed the economic balance, it seems logical that the same or similar capital investment in the cities themselves might have had the better trading result while improving the city infrastructure for the future. It could be argued that if the local shopping public in the conurbation had visited the same style of space in the city (the argument being that the demand for it existed and that it was taken from that place), it could have been retained as developed or redesigned space if there had been an application of more enlightened and farseeing planning policies.

Since the early 1950s, when that great architect Victor Gruen, conceived Southdale Plaza (Plate 4), America has been the leader in the type of enclosed regional shopping centre development we have come to recognise as the model, on a massive scale. Southdale, located in Edina, Minnesota, a suburb of Minneapolis, was opened by Dayton-Hudson in October 1956 and was America's first fully enclosed, climate-controlled mall with competing department stores as anchors. Europeans have looked to the Americans for inspiration and education in shopping centre development ever since. Even the last fifteen years or so, when the European developers were evolving new shopping centres of equal attraction, did not diminish the need to view new centres in America, or to adopt the new concepts, trading styles or general progress of a country in which commerce is a vital market leader in the economy. The glamour of huge regional malls, vast car parking facilities and locations at highway intersections present an ideal which attract the ambitions of Europeans who are themselves restricted by local infrastructures and more stringent planning and statutory regulations. In more recent years, the examples of similar centres have become customary in almost every developed country.

But references to the effects of out-of-town centres on cities can be seen by a look at what I said in a talk at a retail forum as long ago as 1988:

A strange thing has happened in America, in the land which we have so long regarded as setting the perfect example. While the regional out-of-town shopping centres were being developed so successfully, the inner cities – the downtowns – were affected and went into serious decline. Inner city deprivation has contributed to huge social problems.

As we fostered the idea of out-of-town shopping centres and caused controversial debate about the protection of our inner cities, America is now actively regenerating its own neglected downtown areas.

It is interesting, yet so disappointing, that we have increased our concern at the plight of the inner cities and still need to extensively refer to those problems in many parts of the world, not least in Britain. The future use and accessibility of technology by the poorer sector of the population appears to involve a continuation of, and probable increase in, the divide between 'haves' and 'have nots' (see Chapter 10). It seems amazing to me that these situations were clearly signposted for our politicians and planners to see so many years ago, without any likely solution having been accomplished.

At that time I referred to major new projects such as Horton Plaza, San Diego, which had been completed and served as a new example (see Plate 5). Apart from the innovative form of that open air centre in downtown San Diego, designed by Jon Jerdé, something bordering close to a pastiche of an Italian Renaissance street, with spectacular colours and irregular forms, the development by the Hahn Group showed a new belief in the city. The brilliance of the development itself, anchored by department stores of Nordstrom and Robinsons, was that it flirted with the pastiche while being an individual design. What did all these projects represent? They showed a desire to regain a quality for the city centre, which was something that Europeans had never relinquished in a formal sense, although in practice many cities did seriously endanger their future security by starting to accept the policy of out-of-town centres by aiding policies for moves of, at least, bulk trading, out of the town.

Our towns and cities have wonderful advantages of centuries of tradition and historical evolution affording architectural, cultural and leisure opportunities for the pleasure of their residents and visitors. These same features have, however, provided major obstacles to development, in planning terms, to meet the needs of the modern consumer society. Many learned papers have been produced, statistics emanated from researchers and vociferous debates held on the subject of town centre versus out-of-town retailing. I raised the matter in my keynote speech as Chairman of the International Council of Shopping Centres' European Conference in The Hague in March 1986, in order to raise it publicly in the knowledge that it was likely to generate considerable debate, but also in the belief that such airing might provoke considered action to overcome problems clearly arising from lack of thought in certain quarters and lack of clear policies in others. It seemed to be a situation being driven by an amalgam of consumer requirements, retailers' ingrained preferences, developers' entrepreneurial motivation, investors' opportunism, planners' ineptitude, local authorities' fear and bias and, not least, central government's lack of a firm guiding and far-seeing strategy.

Perhaps it is best to firstly see why problems existed in the past. Generally speaking, Development Plans, and town centre plans in particular, failed to foresee, and provide for, the change in the consumer profile, the consumer boom and the response to these factors needed in retailing forms. We all recognise that we cannot operate in a theoretical vacuum, and that consumer needs are perceived and influenced by advertising and the impact of other items. Such experiences as travel and the viewing of other retailing has a profound effect on the way shoppers decide to approach their buying habits. In effect, it has been left to private enterprise in the main to lead the way and create the solutions through better educated shopping centre professionals, including retailers. This has not been an easy task, for all development must comply with planning regulations, which in turn are administered by the very people who appear to be the arbiters of size, usage and style. It is not unusual for this to also include subjective aesthetic preferences, such as brick versus concrete, or even the colour of the bricks! Building control and fire regulations, together with highways authorities, govern the building itself, its siting, mass and traffic generation of cars, service vehicles and public utilities. It is fundamentally true, however, that there is a normal adherence to tried and tested methods, I think mainly due to the PYA[1] syndrome. It can be appreciated that public officers can see no special benefit in approving new methods which will bring major criticism if they go wrong, while bringing no plaudits if successful. There is a good example of building methods during the refurbishment of The Royal Exchange Shopping Centre carried out by my company. We employed Leigh Speakman, an outstanding Canadian Retail Designer with long experience of marvellous projects, who specified tinted mirrors to clad all the internal columns. The English architects prepared a detail which had complicated fixings screwed into the structure, together with fixing beads and anodised aluminium cover strips to hide the fixings to give a neat finish. Leigh was

---

1.   A crude acronym for 'Protect Your Arse', indicating a method of making sure that no blame or liability is likely to fall on the person dealing with the matter.

horrified at the time it was taking to carry out a simple task, but was told that the District Surveyor would not approve another method due to the possibility that the mirrors might fall off the columns. When asked for his usual method in North America, he said 'the glazier takes the mirror, puts fixative on the back, and sticks it up!' Never had he known strong fixative to fail, but he did know of screws coming out. This may not be directly related to the overall planning or concept, but it shows the thought process which might, more profitably, be used at all stages of a development – in other words, a more open and inviting mindset. On the basis that it needed private enterprise to take the lead and design new directions for the overall concept of shopping centres, it is clear that the final decisions allowing such enterprise is left in the hands of a relatively inexperienced or uneducated group of civil servants. Departures from an agreed or well tried and tested set of regulation-based formulae is not an easy thing to accomplish.

The market forces of a massive and rapid increase in the individual sizes of retail units required by retailers to cater for their expanded inventory to meet increased demand from the consumer, variety of merchandise and new sales techniques, placed an unbearable pressure on the existing stock of retail space. This was exacerbated by the spate of mergers between companies, leading to amalgamations of traders, economies of scale and increased trading requirements. In addition, the introduction of new overseas traders added to the numbers and different standards and styles of shop units expected by the customer.

Highway authorities and local planning authorities failed to provide adequate or convenient traffic systems. This has been evident both where new developments have taken place and also where the authorities have acted as a deterrent to such developments. As we have noted, traffic congestion in almost all our towns is a major issue and has led to local authorities seeking the expedient of diverting large generators of car-borne shoppers out-of-town. I say this is an expedient, not as a condemnation of the principle but because many such decisions were as a result of the failure of planning to cater for a signposted phenomenon – the increase in personal car ownership and its use for shopping purposes. There has even been little evidence to support the argument that bulk purchases generate more frequent visits. If this argument is correct, it also means that the consequentially less frequent use of the car on this sector has been diverted out of the town, leaving the more frequent small-item shopping visits to the wider choice to be found downtown. Thus the solution chosen by planners has proved to focus on ridding the town of those who use the facilities least and keeping those who use it most frequently.

There was a failure to provide adequate planned parking in towns for those shoppers who do visit, or else failing to ensure that such car parks which were provided were suitable. They are often ill located, poorly designed and, if not utilitarian, are sometimes threatening or downright dangerous. The recent initiatives to combat inner city crime with grants for town centre CCTV has many references to car parks. The additional cost to the public of these precautionary works could have been avoided by good planning and better management techniques. Indeed, many more recent planning policies have positively operated to the exclusion of parking spaces, in accordance with a general policy to rid the town centre of cars. This serves as another example of the lengths local authorities have had to go, because they have not formulated an answer to the problem by providing an adequate infrastructure needed to maintain a town's trading draw. It almost seems to say that if towns do not know how to cater for their visitors they tell them to stay out. I do not know many enterprises who would turn away custom in that way, but in this case we must assume that civil servants have a different commercial approach to business generation for towns compared to other enterprises. This appears to be at variance with examples in North America. There, a recent panel of mayors from major cities at a major shopping centre convention stressed their welcome to developers to act in a partnership for the renaissance of central areas. They were open in offering to invest a large proportion of public funds toward the infrastructure needed to support major shopping and mixed use developments. It would not be inconceivable for a city to say 'you invest in a major new development and we will provide a car park for 10 000 cars, because we know that our citizens need it to patronise our city'. I add the unstated additional motive and commercial incentive, which is the added property taxes and sales taxes which will be generated by maintaining commercial viability.

Due to the pressures of demand in the central core trading areas, much caused by the lack of sufficient development planning to meet forecast space requirement, rental values escalate. The added service costs and high property taxes in central areas needed to service community facilities are compared to much lower comparative costs of overheads in out-of-town locations. This is aggravated by the high costs of public services due to the maintenance of old infrastructures through lack of planning and general estate management in the past. The urgent repair and renewal works which have been required for antiquated sewers is a typical example. In addition, bad traffic management adds to delays and inefficiencies, causing higher costs to the retailer. Further planning of pedestrianisation has sometimes been carried out without sufficient thought to the servicing problems caused. It appears that the majority of pedestrianisation schemes have had a good effect on retail trading and are generally welcomed by the public. In some cases this has led to restricted servicing hours for deliveries, which also increases costs to the retailer. These are all costs which a retailer in a purpose built out-of-town centre is unlikely to face, because of proper pre-planning and, ironically, the regulations imposed by the town planners for such facilities, the capital cost of which is incorporated by the developer in his project cost.

The commercial thrust and professional education in the basic needs of a retail business is lacking in local authority and planning officers. This is required in order to maintain the competitive advantage of town centres, and the general absence of such commercial cognisance opens the trading attractions of the town centre to attack from competitive locations. It would be easy to anticipate the outrage which these criticisms might provoke, but the fact that we recognise a deficiency does not mean that those given the task of carrying out certain briefs for the town are personally culpable. It is more probable that the general policy for the town has been directed without clear thought for the future based on fully qualified or educated knowledge by minds focused on narrow specialisms. If the responsibility for the work has been delegated to someone whose expertise is in another, probably associated, field even the best endeavours are unlikely to provide the best solution possible. The lack of expert in-depth knowledge, while perfectly understandable, makes it difficult to empathise with external interests who are advocating a different solution. And, before there is further defence and fury that I am suggesting something unreasonable, I reflect that many towns and cities have appointed Town Centre Managers in the past few years. They have a defined brief to manage the town in a similar way to a shopping centre and have grown, at least in Britain, to the extent that there is a thriving Town Centre Management Association. London has its London First group which is a high powered committee set up to do what its name suggests. If it has been necessary to have such managers and promoters it belies the claims that existing and past officers have been the best placed or qualified to look at the commercial requirements as an ancillary consideration to planning and control needs. Rather, it would seem to underline the acceptance that this specialised function and knowledge is not only expert but essential.

I was heartened to note that I am not a lone voice on this subject. In the editorial leader of *Retail Week*, a leading British publication, on 6 June, 1997, the Editor, Kate Oppenheim, offered a similar opinion. I can do no better than quote her words, in their entirety in view of their importance. Under the headline 'Working for a common goal' she said,

> Retailers, particularly Tesco, did not miss the opportunity to lobby local government representatives over what many see as 'abuse of powers' of guideline documents, such as PPG6.
>
> Delegates at the Cities International conference in London this week, the vast majority of whom were local authority representatives, were reminded of the enormous contribution that retailers make to urban regeneration. They were asked to form closer relationships with companies and be more willing to work hand-in-hand, to create a more prosperous future for Britain's towns and cities.
>
> After all, what is the point of retailers and developers working hard to be more creative and visionary in their approach to new projects when planning committees – some of which are made up of people who are totally unfit to judge whether a particular scheme should be given the go-ahead – use Government guidelines as if they were legislation set in stone?
>
> Customers are bored with lookalike high streets and shopping centres. They want to be visually stimulated and entertained and, with the growth in home shopping, this will become even more important for the future success of retailing.
>
> Without planners who understand the retailer's point-of-view, and acknowledge that major companies are willing to make multi-million pound investments in schemes which will provide new facilities for towns and cities, everyone will continue to lose out. Retailers have the largest property development programmes in the country. Indeed, Tesco claims that, outside the Ministry of Defence, it spends more money on property investment than

any other company in the UK. It is also the largest developer of brown field sites, which are hugely expensive to develop for residential use.

The good news is that the new Labour Government appears to be more sympathetic, and hopefully will be more willing to offer retail development a lifeline. But local authorities must still be re-educated and encouraged to stop seeing retailers and their development plans as the enemy, and instead view them for what they really are – 'the goose that can lay the golden egg'.

Although there are some comments which smack of supporting the retailers' camp, the general sentiment is one which should be applauded. Retailers act in the best interest of their shareholders to make profits by selling to the customer. As such, they are providing shopping space in places where their very superior research shows a demand by the consumer. If democracy is the guide, it seems to follow that the public vote is to allow such development. If our local authority officers and committees take a different view to their citizens, it should be based on an expert opinion: such expertise is not generally evident.

Many planning officers have expressed concern that the incredible increase in road traffic has caught them by surprise. This may be a simple statement of fact, but it cannot excuse the woeful lack of applied thought to the clearly emerging trend and the problems which were destined to arise. It was not as if the effects of the motor car were not there to be seen, nor that the results of solutions elsewhere, typified by countless case studies and obvious visual examples were unavailable. An old cliché says that 'today America sneezes and tomorrow the rest of the World has a cold'. Europe, then the rest of the developed world, avidly followed America in shopping centre development, more latterly in the building of Regional shopping centres, both in and out-of-town. In America the construction of out-of-town shopping, and the ready acceptance by shoppers of their convenience, led to what was called 'the doughnut principle'. This was due to the downtown areas becoming empty while surrounded by the migration of population to surrounding areas. Therefore, it could easily be seen, well in advance of actions elsewhere, that a similar policy of moving shopping out of the town centres might provide a short-term solution to the amount of shoppers' cars in the towns, but would with almost absolute certainty denude downtowns of much of their vibrance or life. The situation was even worse in Europe than in America because of the longer cultural and emotional links with the city cores. I have often said that a doughnut is best if it retains jam in the centre.

Thus, in essence, consumer needs have not been addressed sufficiently, or in some cases at all. There has been a steady polarisation of shoppers requiring simple choice, competitive prices, self-collection, good parking facilities and simplicity, versus those still requiring style, comfort, speciality and the pleasure of a cultured environment. Planning should increase consumer efficiency, consumer choice and consumer economy, while, at least, maintaining the environmental standards of our modern world.

As a result of these factors, in particular, a number of things happened. Perhaps the major effect, aided by the planning policies of town centres and the general liberalisation of planning consents and use out-of-town sites, has been that most major bulk retailers have raced to maintain their market share alongside their competitors, by opening large retail warehouses on the peripheries and 'green field' sites. It has been a case of one out, all out. In the food sector, supermarket groups have proliferated, with superstores springing up in almost every conceivable place which might attract the car borne shopper. Often several stores operated by the same group can be seen within the same conurbation, presumably in an attempt to close out its competitors, who would otherwise develop the site and add to the competition. There is substantial evidence that the laws of diminishing return are starting to bite, rather in the same way as the perpetual undercutting and discount wars in food have done. Foodstores have seemingly accepted that the opening of still more superstores out-of-town must have its limitations and 'metro' stores of smaller size are being pursued again in town centres. Full circle, in effect, since that was where the supermarkets started. The irony is that local planning policies encouraged the move out-of-town and now have both out-of-town and the original comparative amount of space in town. This has marked similarities to the comments I made above about decentralisation of business space in offices when referring to the future prospects of outworking. There may even be support for my arguments on that subject from this trend. Supermarket groups usually make huge demographic data considerations before embarking on a building programme and it would seem logical to assume that they would not invest heavily downtown if they thought the working population was to disperse to outwork.

The early days of sites becoming available led to strong competition for those prime areas sought by bulk retailers. As the sites became more commonplace, the appetite increased with the ultimate situation that near-saturation is becoming evident. At each stage of this evolution there has been an inevitable pressure of demand over supply, with the resultant pressure on rents, which have increased. Similarly, investors have accepted that the tenants tend to be large first-rate risks on long leases, with little estate management required. The yields have declined to prime rates similar to town centre prime properties. Consequently, the letting and investment market has been very active.

The design of the early retail warehouse and cash-and-carry 'shed' space has been upgraded, with more grandiose external appearance to satisfy environmental concerns and, in some cases, quite sophisticated and well designed interiors to attract the customer. The overall layouts of retail parks together with the retail warehouse designs, has meant that simple retail sheds have become schemes which are a short step from a shopping centre. The example of the MetroCentre at Gateshead in the Northeast of England is indicative. What commenced life as obsolete land with the prospect of a proposed development of warehouses in an Enterprise Zone[1] with a ten-year freeze on property taxes, is rumoured to have quickly become a conception of a collection of retail warehouses, having a general retail planning use, which could then be linked together into a large area of retail. A short step into an overall envelope, with massive surrounding open car parking and redesigned internal finishes of a shopping centre. With general retail user the result was a superb example of the regional shopping centre.

---

1. Enterprise Zones were set up by the British government as areas for development to encourage employment where there was a high unemployment rate. One of the main incentives was to provide a ten-year property tax holiday, predominately targeted at industrial and manufacturing uses.

8 Out-of-Town and Town Centres

The problems, and the events, which have been described as a small section of the many incidental components of the retail planning process over the past twenty years have had both good and bad effects on town centres. Although some, mainly smaller, towns evoke a character of the market place, and all it should convey, for the sale of such items as food, household goods, etc. it is now generally accepted that bulk food retailing, DIY items and so on, should be located more conveniently out-of-town, but equally could be placed on the edge of the central area. It is true, however, that this has released property for retailers who are more suitable to town centres and that the result has been a greater variety which is more sympathetic to the central environment.

The rush for sites on main roads, and other peripheral and out-of-town locations, has led to a multiplication of similar trades in the same localities, or sometimes even duplication of the same trader in order to keep other competitors out. Stretches of main arteries such as Edgware Road between Staples Corner on the North Circular Road and Burnt Oak in London, or Sainsburys acquiring and developing a second site on the Ring Road around Oxford illustrate this.

Roads such as Honeypot Lane, Kingsbury, NW London, Edgware Road, Colindale and the Tesco Superstore area of Watford are blocked or disrupted by cars waiting to turn from the main roads into retail units of B&Q, MFI, Do-it-All, etc. Right turning traffic and emerging cars, especially on Sundays, cause considerable problems.

Incidentally, the argument that the disbursement of bulk trading units helps overcome town centre traffic problems is an interesting one. Firstly, it would appear that any small gains which may have been achieved in town centres for the freeing of traffic flows, circulatory management, parking and service deliveries, has been negated by a relaxation by local authorities believing that they have solved the problems. Instead of building on the advantages with policies which will make the use of the town centre easier for car-borne shoppers, they have introduced new vehicular and pedestrian traffic management systems. In some cases they have removed parking areas and meter bays, increased fines and penalties, perpetuated hostile parking meter enforcement and increased pedestrianisation and road rearrangement, removing highway access from vehicles, to meet the needs of shoppers wanting to have easy walking access to the shopping core.

The increased pedestrian areas undoubtedly make the town centre more attractive for shoppers than they were before. Shoppers obviously like the segregation from traffic hazards, fumes and feeling of proximity. Nevertheless they also want easy access to the centre from their home together with ease of parking, comparatively cheap or free parking and a secure route from that parking area to the main shopping attraction. Except for those shoppers who use public transport, and in that case the transport needs to be good and reliable, the ability to walk in a town centre in a better environment and greater safety is of little use if the shopper cannot reach those areas in the first place with ease by their own vehicle and have no parking facilities once there.

Therefore, if the purpose of decentralising bulk goods which need cars as the means of self-collection is for the main purpose of easing traffic access and parking, does it work? The real test of all such problems is during peak shopping hours. A casual survey of many areas shows that retail warehousing, retail parks and out-of-town shopping centres are available to provide reasonable access and parking facilities for most of the time. Noted with concern, however, is that even centres such as Brent Cross, in NW London, with thousands of car spaces, has long queues of cars waiting to enter the car parks at peak times. Three weeks prior to Christmas, lines of cars were at a standstill on approach roads 45 minutes before the centre opened. The example of Lakeside Shopping Centre, a few miles north of the Dartford Tunnel east of London on the busy M25, from October onwards clearly shows long delays blocking the inner lane of this very busy motorway for miles in each direction. Although the time nearing Christmas is bad, I recently travelled on the M25 motorway in mid-summer and found the traffic very light until within about 10 miles of Lakeside. I then found a massive traffic jam in all lanes, crawling at a few miles an hour. Nearing the Lakeside turnoff, the traffic was filtering from the outside lanes into the inner lane before using the slip road. After this intersection the traffic continued to be extremely light and normal uninterrupted progress was resumed.

The complaints against planners in general, together with the inconvenience for other non-shopper road users, does not disguise the fact that shoppers themselves may have less passionate views on the specific issue of the planning environment. For all the queues, shoppers obviously love the Lakeside Centre, and are prepared to put up with the inconvenience to get the reward of being in a major venue to shop, eat, stroll and enjoy the environment. Perhaps the perception of the wait, in a car on a slow moving motorway, is that it is worth it because, well, it's not so much worse than waiting to find a space in smaller car parks in the nearest town, or a fight for a meter which gives limited time and the possibility of a large fine, clamping, or ultimately, removal. And there is the added time to travel through crowded roads with traffic lights, one-way streets and pedestrians. Oh, and once there we can walk to all the shops without getting wet. And so on . . .

The message is certainly getting across. Many areas of Kent are already under threat as a result of this major centre, which is the other side of the Thames Dartford Tunnel in Essex. But now Bluewater is coming toward a completion on the Kent side of the river. This massive centre, with about 1.6 million square feet, will be anchored by department stores of John Lewis Partnership, Debenhams, Marks & Spencer and a large number of chain stores. Old established shopping towns in Essex and Kent, some containing relatively recent town centre schemes, are having to consider how to combat the threats of these developments. Huge free car parking and just about every high street name shop under one roof, is a formidable competition. These developments do not happen overnight, as we have seen. There are years of planning consultations, followed by the gestation period and then the building period, letting and fitting out period, promotion and acclimatisation by shoppers. In all, a very long time. One might wonder, that if all this can be achieved from the start by a developer making compromises and negotiating in almost every direction, with the planners, environmentalists, highway authorities, fire officers, building contractors, financiers, and many more third parties, is it not possible for single local authorities to have sufficient time to promote plans to combat the obvious danger to their town centre's prosperity? When one looks at the progress of a number of towns so obviously in the firing line, the lack of concrete action is, at least, surprising.

A fast ride from the Dartford Crossing, along the M25 and down the M20 brings one to Maidstone, the county town of Kent. A quick journey, but conversely, exactly the same the other way, from Maidstone to Lakeside! The problem of this well established and thriving town is not only the question of how to provide modern competitive shopping but, as seen with others, how to deal with the car-borne shopper. Maidstone District Council appeared to have every intention of beefing up the shopping provision with the development of the former Fremlins Brewery site at the bottom part of the High Street adjoining the River Medway. This site already has planning permission for 370 000 square feet but a detailed planning application is still awaited from the alleged developer, who has replaced Hammerson, who withdrew. Although the Fremlin site is, in my opinion, off prime pitch it could make a good focal anchor for the town by being situated at one end of the town's shopping centre, whereas the Chequers Centre is at the other, with the established prime Week Street and other smaller shopping in between.

The Chequers Shopping Centre, with 350 000 square feet, has 1000 car spaces and now intends to add a further 420 to that number. It seems that Maidstone accepts that the car is essential for modern shopping success. They knew that the Fremlin Centre was unlikely to succeed unless the road access was substantially improved. Perhaps ten years ago, when I viewed the scheme, the restricted road via the bridge over the river, and the long delays in entering the town, caused considerable scepticism about viability. There still appears to be a grave doubt that the funds for the road improvements around the main entrance over the bridge, and adjoining what was the Fremlins Brewery site, will be available before the year 2000. It is to the credit of all parties that a scheme appears to be getting nearer, but again the time taken to get to this stage is alarming. If the town truly saw Lakeside and Bluewater as real competition, why has it taken until now to programme a local road system and think, only think, about detailed plans – let alone build and let a shopping centre which would seem to be a crucial part of Maidstone's strategy to retain its market share, after the opening of Bluewater.

If Maidstone accepts the need for cars in the town, the nearby famous tourist cathedral city of Canterbury appears to deny a welcome. They do not pretend that shoppers will not use cars, nor do they ignore the problem. They simply have a different approach. Basically, Canterbury wants to protect the heritage of its town centre. With an existing out of date car park capable of taking 1000 cars in the town centre, the Council now plans to halve that number when a new shopping development takes place. The development of the Whitefriars Centre by Land Securities will provide about 300 000 square feet of new retail space. In other words, the town has an existing traffic problem and insufficient spaces with its existing amount of retail floorspace and will increase that total retail area significantly while removing many of the present car park spaces. Is it just me who sees this action as strange, or have I missed something? It seems perverse that the Council wants to actually reduce the number of cars when they might have had an opportunity to at least maintain the amount in better arrangement or circumstances for shoppers. The Council says 'the Whitefriars area must be considered an integral part of the historic centre where the encroachment and impact of vehicles must be minimised'. How idealistically simple! Thus the Council's objective is to cater only for traffic which must be in the area for servicing or access and restrict on site car parking to an absolute minimum. This is endorsed by Tony Parker, Assistant Director of Architecture and Engineering, who says 'There's a positive discrimination against providing parking with office developments.'

The method employed by Canterbury to get shoppers to the shops is Park and Ride. These bus ferry schemes are seen by Canterbury as a means of keeping the traffic out of the centre while protecting the shopping viability. The Council is also anxious to see bus priority to ensure that buses will be able to enter the city before cars. Statistics are said not to be available. It seems reasonable to think that park and ride systems are very popular with everyone during summer months, but will they be so popular in the winter rain and cold, when the shopper is weighed down with several heavy bags and a couple of children in tow? It may be case of the City of Canterbury relying on the fact that it is one of the most sought-after locations for multiple traders, being a wonderful trading centre. As in all commercial situations, anyone who has a tremendous success should look to the future and guard against competition from similar offers elsewhere.

It can be seen, therefore, that attempts at decentralisation in order to avoid town centre traffic problems can, in some cases, cause corresponding traffic problems in tertiary areas which may have more far-reaching effects on general traffic patterns for a wider public than solely the previous town centre shopper.

If a shopper visits an out-of-town retail park and fails to locate convenient parking, perhaps in bad weather conditions, a decision may be made not to stay. Apart from the frustration which will probably lose that customer for ever, the shopper has the alternative of seeking another retail park, even though the first may have a solus trader not to be found elsewhere, but the shopper will have no greater certainty that the second will offer any better parking.

At shopping centres which do provide large numbers of car parking spaces shoppers may have to settle for spaces at peak times which are at a considerable walking distance from the retail destination. Milton Keynes Shopping Centre is an example where it has been known for visitors to tour the inner ring car park followed by the outer ring car park without success. Even if they find space and assuming that the weather is fine, a walk to the centre itself would take several minutes and once inside a walk in the malls can be a distance of up to a quarter of a mile. One is forced to wonder how this is more convenient, even compared to the less than ideal situation of parking on the edge of a small town, taking a bus or underground and facing a similar walk in more acceptable and pleasant environmental surroundings. The further extension of the centre may help to overcome this problem.

Attempts to tackle the traffic congestion and pollution problems show that the solution to one may be logical and acceptable in theory, but gives rise to other aggravations of the remaining situations. For example, the former British Environment Secretary John Gummer announced a ten-year plan for a reduction in pollution directed mainly at vehicle emissions. All local authorities will be required to monitor air quality in the same way that many do already. Stricter vehicle emission rules will encourage people to buy new cars. But the New Labour Party point out that the real cause of traffic generated pollution arises from greater dependence on private cars and the gradual decline in public transport. On the face of it, the measures will probably make users upgrade their cars or, with the passing of time, simply exchange them for newer models which conform to the requirements; it is unlikely that the dependence on the convenience of the private car will be given up, simply in order to comply with a measure which can be overcome quite easily. The fact is that the convenience of private transport is unlikely to be forsaken for inadequate public transport, unless and until circulation seizure is commonplace. Even then, such conditions will probably apply almost equally to public transport using the same road system as the cars. The underlying possibility of the New Labour Government's comment, made by them when in opposition, is that they may introduce direct taxation on car users as a means of control and redirection to public transport use, inadequate as it is.

To underline the comment that proposed solutions to one problem create others is seen by the probable effect of the anti-pollution measures on another policy issued by the very same Department. Planning Policy Guideline 6 (PPG6) was issued in order to discourage retailing in out-of-town locations. Planning Policy Guideline 13 (PPG13) directs new development to existing urban areas. The increase in development in this way would increase the concentration of congestion and pollution there. The policies are to limit out-of-town development and restore the vitality of the town centres, but there are opinions saying that more edge of town development could be the answer. Rory Joyce, of Chartered Surveyors Drivers Jonas, thinks that a superstore built in the suburbs can significantly reduce the length and number of car journeys. There should be a readily acceptable logic that a trip to a local or neighbourhood retail area will reduce the overall usage of cars, if the alternative is to drive fifty miles or more to a super regional centre. At least this is a sensible approach to bulk trading situations which I have supported elsewhere in this book, but again there is a hitch. Out-of-town developments actually increase car dependence, because there is usually no other convenient way to reach them. It also fights against the Government's desire to improve the quality and market attraction of the town centres. It is strange, and another example of the conflicting solutions to the problem, that the ways introduced to make town centres more attractive, such as pedestrianisation, parking and access, have increased congestion.

The Government's retail planning guidance, PPG6 Revised, was published in July 1996. In general, the document re-emphasises the contents of the draft PPG6. The effects of the guidance on various types of retail development follow the outline given in this section, but it may be useful to restate some of the most important thrusts:

- It is recognised that there may be circumstances where Regional Shopping Centres could fulfil an important retail need, but generally this is unlikely to be in accordance with the guidance criteria for new retail development. Where there is scope for such an argument, it must be identified in regional guidance, with proposals being progressed through the development plan process.

- It also recognises that large bulk stores may be unable to locate suitable sites in towns or edge-of-town locations. In such cases, it is for local authorities to ensure that they are located in places where they will still be easily accessible by a choice of transport means.
- Superstores are often an anchor in smaller town centres These are thought to be best situated on edge-of-town locations, allowing linked trips by shoppers. Here, the definition of 'edge-of-town' is to be determined by reference to easy walking distance, with most shoppers being unlikely to walk more than 200–300 metres from the primary shopping area.
- Factory Outlet Centres are seen as centres which draw customers from a wide catchment area, mainly by car. In the Guidance, they are, therefore, unlikely to conform to the criteria for new retail development, but they may be seen as a means of revitalising a declining town centre. An indicator of the impact of factory outlet centres can be acquired by looking at the statistics of Sawgrass Mills in Northern Florida which claims to be the second largest attraction of people after Disney.

According to a report in *Property Week* magazine in September 1996, the Government's planning guidelines are being used by Newcastle City Council as reasons to object to the proposed extension of Gateshead's MetroCentre, by Capital Shopping Centres. The proposal is for an additional 372 500 square feet and involves the construction of an Asda Foodstore and an extension to the existing mall to provide increased floor space for a Debenhams department store, 27 new shops and a new multi-storey car park for 1650 cars. The traffic impact report, submitted by Capital Shopping Centres, claims that the number of cars visiting MetroCentre would increase by 3000 a day, but according to Newcastle City Council, the A1 western bypass is operating above design capacity and any additional traffic would undermine the strategic role of the A1 through Gateshead. The arguments I have used elsewhere, that relocation of major retail out-of-town does not necessarily ease traffic congestion, but merely concentrates it in another place, is supported by the announcement in late June 1997 that Asda is to quit the MetroCentre to move to a larger store a quarter of a mile away. They claim that part of the reason is the failure to resolve the problem of day trippers forcing its shoppers to park too far away.

This situation is not unique to Britain. France has enforced a strict policy of control on shopping centres and retail development over a quite small space expansion for some time. Belgium has a system of both planning control and a socioeconomic permit which is considered by a separate group in order to allocate the actual trade uses of the proposed development. In Germany, there have been stringent controls over out-of-town development for some time. The recently opened, and very successful, CentrO Shopping Centre at Oberhausen may be the last centre to be developed out-of-town for a long time. Although the town of Oberhausen was not a thriving retail centre before CentrO, reports now indicate it is dead. There have been unsubstantiated statements that a more drastic order from the German government has now almost totally restricted the development of Factory Outlet Centres, which are seen as another major threat to the downtowns.

The attraction of Factory Outlet Centres to shoppers, and the effect they can have on other shopping may be seen from the success of Sawgrass Mills, which I refer to elsewhere. Situated in Northern Florida it is reported to have over 20 million visitors a year. Within 15 minutes drive at Plantation, there is Fashion Mall. This three level centre is a fine example of a good, modern and attractive centre anchored by two major department stores. Recent inspections showed, that contrary to the previous visit when it was busy, the top floor is virtually vacant and the second floor has many shops empty. The cause attributed by tenants is the effect of Sawgrass Mills, which now incorporates a fashion mall.

What I find so disappointing is that the problems of our town centres, and the clear signs of the effects which out-of-town shopping has on them, together with the need to address the traffic problems against the considerable data in the possession of the Department of Transport and the Department of the Environment, has taken so long to be addressed. As a developer, with the limited resources of a small company, even I gave a warning of the probable disasters which were emerging, many years ago. Over a period of seventeen years of continuous government, a period of such length that planning to avert the failings so obviously appearing was entirely adequate, the guidance now issued is simply too late. I am not arguing the merits of the policies in detail, other than to say that they seem to be a patchwork of trying to recover ground lost for ever, but to illustrate that planning, in the broadest sense, was always, *per se*, essential to find any solution for our future. It was as essential as planning policies must always be if problems are to be objectively viewed, trends assessed and solutions found. It is another lesson that planners are trying to seek emergency solutions to the problems caused by their lack of previous planning foresight.

For that reason, and not for any political argument, I found it profoundly disappointing to see the announcement in September 1996, that a Labour Government would change the planning system within months of being elected. In my opinion, the planning system allows a good framework, but it was the implementation by short-sighted officers which could be faulted. Keith Vaz, the Member of Parliament then speaking as Labour's Planning and Regeneration spokesman, unveiled details at a speech to the property industry, following a fourteen-month planning review called 'Planning for Prosperity'. The thirteen-member panel which conducted the review included representatives of the public sector, private sector and leading members of the profession. The main recommendations included a relaxation of the restrictions on out-of-town developments. It was proposed that there should be a priority review of the PPGs to permit the wish for consolidated PPGs that are not in conflict with each other, or in conflict with the overkill objectives of the then government. The review of PPGs, it was claimed, would allow a Labour Government to introduce what may be seen as the most controversial change in planning policy. This would be an announcement that decisions as to retailing were best left to local councils. Rather bizarrely, Mr Vaz said 'The food retailers have done a fantastic job in making shopping a leisure activity and we do not intend to stop that.' Labour also planned to explore the possibilities of tax incentives to attract the private sector back to town centres. As a personal comment, I cannot see how any tax incentives will be really attractive in a situation where the development is for an area of decline unless there is a real prospect of reversal. Tax is a small element in the matrix of consideration of a successful outcome. The most important feature of any consideration is the likely success and profit, on a long-term basis. Town centres which are attacked by competing out-of-town growth and the vacating of shops, due to planning infrastructure and traffic congestion, are simply not stable long-term secure investment options. With a General Election in the offing at the time of the new announcement it added uncertainty to a situation which had been too uncertain for too long.

At the planning conference where the Vaz announcement was made, Kingfisher's Sir Geoffrey Mulcahy said that the then Government's clampdown on out-of-town development ignored the diversity of retailing: 'There are many different types of retailer and many different types of shopping trip. Different types of shopping need different types of locations,' he said. Delegates at the conference heard that PPG6 may force unsuitable retailers to locate in city centres and that retail developments may locate in unsuitable sites, simply because they are available. The use of the planning system to reduce car usage was not the best way to achieve this objective. David Sainsbury, Chairman and Chief Executive of J Sainsbury, largely supported these views: 'The credibility of the system is now being called into question,' he said. He thinks it is simply wishful thinking to believe it is an option to locate stores in city centres which have inadequate car parking.

Even taking account of the fact that both these very experienced and successful retailers are members of the group promulgating the new policy document, their views are rather strange. To directly link the statements to the interests of the companies they represent may be slightly unkind, but it is a fact that Kingfisher's Comet and B&Q, and Sainsbury and their subsidiary Homebase are well represented out-of-town and have a preference for that type of location, for obvious reasons. They are also supporters of the out-of-town big business lobby. However, some of the other comments are also somewhat surprising. To suggest that different types of retailers need different types of locations is all very well, but ignores the trend that large out-of-town centres have had almost the same retailers as the downtowns in recent years. Factory Outlet centres, retail parks and concessions in bulk warehouses have become locations for high street names. I see no suggestion that there should be a selective restriction on planning use, and neither would there be any justification for such a proposal. The end conclusion of the statements made at the conference is that there should be a market forces policy, with the major stores, including Kingfisher, Sainsbury, Tesco, etc. being able to compete with the town centre. Is this not exactly the situation which has been in force in the past? I thought that the effects of that – comparatively – free for all policy was the reason for more protection of the town centres. Now, at the same time as PPG6 is being lambasted, it is argued that the status quo should be maintained.

Yet, we must wonder whether that is a correct assumption. It has been interesting, although frustrating, to try to see where we are likely to be with planning policies in the future. The arguments put forward by Mr Vaz, seemingly with authority of a policy statement on behalf of the New Labour Party, and the supportive arguments of industry leaders, comes to naught if the uncertainty of the past, the dithering, the dichotomy of the interests of towns and out of town, together with the traffic problems, remain without direct and constructive actions from central government. Almost immediately following the statements by Mr Vaz, Michael Meacher, then New Labour's Shadow Environment Protection Secretary, spoke to the Party Conference. He said that a Labour Government would stop the sprawl of out-of-town shopping and other developments. He told the Conference:

> We will not allow the precious green space of our countryside to fall prey to developers and speculators – not while we have thousands of acres of derelict urban land in areas crying out for new investment and new jobs.

In another part of his message he said that Labour would base its transport strategy on quality public transport to provide a real alternative to car use, and would 'clamp down on the belting monsters'. It should be noted that production of motor vehicles in Britain climbed steadily through the last decade with a total of more than 1 700 000 cars and commercial vehicles being recorded for 1995. This was the best performance since 1977!

It appears that Shadow Ministers were alarmed by Vaz's statement, which had given the impression that Labour would relax the present PPG6 and PPG13 policies. Vaz himself, speaking to a fringe meeting, described Labour as the 'town centre party' and added 'We have to make sure there is adequate investment and support to ensure that town centres remain the hub of retail and other activities.'

In another bizarre twist to the political outlook, Labour was expected to perform another U-turn on out-of-town shopping. Shadow Environment Secretary Frank Dobson was reported to intend to make plain during a Parliamentary debate that a Labour Government would adopt a policy of presuming against out-of-town development unless there were exceptional circumstances. He indicated that Labour wanted to see maximum effort given toward restoring existing town and city centres.

Annual Conferences of the political parties give an opportunity to hear approaches to many topics which may not otherwise be aired. I have referred to the planning policies of the Conservative Party when in government and the Labour Party, with the latter exposing two opposing views from authoritative spokesmen. What of the Liberal Democrats? Their local government spokesman, Christopher Davies, told a fringe meeting at the annual conference in Brighton in September 1996 that the Government should block all out-of-town schemes now in the pipeline. Davies said that the onus for refusing out-of-town developments should change, so that local authorities should not be required to prove that it would affect the viability of an existing centre. Instead, developers should have to prove that their proposals would not harm traditional town centres.

After the confusion, in an address which might have been thought as certain as it is possible to be when reporting the statements of an opposition spokesman on policies to be pursued, before his party was elected to government in May 1997, Mr Vaz announced a ten-point plan at the annual conference of the British Council of Shopping Centres in Edinburgh in November 1996. Much of this may repeat what has been stated earlier in this section, but while highlighting how attitudes can change rapidly over a short period, it may give a conclusive idea of the path ahead. This, of course, depends on the usual chance that policies of governments, once on power, may not totally coincide with pre-election manifestos. I am grateful to my old friend, Eric Williams, Editor of *Shopping Centre*, to be able to repeat his report in that paper of the proposals:

Mr. Vaz put forward a ten-point plan for the regeneration of Britain's town and city centres. He said that the adoption of them would mean that there will be no need for any out-of-town centres. The proposals were: (1) introduction of stronger land assembly powers for public/private partnerships in town centres, (2) the targeting of dedicated public funds and specific grants for town centre improvement as an alternative to the competitive bidding process, (3) encouraging residents back to town and city centres, (4) further developments of the concept of networks of town centres, (5) exploring new ways to provide incentives for private-sector reinvestment, (6) greater integration of national retail and transport planning policy guidance, (7) strengthening the identity of individual shopping centres and key shopping areas, (8) enhancing the role and quality of shop service through investing in people, (9) [giving] greater attention to crime detection and prevention, (10) support for the concept and practice of town centre management. Mr. Vaz said that his Party had welcomed the Government's 'belated recognition of the damage its planning policy was inflicting' on retailers both rural and urban. He said 'we continue to believe that town centres should be the preferred location for major retail developments, whilst recognising that some out-of-town developments may be justified in particular local circumstances'.

Mr Vaz went on to point out that 74 per cent of Britain's shopping space was still concentrated in town centres.

This, of course, means that a staggering 26 per cent is out-of-town. In another passage he said: 'Surely, there is by now general agreement that the planning appeals process, in particular, has become too slow and adversarial. Our "Planning for Prosperity" Review committee concluded the whole system was in need on rationalising and streamlining.' I reflect on my comments made earlier in this passage with reference to the statements made at the announcement of that committee's findings. From my readings of that committee's recommendations, it seemed that they were much more pro-out-of-town than now indicated. There are several other anomalies which you will observe.

There was a call for a car parking levy on out-of-town centres to provide existing town centres with funds for the improvement of their centres. This is an interesting concept and does appear to give some compensation which may overcome the major problem of providing a town centre infrastructure to combat traffic congestion. Ironically, many superstore planning consents are won by offering planning gains to help with road improvements and overcome objections based on the generation of the traffic increases caused by the development. Effectively, local authorities are obtaining financial input from out-of-town developers or retailers to improve tertiary roadways while the inner roads and town centre parking provision is starved of investment, with the result that they deteriorate and become less attractive to shoppers.

The best methods of overcoming traffic congestion are thought to be better traffic management and improved public transport. Even if the use of buses by the public were to double it would only reduce the cars on the road by 10 per cent. Rachel Christie, of Birmingham's Environmental Protection Department, says that sometimes pollutants such as ozone are highest in rural areas. Similarly, congestion in rural areas is growing in many places, with the Council for the Protection of Rural England predicting that traffic levels will more than double by the year 2025.

There remains the argument that the exclusion of food supermarkets, furniture stores and DIY from town centres is correct because there is no place for them in a modern comparison shopping centre with traffic problems. The argument continues that the town centre will replace these trades with more speciality trading and will thereby benefit. This argument is too generalised, however, because some towns, most particularly market-type towns, rely on food and household shopping facilities for their character. Some towns are also not suited demographically and economically for speciality shopping centres or highly stylised shopping. In addition, if the argument is followed that the release of space in town centres caused by the relocation of bulk traders can be utilised for more suitable traders, it follows – except in the case of huge demand and under-supply – that the secondary and peripheral areas of the town will show vacancies. There may, therefore, be a substantial case for relocating those bulk retailers not to out-of-town locations, but to edge-of-town areas, thus supporting the town without the necessity for them to go out of town as free standing units.

Transport consultants Symonds, Travers, Morgan presented a study, carried out for Marks & Spencer, at a conference in London in October 1996. The study involved travel diaries of shoppers in a catchment area for a new 40 000 square foot store in Brooklands, Surrey, England. The diaries were kept for a seven-day period before and after the store's opening and show that, instead of an increase in traffic, there were no significant effects on overall travel habits. According to the study, shoppers at the new Marks & Spencer store were already in the habit of shopping more often than the average, and also shopping by car more than the average, before the store even opened. Peter Mynors, one of the authors of the report says: 'If trips to the new retail location replace trips to other retail destinations, the total number of trips may change. For example, a larger number of low spend trips may be replaced by fewer high spend trips.' Peter Jones of DTZ Debenham Thorpe argues that the findings are what people suspected. In other words, that new stores do not necessarily generate new car trips, but merely redirect them.

There is another anomaly to the out-of-town bulk retailer question. Although car ownership has grown substantially, many of the out-of-town retail parks prosper on budget pricing policies, sometimes aided by cheaper building design and less sophisticated shopper amenities. If their market draw is price-related, rather than the pleasure of a shopping experience, they are more likely to attract the income group statistically with the lowest car ownership. This is a feature which I find most puzzling since the out-of-town locations, presumably giving ease of car access and the biggest car parking facility, usually without correspondingly high public transport connections, is seeking to attract shoppers of whom a proportion are least able to take advantage of those attractions.

To combat these criticisms, the developments of retail warehouses have been enlarged to provide bigger sales space and more car parking. To provide the variety and overcome the solus visit objection, several retail warehouses are usually grouped together to form a retail park. The visual design has been upgraded and shoppers' amenities extended. Leisure activities, including multiplex cinemas, garden centres, petrol stations, auto centres and children's attractions, have been incorporated. Greater emphasis on catering is being introduced, whether in the form of stand alone or drive through McDonald's, or in-house catering as in Tesco's superstore at Neasden. I spoke earlier of this being a short step toward a shopping centre, and it would be a fairly easy extension to see separate units or a retail park joined into one by a canopy or enclosure, to become, in effect, a shopping centre. As an absolute extreme we could visualise long stretches of the Edgware Road from Staples Corner to Burnt Oak, which I mentioned earlier as having many separate bulk merchandising stores, being a series of long strip-shopping centres!

Finally, John Prescott, Deputy Prime Minister, has claimed to have cleared up any doubts about Labour's attitude toward out-of-town development. In June 1997 he stressed that he will closely follow the former Conservative Government's policy to curb it. He said he was committed to revitalising town centres: 'I will therefore expect local authorities to apply a sequential approach to selecting locations and identifying sites for key town centre uses, and will expect developers to apply this approach when selecting sites,' he said. This sequential approach would involve consideration, firstly of town centre sites, then edge-of-town, finally out-of-town as a last resort.

9 Town Centre Economies and Planners' Attitudes

Shopping centres, in particular, are quite different to other forms of property, and their development and management needs specialist knowledge and experience. In the past, the failure of both developers and architects to apply such specialist expertise, together with many retailers looking only to their own individual shop interests to the exclusion of the effects on the greater entity, has meant that many shopping centres in the United Kingdom and Europe in the past were less efficient and attractive than the best centres in America. During the past decade or so, European centres have become so attractive that we now see Americans looking to this side of the ocean to gain new ideas. The effects of cross-border retailing, with many American retailers such as The Gap, Tower Records, McDonald's, Crabtree & Evelyn, and others having increasing representation, has helped this harmonisation.

Shopping is different to other types of buildings because offices, factories and houses are built for the occupiers, whereas shopping centres have to be attractive to the occupying retail tenants, however, the success of the centre is ultimately decided by the shopper. The shopper has a wide choice of shopping venues to visit and if they are not satisfied with the attractiveness, design, convenience, retailers, ease of access, parking or management, they will go elsewhere. In bygone days, as explained earlier, shoppers went to the market or shopping area of their locality to purchase goods. These were, in effect, the only places available which offered a range of the staple and luxury goods needed, because transport and communications were limited to short distance trips.

A valuable research report was issued by the British Council of Shopping Centres (BCSC) in November 1996 under the title 'Town Centre Futures: The Long Term Impact of New Developments'. The key findings included the important point that

> the study shows clearly that the future for our town centres does not depend solely on whether or not they have out of town shopping to cope with. Although new competition clearly can

affect business in the short term, it can also stimulate new investment. Equally, early and effective action by local Councils can be a
major influence in supporting the future of centres.

My comments about the policies adopted by Maidstone (p. 65) are
relevant to this very apposite conclusion.

The BCSC research is unique because it addresses, for the first
time, the question of the impact of out-of-town retailing. It considered a selection of the larger towns and cities in Britain where there
have been major out-of-town shopping developments over recent
years, and examined changes over a fifteen-year period between 1980
and 1995. It then assessed whether the impact of out-of-town
developments on the shopping provision and sales levels in the case
study centres since 1990 can be considered significant in the context
of the longer-term structural changes occurring on the high street.
The research also analysed whether those high streets that have
benefited from active town centre management, as well as new public
and private sector investment projects have been able to gain trade
and withstand competition better than those that have not.

The key findings are summarised as follows. Many changes in the
high street reflect some of the more general long-term trends in
retailing. For example, there has been a long-term decline in the
representation of footwear, men's clothing and bulk goods across
most of the case study centres between 1980 and 1995. This reflects a
greater dependence by men in particular on multiple chains, rather
than independents, for clothes and shoes, the rationalisation of these
shops by the larger chains, the decline of the independent retailer and
the growth of out-of-town retailing.

Imbalance generally occurs at the point between centralised and
decentralised shopping, where it depends on changes in overall
spending power. Over the short term, the opening of five major
new out-of-town centres coincided with a major economic recession.
It is, therefore, difficult to determine if the effects on the town centre
is as a result of the recession on trading patterns, or of the competition.

In some cases there has been a growing concentration of retailing
and investment along the prime pitch at the expense of secondary
shopping areas. Therefore, although out-of-town shopping facilities
may have accelerated the trend of decline, they did not initiate it. In
general, those centres that already enjoyed long-term investment,
backed by proactive and far-sighted planning policies, have contin-

ued to enjoy growth, despite any short-term fluctuations in the local market and national economy. On the other hand, centres that already had poor shopping provision, or were declining over the long term, have continued to lose market share. For those weaker centres that were suffering from long-term decline, out-of-town competition has tended to accelerate their problems. These problems were accentuated where town centres have suffered from reactive rather than proactive planning policies. This can be illustrated by looking at centres that have large, attractive and modern shopping centres. They have generally been better placed to withstand the competitive effects of major new out-of-town retailing. This view is strengthened by cases where new shopping development has taken place in town, and has boosted the attraction and made them more competitive.

The research shows that early and sustained town centre investment can reinforce a town's resistance to competition. This is especially so if undertaken within the framework of a planned stategy, but it must be implemented early. Unfortunately, many initiatives have tended to respond to competition rather than precede it.

Shopping trips are most regularly made for food and other household items such as cleaning materials, toiletries and magazines. The supermarket is the largest destination for this type of convenience shopping and it is usually done on a weekly basis. A comparatively short time ago, this shopping was a combination of personal 'shopping basket' visits and partly use of delivery service. The home freezer has made the need to shop quite so frequently less important, although the amount bought on each visit has grown considerably. During this period, the supermarket has grown in the size of each individual unit and has become the eponymous superstore in almost every locality. The corner shop has almost disappeared, with the strange corollary that more local convenience stores, operating long hours, have emerged in strength based on personal service, smaller environments and targeted merchandise, available without long travel distances for the shopper and the absence of waits at checkouts behind piled trolleys.

The other type of shopping trip is usually to buy fashion goods, shoes, electrical appliances, jewellery or furniture. Because this is not for weekly or daily essentials, the visits tend to be less frequent and are to places offering a large range of such goods. This is likely to be a major shopping centre, such as the high street or regional centre, with the usual brand name multiple retailers well represented.

With the increase in leisure time, and the growth in family income due to general affluence and multiple family earnings, the shopping visit continues to be a form of family entertainment for many. The householder has come to expect a wide choice of many items to see, browse and be enticed to buy, during a shopping visit. Sometimes the window shopping, in itself, is the leisure experience, without any actual purchase being made. We are in an age of using short-lived consumer articles, and a change as a result of style, fashion, not simply because of age or failure, is now taken for granted. Greater leisure time is opening the prospect, already in clear evidence, of a trip to a shopping centre, high street or other retail experience, being used as a form of recreation. Attractive places, with interesting environments and the added features of entertainment, eating and meeting places, are epitomised by shopping centres in their many guises, fulfilling the description.

There is always some confusion about the term 'Shopping Centre'. Generally a shopping centre is defined as a *group of retail and other commercial establishments that has been planned, developed, managed and owned as a single property*. Of the 42 000 shopping centres in the United States, most are smaller neighbourhood centres and only about 2 per cent of the total are classified as Regional Malls, but these large centres account for more than 30 per cent of all industry sales.

In this book the term 'shopping centre' has been used liberally. Therefore, it is not meant to describe a purpose built enclosed shopping centre *per se*, but a place where shoppers may go to find a collection of shops meeting their needs. It may be helpful to differentiate between the differing descriptions of shopping centres at this point.

- The *Neighbourhood Centre* is a small centre, usually with a super-market as the anchor trader, which has a good variety of con-venience goods as well as personal service trades, such as dry cleaners, laundrette, bank and betting shop. It normally has an area of about 50 000 square feet and serves a population of 5–10 000 people in a radius of about five miles.
- The *District Centre* (or Community Centre) is often developed around a small department store or variety store as its anchor. It

usually has between 100 000–300 000 square feet of retail space, and serves a catchment area of 10 000–15 000 people. In addition to convenience goods, there will be a range of comparison goods and personal service trades. This type of centre can often be seen in small towns which cannot support a regional centre with department stores and several variety stores.

- The *Regional Centre* may be in the centre of a town, or be the downtown area itself. It comprises a large collection of comparison trading units including fashion, shoes, furniture, and offers a large range of price comparison as well as selection of a range of items, often not stocked by smaller shops and localities. It may serve a large catchment area of up to 25 miles, depending on local roads and transport. There are usually one or more department stores of size, offering the widest range of goods, services and leisure activities. A regional centre will have a lettable area of at least 300 000 square feet and a draw of at least 150 000 people. In recent times it has not been unusual for a regional centre to have an area of 1 million square feet, and in America 2 million square feet is commonplace. It should be recognised that many of our existing shopping centres within towns have all the essential ingredients of a regional shopping centre, and perform the function of providing the shopper with all the range of comparison goods, but they have developed gradually over a long period of time and have characteristics which vary greatly.

- The *Out of town*, or Suburban Centre (often referred to as a Regional Mall) was established in America, France and Australia before Britain. They need large areas of land, a good road system and a mobile and affluent shopping public in a radius of, say, 25 miles. Regional shopping centres of this type usually have at least two department stores and several variety and specialist stores. They usually include a large supermarket and food traders. They must provide large and easy car parking facilities on ground level.

- *Speciality Centres* are smaller centres which contain niche traders and, as a result, units are generally smaller than in a standard shopping centre. A speciality centre succeeds as a result of its distinctive tenant mix and has no anchor or major trader as the main draw. It is successful as long as the total mix of retailers constitutes a complete whole attraction greater than the individuals themselves. In other words, it is a place which attracts because of its special character and environment, rather than a place where everyday items can be found.

- Finally, *Theme Centres* is a term used for centres which are promoted around a particular type of activity. This can be a small waterside development around the theme of boating, an old English village decor, or a type of eating or entertainment theme.

There seems little doubt that the great difficulties experienced by developers with planning authorities some years ago to obtain change of use for retail sales, even on a cash and carry basis on industrial estates, is no longer so extreme. The spate of consents granted either for food or specifically non-food retail warehousing out of town again echoes the enthusiasm by local planning authorities for the policy to take bulk goods out of town centres. The conclusion one might like to draw from this movement, is that local authorities would like to see more apposite development in the towns, if only to protect the cores from the very competition they are themselves creating by the out-of-town consents. As an extreme comparison, this may not be dissimilar to the way retailers are promoting their own competition by use of the Internet while, at the same time, increasing their promotion of new stores to combat the threat and increase sales volume. The difference may be that retailers have the option, as a class, of withdrawing support from the Internet in the future, whereas out-of-town or alternative development in bricks and mortar is relatively permanent.

While the evidence of the consents and growth of out-of-town development is there for all to see, there seems to have been no discernible change in attitudes by planners to town centre development. There are, of course, more theoretical reasons to exercise stricter control in town centres. There are more intrinsic historical and environmental features to protect, although ironically, environmental protection groups and lovers of the countryside may have similar views on out-of-town development. Thus, the planning theories continue in conflict with commercial realism and experience. The move to 'lifestyle' and the quality of life, giving everyone the choice to enjoy the pleasures of a fulfilling experience, once again shows signs of conflict. Those who wish to enjoy the varied scene of the town centre with its total civic and commercial environment, or those who want the convenience and more controlled planned dedicated shopping envelope, compete for that choice with those who want to choose the natural environmental habitat.

Earlier, I said that education is sorely lacking amongst planning officers with regard to modern retailing practices, methods and experiences. I do not make this comment lightly, and I certainly do not intend to insult officers who are expert at planning law and the application of both practical and political wishes of their own authorities. It is a regrettable fact, however, that personal inspections of case studies and knowledge of successful developments completed elsewhere do not feature highly in planning discussions on proposed central area development schemes. Even where there are enlightened planning officers or encouragement from town councils, other members of the officers team (engineers, fire officers, highway engineers) often fail to take advantage of the development team's expertise, insisting on imposing their own tested and tried methods or safety first standards. These often include a great deal of over-design or over-specification as a precaution against liability risked by new methods or ideas, severely restricting imaginative schemes which are usually based on actual practical working experience and similar examples of success. There are many examples which could be used to illustrate this statement. It may suffice to refer to servicing arrangements for delivery trucks to shopping centres where the norm is for both building control, planning officers and highways to impose standards for articulated vehicles with maximum turning radii and standing areas. Sometimes these vehicles will never be used and often the amount of space required is grossly over-estimated. One medium-sized centre in a London suburb has a two-lane roadway ramped into a basement service yard with loading docks to the rear of almost every shop. The capacity of deliveries which could use these facilities at one time is enormous, plus the number of vehicles which could park and wait. The reality is that most days the entire road is empty and the basement has no more than two or three vans delivering.

As stated, the changing, and ever faster changing, consumer profile must be addressed by planners. The consumer is spending less time at work and has more time for leisure, including shopping. According to the famous American author John Naisbitt in his book, *Megatrends*, the shopping centre is the third most visited place after home and work. The consumer now has a greater spending power than ever before and there is a growing resistance to 'chore' shopping. There is a trend toward companion shopping, with participation by the whole family. To provide for this, shopping must incorporate merchandise, pastimes, attractions and leisure, to capture and entertain all the individual members of the family, at one locality and at one time.

This has been attempted in full out-of-town shopping centres by the inclusion of catering, in the form of foodcourts and restaurants, a wide variety of shops and some occasional ancillary items. Metro-Centre and Merry Hill incorporate multiscreen cinemas and other attractions. In the case of retail parks or retail warehouses some catering has been introduced. Indeed, at the two centres named, extensive retail parks with major units are adjacent to the centre itself.

There has been much reference to the 'leisure box'. The imagination of developers was first energised by the development of West Edmonton Mall outside Edmonton, Alberta, Canada. This huge centre, with a floor area of 5 200 000 square feet incorporates a major shopping mall with a major collection of leisure activities. Within the mall is a full size galleon, a submarine ride and a white-knuckle ride. Adjoining, is a huge glass domed covered wave pool on which one can surf and a beach, with changing huts for swimmers. This amazing development, during winter in the snowbound area outside a rather remote town, became a place attracting visitors from all over the world. Charter planes of tourists and shoppers made special visits. Reports of the economic success of West Edmonton Mall are mixed, but another, Mall of America, is owned by the Simon DeBartolo Group, Triple Five Corporation and a large pension fund at Bloomington, Minnesota, and is of similar size (4 200 000 square feet), planned around a Camp Snoopy theme and containing an indoor aquarium. The retail space amounts to approximately 2 500 000 square feet. It is said that the owners plan to build a second phase which could eclipse the first in size and scope. One of the proposals put forward for a contender to occupy the second phase of Mall of America is the Hyperport. This would be a complex futuristic enterprise that its developers claim would make the it a centre of influence in the information age. Already they have been calling it the Info-Mall and it is said that it would have a satellite–computer network which would be the 'information power plant'. Surrounding the power plant would be a range of tenants who would use their technologies as a permanent trade exposition. Although not strictly comparable, we could refer to my ideas about the introduction of technology into the infrastructure of shopping centres, which is a similar projection of the future.

Nevertheless, any possibilities of incorporating the leisure activities of West Edmonton Mall, Woodbine in Ontario, or Mall of America, in shopping centre developments in the United Kingdom, is now perceived as unlikely even on a very scaled-down basis. Apart from the cost of providing such leisure experiences and the uneconomic returns likely, it is now recognised that large-scale leisure specifically located within the retail area of the mall, can have an effect on the consistency of the retail element in a centre. The disadvantages of having to give Johnny a ride at additional cost every time the centre is visited assumes a special significance to a cost-conscious parent. In addition, some of the rides and events are pieces of showbusiness, attracting the total attention of shoppers. These shoppers will line the edge of the mall during the performance, during which time they turn their backs on the shops and sales activity drops dramatically.

The retail element attached to major leisure developments tends to be closely associated with that draw. Universal City Walk in Los Angeles is an open shopping street leading to the main Universal Studios presentation and features shops which sell mainly items related to Universal Pictures (see Plate 6). It contains a large multiplex cinema and several well known restaurants and cafes, with the whole project having a movie theme with an oversized gorilla clinging to buildings, cars through first storey elevations and a twenty foot guitar at the entrance of the Hard Rock Cafe. In effect, the main function of the development is leisure with retail being an added, but associated, attraction and sales generator.

The latest project to be announced in the United Kingdom is the proposed development of the former Battersea Power Station on the South Bank of the Thames in London. With interiors designed by the architect responsible for Planet Hollywood it is a large entertainment centre with ancillary shops. Taking note of the amazing leisure offering at the Stratosphere Hotel in Las Vegas, which has atop its spectacular tower an open air white knuckle ride and a reverse bungy jump, one of the alleged attractions was to be a ride up the inside of one of the power station chimneys, round the outside of the top with views over London followed by a fast drop to the bottom. If true, it would be interesting to see whether the building control and safety officers employed by the local authority might ever permit this to go ahead.

Other than in huge mixed leisure–retail malls, such as Mall of America, which become more than retail centres but rather big tourist attractions, large leisure provision tends to be used as the leader, as in Universal City or the Trocadero in London, with the retail as a support. Where large leisure is being provided at a main line shopping centre, such as MetroCentre, it is being added as a separate leisure box adjoining the shopping mall, but not directly integrated into it.

It should be recognised that the town centre already possesses most, if not all, the features being contemplated by out-of-town centres. Parks, cafes, museums, galleries, cinemas, theatres, architecture and the varied street scenes, together with people of different types and on diverse journeys, create a special environment which is often taken for granted.

Unadventurous, poorly educated and greedy developers must be blamed for developing shopping centre investments which merely provided shop units as simple boxes to meet the demands of retailers, without any associated attractions or excitement. Hoping to pander to the end investment aims of major institutional purchasers, they wanted to produce relatively management-free properties. But the institutions also have a lot to answer for. The general policy of seeking management-free investments or full repairing and insuring leases and four cheques a year without undue involvement meant that shopping centres were regarded as prime only if management was not by any stretch of the imagination thought to be intensive. As a result, high street shops were sought, but centres only if they were simple and trouble free. Thus 1960s centres tended to be open paved precincts with, if possible, even the public areas dedicated to the local authority to avoid maintenance, cleaning or policing. At a time when America was recognising public consumer requirements, we and our funding institutions, were unable, unwilling, or too short-sighted, to provide managed environments for that time, let alone the future.

Fortunately, things have changed. In the last few years new centres have been designed and built to the latest standards. Institutions are aware of the long-term advantages of good management, and the more professional and educated approach by all concerned has evolved a specialist industry founded on more secure bases. This acts to the advantage of investors, developers, retailers and, above all, consumers. It cannot be stated too often, or too loudly, that it is the consumer, the shopper, the provider of turnover and sales, who drives the success rate, or failure rate, of a shopping centre.

High streets are boring! We have all heard that said. Standard shops with standard shopfitting and the same Woolworth, W.H. Smith, Boots, Tesco, Sainsbury, Benetton sign everywhere. Yet, most developers want these same names in their centres. That is because they are huge draws, as long as the image is not, again, identical to the very street they are meant to eclipse. The other main reason for trying to attract these traders is that developers recognise that institutional investors want these chain store tenants and it is accordingly reflected in the price they will pay.

An argument put forward for the success and attraction of the shopping centre is that the environment is better, often weather-protected or enclosed, traffic-free, bright, clean and secure. But we must be aware that the British shopper is no less conservative in their outlook on this than in other matters, when it comes to change. The shopper has got used to the high street, a high street which has evolved and adapted. It has familiar sights, signs, well trodden pedestrian routes, noise, smell and feel. Variety of street scene, people and yes, even crowds and crush. As strange as it may seem, many people feel happier in such surroundings and while critical and complaining, would decry any major change. There is no explanation. It is inherent and inexplicable. It is a subconscious human feeling of having got used to the present and mistrusting the unknown.

For centuries shoppers have thronged to the busy market stalls – Petticoat Lane on Sunday, to me an abomination of noise and crush, to others a joy. To the souks and bazaars. To London's Oxford Street at Christmas. John Naisbitt, in *Megatrends*, says people need contact with other people. He cites the crowded atmosphere of rock concerts and discotheques. Why would anyone endure the crush, heat and noise unless personal contact overrode these discomforts?

An average pavement is 10 feet wide and can accommodate 10 000 people per hour on it, despite being edged with tremendous vehicular traffic. You will, therefore, perceive that I am proffering an argument that shopping centres must react to the shopper by providing a convincing alternative and acceptable environment. Have we done that so far?

I remember when I built the first covered centre in Holland, the 75 000 square foot Ridderhof Winkel Centrum at Ridderkerk near Rotterdam in 1969–1970. I agreed that the scale would be determined by the width of the Mall, which I argued should be 12 feet. The architect and letting agent quoted a minimum of 25 feet preferably 35 feet. On my visits to the United States and Canada at that time I noted such widths in 1 million square foot Regional Centres, but also saw narrow malls in the very successful and revolutionary St Catherine's Place in Montreal. To resolve the problem in my own mind, I stood in Burlington Arcade for hours, knowing how successful it was and noting the extremely narrow arcade. More rewardingly, I stood in the terminals of London Airport. Having paced out the width of the access ways to the aircraft departure lounges, I assessed, first, how many more people had to use these walkways than could ever be expected in a shopping centre. The result – I insisted on a compromise of 14 feet which proved more than adequate. At the Royal Exchange Shopping Centre, Manchester we had 12 feet malls. The Plaza on Oxford Street had 15 feet at the entrance and down to 12 feet and 9 feet around the Atrium. This, for a Centre which had a pedestrian flow of over 35 000 a week, on a street with 37 million a year! The new owners of the Plaza have carried out a refurbishment which was sorely needed after nine years. As part of this, the ground floor has been rearranged to remove the central opening to the lower ground floor and create a wide area giving excellent sight lines to the shops and the upper levels. One thing which has not changed, however, is the width of the entrance and the mall from Oxford Street, being the main traffic generator with 95 per cent of footfall; that still remains at 15 feet and, continues to work well.

Again, I say that people want to be where many others want to go. They see success as being popular. Many people means popularity, in queuing for the cinema or for the sale.

Today architects and planners still dictate 30–35 foot mall widths creating acres of space and a feeling of leisure. They also create cost, loss of revenue, but most important, a shock to shoppers' perception of a busy shopping area. To compound the problem, the one great disadvantage of the high street is accentuated. With over-large malls only one side of shopping can be conveniently visited and viewed, just like the pavement, whereas narrow malls, even when crowded, allow the shopper to wander from one side to another and be aware of each attractive shop and all merchandise.

At my company, Glengate, we distribute a unique-to-the-centre Tenants' Manual to all prospective tenants. This gives not only a copy of the Lease, but Rules and Regulations for the operation of the Centre to maintain quality. It contains Design Criteria for shop designers with basic details – what is provided by the landlord: services, colours and materials. What is required from tenants: signage, lighting, stuck glass or frames. Submission of drawings, details, approvals procedures. Traders' Association Bylaws. Deliveries and working regulations, etc. Most good shopping centre developers do this and we are certainly not unique. But, at the time of the Royal Exchange Shopping Centre development in 1978, I had not seen a Tenants' Manual produced elsewhere in this country. It was shown to me in Canada and seemed so helpful and logical that I thought we would introduce it in England. After all, a service manual is provided for a car or washing machine, so why not for a shop and shopping centre? Strangely, although there was a muted welcome, most retailer tenants did not think that the contents of the manual actually applied to them. It was a good idea to regulate everyone but surely their shop front design was good enough for the high street, and therefore was good enough for a shopping centre. It is a reasonably accurate statement to say that very few tenants either passed on the design criteria sections, which incorporated essential basic data about construction, dimensions, services, etc. to their designers or shopfitters. Those who did mainly allowed the designer to dictate to the landlord. It has become easier to convince tenants that their future success in a designed centre has a great reliance on the similar success of other retailers. Together they generate not only their own sales attraction, but also a combined and harmonious attraction held together by the overall management of the centre and application of the fundamental promotional policies. As a result, acceptance of a considered set of design parameters and regulations for the general maintenance of standards leads the retailer to abide by pre-set reasonable criteria. Within such a framework, we urge designers to be original, although many retail clients are reluctant to depart from their usual standard style of units.

By doing this, we are trying to recognise that old habits die hard. We are trying to recognise that the shopper will visit our centres only if they prefer them to the environment in which they have been comfortable, in the broadest sense of the word. We cannot replicate the street scene with churches, museums, bus stops, pavements, noise, crush, wind, rain, sky, so we must provide design, weather-protection, climate control, cleanliness, security, leisure, food and catering to compensate. We hope that the habit will become one of continued repeat visits to our centres because they are found to be good, clean, enjoyable experiences and by doing this the old habit of the open, noisy, dirty and sometimes dangerous high street will be replaced.

Standard shops, standard multiples, boring high streets. But will we say the same about shopping centres in the future? My present fears are that we will. 'Clones of clones' are being produced by expedient designs from both experienced and educated architects and developers, and more so from architects and developers who have suddenly become interested in retail, not as a specialised studied subject over years, as is necessary, but because it has recently been a profitable and fashionable part of the property scene. These developers will surely evaporate from retail as quickly as they appear, once they burn their fingers or any boom dissolves.

I do not want to imply that only design, or only leisure add-ons, or only shopfronts and merchandise, is sufficient. The shopping centre, unlike other forms of property is a living, ongoing, managed, promoted venture. It is the experience of the senses as well as the physical which attracts and succeeds.

The message is clear. Shopping Centre development and management is extremely complex; it needs 'gut feeling' as well as market research evidence. It needs flair and courage. It needs institutional backing for large sums based on educated assessments. Above all, it needs an open, searching and fertile mind to succeed in the future.

Part III
Living with Technology

10   Technology: Creating 'Haves' and 'Have-Nots'

Shopping centre development, management, marketing and promotion are not alone in having to depend on social attitudes. In architectural terms, in the broadest sense of the definition, society's requirements have to be taken into account. There have been many examples throughout history of society being provided with what is the perceived architecture of the times, only to be disillusioned some time afterwards. In building, the 1960s industrialised building methods for residential flats, giving rise to large soulless concrete slabs, is typical. This panacea for the housing shortages was hailed as a great advance. Later it was seen as the creation of ghettos of misery, lawlessness and mediocrity. It produced many no-go areas where normal residents lived in isolated fear, devoid of many features and advantages of normal community life.

There were the 1960s office blocks which many current architectural critics condemn as eyesores. It is ironic that such luminaries as English Heritage have decided to list some such buildings as being examples of the [bad] architecture of the period. Shopping centres were also very basic. The pedestrian centres were referred to as shopping precincts and were open with small canopies offering weather protection and pedestrian walkways which were usually paved with local authority-type slabs.

Why do I speak of these historical events? Because it is necessary to take account of what the shopper, the consumer, the resident or anyone else using a product wants, when designing for today and for the future. It has always intrigued me when I hear of the 'new' product which will be an outstanding success, and realise that the producer has not bothered to research whether the same, or similar, items were produced in the past. It seems an essential requirement for us to know about historical events and trends, and use that information to judge the likely success of the same matter now. Buildings have been constructed for centuries. Shopping habits have been roughly the same throughout that time. The advent of the motor car as the predominant amenity may have had a great effect, but the basic shopping habit when at the shops has been reasonably consistent.

So, following this line, how can we use historical research to help us consider whether the new electronic technology will change habits, be acceptable to that shopping public and, as a result, be successful as a medium for retailers and providers of the systems? There appears to be only one logical avenue,which is to study how technology has been adopted or declined by society in the past. We need to see whether the promises advertised for such technology have been realised, whether the advantages have been achieved and the good and bad effects which have emerged. I have pursued this line with much trepidation, because I am the first to acknowledge my shortcomings as a social historian or commentator. However, I see no alternative to providing some of the information I have gleaned and then applying my own experience as a shopping centre developer and manager to reach an estate-based conclusion, as far as possible at this time of great change.

Firstly, I have been very impressed by a series of seminars in March 1996, under the rather forbidding title of 'Colloquium on Advanced Information Technology, Low Income Communities, and the City' at the Department of Urban Studies and Planning, MIT. Leo Marx, whose field is cultural history, gave a fascinating paper on 'The Critical and Historical Perspective'. He is in the programme in science technology and society, and has spent a lot of his professional life studying the inter-relations between science and technology and the rest of society and culture. One of the questions he addressed is why we are assuming that information technology could be a decisive factor in resolving the problems of low-income city populations and inner city populations. He said that, on the face of it, the proposition that information technology could be a really significant or decisive factor in resolving problems of the inner city seems to be, as they say at MIT, counter-intuitive. The new technology is particularly demanding in its qualifications for access – [that demand is influenced by] the amount of education, language and other skills needed to use it. One is thinking about it as an instrument for solving the problems of a population which has been particularly deprived in precisely those categories of skill, and which is a generally stigmatised population. Here, again, you will note the doubts being raised about education to the necessary level and the logical extension of the argument about haves and have-nots.

In recent times we have become accustomed to living in an economy which assumes that unemployment is normal. It is reasonable to assume that the unemployed will be less able, or unable, to avail themselves of the required access to new technology as a result.

Leo Marx points out that one general inference that can be drawn from the history of responses to technical innovation is that they invariably trigger excessive, unrealistic, utopian expectations. He cited a few examples from American history. The first two come from a not unrelated technology, the introduction of electricity. Marx gave quotations from the book *Electrifying America* by David Nye, who told of Edison expressing utopian ideas about the uses of technology which were characteristic of the popular press. He predicted that electrification of the home would eliminate the distinction between night and day, speed up women's mental development, making them the intellectual equals of men. Constant light might lead to the elimination of sleep. In later years, he hinted that he was experimenting with electrical ways of communicating with the dead. By such predictions, electrification became bound up with ideas of social progress in the transformation of human nature itself. Similar predictions became a common element in late nineteenth-century utopian writing. Beginning with Edward Belham in about 1890, more than 160 utopian books appeared in the United States in a twelve-year period.

At the end of his book, Nye sums up some of the general expectations:

> In the beginning, Americans believed that electricity would free them from toil as prophesied in the popular press utopian works, feminist proposals and back to land movements. Extravagant predictions about the electrified future were an integral part of the new technology social meanings. Americans learned that they might use electricity to abolish sleep, cure disease, lose weight, quicken intelligence, eliminate pollution, banish housework and much more. But few of the predictions of amateurs and experts from Edison to the technocrafts were realised. As the actual development of electrical technologies lived up to expectations, electric trolleys did provide economical mass transport. But they did not lead to urban deconcentration into a pastel utopia. And in any case they were abandoned in favour of automobiles. Productivity rose in the electrified factory permitting shorter hours, higher pay and more consumer goods. Yet pressures on the job also

increased as managers achieved greater technical control over work. And in contrast to the dream of automated factories eliminating human toil, came either a stepped up piece work system or the assembly line.

Even today, when we take for granted the fact that computers and other technological aids help us all to do our jobs much more effortlessly and efficiently, we continue to think that the work amazingly conducted so quickly must be saving us time. This effort should be allowing us the benefit of more spare time to enjoy our chosen lifestyle, and have the time away from work to pursue leisure activities. Yet the modern description of 'time-poor' continues to typify many workers, whatever their financial and power status. Rather than saving time, a survey by Motorola finds that technology seems to make people work longer hours. People who use the most technology work the longest hours per week, amounting to 43.7 hours. Those who use 'no technology at all at work' work only 33.7 hours per week, the lowest. Surprisingly, the survey did not consider telephones within the definition of 'technology'.

Limitless free energy was predicted when nuclear power was introduced. We are all aware of the history of that and the more recent impact of environmentalists.

The word 'technology' itself, and the concept of technology, is of relatively recent origin. In cultural history it is believed that when new words come into being they usually indicate important changes in culture. The traditional words were mechanical arts, useful arts, practical arts and inventions. The word 'technology' was not in general use until about the time of the First World War, having started to become used during the period after 1900. Our assumptions about the mechanical arts are closely associated with the idea of progress. But, to refer to progress may be trivialising what is a decisive idea, the fulcrum of a whole way of looking at the world which came about at the end of the eighteenth century and coincident with the age of revolution – the French, American and Industrial Revolutions, for example. These all happened around the same time and make up the great change between the era of feudalism and modernity.

In the 1780s and 1790s, they began to say that we live in a world where the dominant characteristic was history. This meant that history was viewed as a record of the continuous, cumulative and steady expansion of knowledge and of control over nature, resulting in the improvement of the living conditions of everyone. The idea of progress became the pivotal point of a whole world view. The reason why history became so important was that people stopped believing in traditional cultures, about myths of origin and religious myths. There was a growing sense of who they were and where they were in time.

The *New York Times* has recently carried a series on the effects of downsizing. Repeatedly, people have said 'I'm losing my faith in the American dream. I used to believe that my children would be better off than I was'. That is an example of the residual element of the idea of progress. Thus, progress was attached to history itself and when people wanted to show that progress was occurring, they mainly used an example from the mechanical arts. John Stuart Mill pointed out that when you see a train moving across the landscape, it is a wordless argument for progress, because you know that it was a mode of transport unknown to your great-, or great-great, grandparents. It is now here and therefore makes the concept of time and space much shorter. To put this in a different way, technology transmits the belief in progress wordlessly.

Of course, if we think about the past, there were many people and groups who were oppressed or disenchanted and who did not support the argument of progress being good for them. Leo Marx gives an interesting story of people who were sold the idea and then were disenchanted. In the nineteenth century Boston Associates set up a group of textile mills in Lowell, Massachusetts. They had the brilliant idea of recruiting pink-cheeked farm girls with an average age of 19.7 years, to work in the mills on a twelve-hour day. This was an incredibly hard and noisy job. They built housing with chaperones and what was considered a showpiece of modern technology. People came from all over the world to see it. These young girls from the farms were eager to come and work. They came because they thought they would work for two or three years and make enough money to buy a dowry and then return home. The mills allowed them to escape the farms for life and they were excited about coming to a city and meeting other people. They found it socially interesting and even started a newspaper. But things did not work out as they thought. Firstly there was a recession and the owners were pressed. The girls had to work more machines at a faster rate. Because the owners could not compete, wages went down. As the girls were disenchanted, they went on strike and tried to organise a union. Then in the 1840s, with the sudden wave of immigration from Ireland, Irish males offered cheaper labour and the girls were sent back to the farms. This story, and the whole experience, is typical of what happens when new technologies are introduced. Nevertheless, a new technology is unquestionably seen as a benefit.

Then there is the change in the equipment itself, together with the convergence of science and technology, particularly in the fields of chemicals and electricity. This change of character is also shown by the railways. Previously the items of the mechanical arts, the inventions, were free standing items such as the spinning machine, the power loom, the steam engine. These were literally single objects. But with the railways something new came into the scene, what we now call 'technological systems'.

In Alfred Chandler's book, *The Invisible Hands*, about the origins of professional management, he uses the railway to show why the family firm went out of existence as the dominant commercial organisation and was replaced by the modern corporation. A railway is not just a train. It is thousands of miles of track that have to be controlled, day and night, in all kinds of weather. It involves personnel, experts and expert management. Increasingly the new mechanical arts were systems and not single entities. They incorporated elaborate systems, like the railway, the electrical power system, or the mass production assembly lines in the automobile industry.

And talking about the automobile industry, the internal combustion engine is a technology which absolutely changed the world. Where is the technology there? It could be the assembly line itself. Or the Ford Motor Company. Is it the glass, rubber or steel manufacture which goes into the car? Is it petroleum or road building? When you think of the components of what we call automobile technology you have a large segment of society in culture. In America, some people have estimated that about 20–25 per cent of the work force is somehow attached to it.

Therefore, when we think about the impact of technology on society it is often a little misleading, because we live in a society where technologies are part of the framework. In the end, the technological aspirations of the Lowell mill girl venture did not fulfil the utopian dreams. But on the whole, the new technology, like almost all technologies, ended up reinforcing the established order. The view in the dominant culture and the view which is sold to the population, is that history is progress. Those who invented the concept of history as progress were absolutely clear that science and technology were a means to an end. The end was a more just and equitable society. It was based on one which had the idea of government and the consent of the governed. Thereafter, little by little, the idea of science and technology as a means to an end disappeared. By the mid-nineteenth century, the advance of technology was seen as an end in itself. It was a good without question. Even today, it is rare that we ever refuse the option of a new technology. Today, we talk all the time about technology changing things. Television series, the computer: we constantly use sentences in which technology is causing things to happen.

But there is a strange paradox in the way we think about technology today. If you ask people to define it, they say, 'It's a thing, a device, a mechanism'. Therefore we have the strange situation that what is now so deeply part of social life, power and structural meaning is still seen by many as a kind of magical object. That may be the problem and once again leads us back to literacy. Maybe the reason we think that the computer and such interactive media associated with it can solve our problems is because we think in this way. Apparently, Nicholas Negroponte told Newt Gingrich, the Leader of the House in Washington, that the way to solve the problems of the poor inner city was to give everyone a lap top computer! That is the quality of thinking connected with technological utopianism.

Leo Marx believes the truth to be that there is no settled opinion about what kind of entity technology is. That is one reason why it is so susceptible to mysticism. The conclusion is that there is considerable scepticism about the capacity of a technology to resolve complex social and political problems. It is thought, however, that the role of the new technology is, instead, a valuable form of capital. The financial press refers to technology stocks, and are referring to hardware and software. On this assumption, supported by a great deal of factual evidence, the people who benefit most from technologies are those who are most closely related to those who own and control them. The primary significance of information technologies now is their role in creating the era of post-modernity, which is sometimes called the 'new world order'. My further comments on the advantages of promoting the Internet as a means of commercial trading, and for retail sales in particular, for the developers, providers, manufacturers and other ancillary products, will be predicated on this premise.

The new technologies are the means of transmitting mass produced global popular cultures of infotainment. The effect that this is having on employment opportunities of highly qualified, experienced, well

educated, upper middle class employees, makes it seems wildly
unrealistic to rely on these technologies, as such, to solve the
problems of the people in the inner cities. What is another potential
problem is that the information available to the better educated,
skilled or executive classes is not readily available to the poorer
sector. Again, the have-nots!

The means of access for the poorer person is presently reliant on
use of computers in schools and other public areas, and therefore also
depends on information being public. With the huge profits poten-
tially available in the future, what is now happening in information
revolution is that those people who are most likely to benefit
financially are determining how to shut off a substantial part of that
information, which has been public until now. It is a little like the
access everyone had to television programmes through the BBC and
ITV, before the coming of Sky. Now you cannot get a lot of live
sports transmission unless you subscribe and pay for it. The Tyson
world championship fight in 1996 was a further example of how
subscription to Sky still did not allow viewing without further specific
payment. The press has being talking about pay-as-you-view subscription for Premier League soccer matches and Manchester United
are investigating a separate viewing channel for their own matches to
satisfy their large supporters' club who cannot get tickets. Bearing in
mind that soccer is a mass enjoyment for a large sector of the working
men and women, this is a further trend toward making access more
limited and available only to those who can afford it. In the World
Wide Web many are trying to think of ways to cut off what is
presently public, which means what you can get at the moment as
long as you have the tools. It is, therefore, a strong possibility that by
the time the poorer user can afford to access the system available to
the richer section, the information will not be as extensively useful as
it is at the moment, or will be only if additional payment is made. My
son-in-law who was a Veterinary Surgeon at a famous Royal College
of Veterinary Medicine, to which referrals are made by general
practice vets, tells me of owners of pets who say that they have used
the Internet for advice and ask if this can be utilised. There seems to
be reasonable doubt that free advice of this type will continue to be
given in the future over a free medium by those who rely on it for
their living. Payment for such information, of course, goes almost
directly against the original purpose of the World Wide Web, which
was put together very explicitly as a device for high energy physicists

to share data. Then the browsers who recognised its use were put together, again with the purpose in mind to allow academics to share information. The whole thing had now assumed a quite different proportion and has been appropriated for a very different set of purposes. There are now a whole range of subject matters, even to the extent of pornography.

Peter Cochrane, Head of Research at BT Laboratories, who is quoted later on the almost sci-fi advances which will be seen in the next twenty-five years, wrote a revealing article in the London *Daily Telegraph* (13 August). I think it is revealing on two main issues – literacy and sales hype directed at those who can afford access, without any reference to those who cannot. This is a prime example of another promoter of electronic services, a manager of a telecom company, who adds a strong sales pitch which directly serves the company's profit objectives, while purporting to give an objective and balanced research statement. Not that what is said is incorrect, rather that which is left out makes it slanted.

Mr Cochrane rightly refers to the children who have been born into a world of computer technology and the older population who perceive technology as unfriendly, complex and expensive, in terms of money and time. He echoes the opinion of many, and my own given in this subject, that if we are to combat the information division in our society we must make available and easy access vital. He thinks that competition from the brown goods sector may soon change this, with the first integrated television and personal computer units having been announced 'at a price little more than a top-end TV'. There is no reference to the cost of a new television, or the affordibility of this to a large number of poorer people.

However, he feels that the biggest hurdle by far to success is technophobia. He believes this is age-related. The answer is to get onto the system and use it by trial and error. But finances are not totally ignored when there is reference to the distribution of wealth in terms of the number of TV sets, video recorders, hi-fi systems and games machines in the average home, along with the money invested in transportation, designer label and luxury clothing. He sees that it is really a matter of how much people value technology and how useful it is to them that dictates investment patterns and access to the information world. The conclusion reached is, that once people discover the usefulness and power of this new world, money is quickly directed into purchasing equipment and software.

One challenge which hits both rich and poor, he says, in this IT world is to keep up to date, for within three years a top-end product will become outmoded. Then there is the cost of connection and communication, with such cost being compared to the cost of purchasing or renting videos, or running a car: 'None of this technology is really that expensive,' he says.

In this real world, why do we completely ignore the poor sector? The mass marketing philosophy of major players being directed toward the sale of goods solves none of the problems foreseen by the socioeconomists extensively related in this book, nor do the seemingly objective comments of a market leader offer any constructive pointers, other than to suggest that it will 'not be that expensive'. The 'haves' are the targets, the 'have-nots' will have to sacrifice other essentials, which they may be able to barely afford, to achieve a dream world scenario.

Mitch Kapor, an Adjunct Professor at MIT and one of the founders of Lotus, also spoke at the same sessions as Leo Marx, on the problems of closing the gaps between the 'haves' and the 'have-nots'. In the course of his talk, a number of interesting observations emerged. He set the scene as at present. Without covering ground which is stated elsewhere, and most of it repeated by almost every commentator everywhere, I was impressed by some added parameters introduced by Mr Kapor. For example, he referred to radio as a very significant medium. Although its importance has reduced because of television, there are still billions of hours spent listening to it and programmes such as Talk Radio have become an incredibly important political force. The radio stations are limited by licences, owners have a tremendous power and, often, it is a generator of profits not available to anyone else. Conversely, those without a licence do not have those advantages. But, says Mitch Kapor, the Internet changes all that.

Today there is a technology called RealAudio™,[1] that allows the transmission of voice and music over the Internet, in a way that any user with a computer and a phone line can access. There are at least 3 million people who have downloaded a free copy of the Real

---

1. RealNetworks™

Audio player which integrates with the World Wide Web. There are already over 1000 sources of audio information from ABC radio and small obscure sources of information. But as a function it is about the same as radio because it has audio, and starts playing within a few seconds of clicking onto it. There are live events being broadcast, but it is not going out over the air. It is going through the wires, through the Internet and therefore there is no limit on the number of people who can operate as realaudio servers. Each of these servers can be the equivalent of a radio station, but one which is not a local station, but rather one with a global reach. The radio station is one which can broadcast live, or store its information so that people can get it whenever they want. Conventionally, if you miss the time a pro-gramme is on, you may be lucky enough to catch a repeat, if not you've missed it. Not with the Internet, because you can get the programme any time to suit you and in addition, if the phone rings, you can use the pause button and resume listening after your call. This may revolutionise the radio industry, because a licence will no longer be needed.

This example and glimpse into the future – although according to Mitch Kapor it is already here – does not directly impact on shopping habits. What it does, however, is reinforce the gulf that not only exists, but is likely to increase, between those who can access the power of the Internet as a result of having the few thousand dollars to get the specialised software and operational costs, and those who will struggle merely to become wired at the most basic level. Some have access to information and political involvement on a wide scale, other do not: the 'haves' and 'have-nots' again. Or, as Mitch Kapor puts it, the 'Amplifier of inequality'.

He illustrates this by forecasting that key information for people to get ahead economically comes out of the Internet first. For instance, there is a steady migration of employment and professional help-wanted advertisements being directed onto the Internet and away from newspapers. He thinks this is much more efficient, because searches can be made in a particular area of interest, but if someone is not connected they will not know about it and be left out. That is a paradox, because the Internet is designed to bring more people with a similar interest together, yet it really highlights the divide between those who are connected and those who are not.

Interestingly, he also talked about the difficulty of using personal computers and the slow speed of telephone lines. Without going into the great detail he did, the summary is that the increased speed forecast by the use of ISDN[1] as a high-speed access, and cable modems, are both seen by this expert as not being immediate-term events. This led him to the idea of the Internet appliance, which I have discussed elsewhere. This is the device which is cheap and simple. Mitch Kapor thinks that it is the sort of thing people wish exists, so they pretend that it does! He sums up:

> The point that I just want to get across is that people who are counting in the technology environment being really different tomorrow than it is today and who are doing their policy planning on that basis, I think are going off onto an improbable scenario.

As a developer, investor and manager of shopping centres, I have to deal with the realities of the market place. This means that the likely trends of customers' behaviour and their effects on retailers' decisions, to take shops and trade in centres must be viewed on a similar feet on the ground basis. We cannot afford the luxury of being idealist dreamers, other than at the conceptual stage. Effectively, I am reminded of the frivolent definition of an economist who says 'I know that it works in practice, but will it work in theory?'.

That is why it is so important for the references to utopia to be placed into a realistic context. We could ask whether we have heard talk of being liberated by technology before. As can be seen from several references, the old system of capitalism was supposed to collapse as a result of its own contradictions. The, then new, system of communism was supposed to have been born in a traumatic revolutionary transition and we were going to eventually progress to the higher stage in history, when people could live freely in natural surroundings.

Karl Marx mused that we would be able to 'hunt in the morning, fish in the afternoon, rear cattle in the evening and write literary criticism after dinner'. One of the driving forces of these historical changes would be the perfection of industrial machinery, which would liberate people from the drudgery of factory work and allow them time to do whatever they wanted. That was the general idea for

---

1. ISDN (Integrated Services Digital Nework) voice and data method. In the USA this is referred to as Broadband.

generations of Marxists, communists and socialists of various kinds. But it did not work out that way.

Everyone is in favour of the idea of technological advance, and from early days have made the connection between new technologies and better democracy. The telegraph and television, to name but two, were seen as tools for a more democratic system and an empowerment of the citizens. Unfortunately, none of these items proved to live up to the hype advanced.

That opinion is voiced by Howard Segal, a historian of technology at the University of Maine, and the author of *Technological Utopianism in American Culture* and *Future Imperfect: The Mixed Blessings of Technology in America.* He says that Americans' belief in technology, and the trust that technology can solve our problems, is naive, shallow and seriously misplaced. Europeans were cured of their enchantment with technology after they saw some of the effects in the horrors of the First World War. Americans began to lose their enthusiasm as they realised the appalling effects of atomic bombs and the real dangers of nuclear power.

But again we are embarking on another round of promoting the elusive ideal of a more decentralised, democratic, wired world. Perhaps it is no coincidence that the allure of technology is so powerful again today. The position of Phil Bereano, a Professor of Technical Communication at the University of Washington in Seattle, is that this allure is bound up with a frustrated sense of manifest destiny. He explains: America is not a society that deals well with limits. In the nineteenth century its people could head West and gobble up land. Through most of the twentieth century, Americans could carry a big stick around the world and get much of what it wanted. However, for the past couple of decades its relative economic strength in the world declined and the country has had to face up to its limitations. As a result, America had to frantically look for its new frontier or a limitless expanse in which it could pursue its destiny. In other words, says Bereano, it is primed for a technological quick fix.

This may bring us back to Marx. It has been remarked that there is an eerie similarity between the basic gist of his theories and the historical vision of Alvin Toffler, the popular futurist who advises one of the most powerful people in America, Speaker of the House Newt Gingrich. This point was made in a scathing article originally in the *New Yorker* magazine by Hendrik Hertzberg and updated in the *Star Tribune*, who says that both Marx and Toffler see history divided into three progressive stages. These are agrarian, industrial and post-industrial, and both see a nearly irresistible force of history driven by technology. Both see a very painful dislocation as society shifts between ages, and both project a vaguely defined decentralisation future: a techno-utopia. Now that we know what happened when Lenin, Stalin and their followers tried to turn the theories of Marx into a better society; we must ask what disasters might emerge if we follow today's utopian dream, as advanced by its modern disciples.

Peter Cochrane, to whom reference was made earlier, expects that technology will develop in the next twenty-five years to the extent that 'Computers equal humans'. They will become much more intelligent, powerful and autonomous machines, which are more of an assistant than a tool. He believes that the keyboard and the mouse will be replaced by a voice-responsive, talking computer so that you no longer have to read everything or type instructions. Speech will be able to be converted to text. The hand will be able to be put into the screen and feel hard and soft data that can be adapted or modified. There will be head- and eye-mounted displays and cameras taking you into two or more worlds at the same time. This is a vision of the future and may be quite accurate, although frightening to many. But, in reality, what advance does this portray over and above what we have as human beings at the moment? We have our own senses which are operated and dictated by our own wishes. It seems to me that the advantage would be that we would be able to associate with a larger world, faster, but still in a second-hand virtual reality sense, instead of our own. The disadvantage is the prospect that reliance on new systems as outlined will make us the slaves of technology, and susceptible to third-party direction of our thoughts, privacy and independence.

Earlier I referred to the utopian fantasies that are presented by the people who promote or sell technology. A guide to the thinking is given by another senior person at BT. Raj Kanthan, Product Manager of Internet Access, says: 'BT approaches the Internet as a global communications company. However, our customers want to communicate today and in the future, we want to be there with services which match their needs.' Whilst the message is what we might expect from any progressive technological company, it serves as a further indication that BT, as well as many others, wish to exploit the commercial advantages of the market of the future, as they see it. It seems clear, from many of the arguments in this section, that they will benefit or profit most. As new means of increasing profitable exploitation are found, the cost of joining the club will rise, and the less advantaged person will find it harder than ever to participate. Someone has used the analogy of an alcoholic parent, who makes empty promises to their child and actually believes them to be realistic, only to fail to come through with them because of their illness. Much of the promise to everyone is for the Internet and interactive media to solve the convenience and cost features for the future. Is that likely without further cost?

11 Is Shopping a Chore? Being Digital and Big Brother

Many shoppers regard general shopping as a chore. That has been one of the reasons why shopping centres have received so much attention in recent years in efforts to make shopping a more pleasurable experience. However wasteful of time shopping for everyday articles is, shoppers, up to now, have found it a necessity. I firmly believe that they dislike even more the thought of staying at home for hours on end surfing the Internet or watching television, when they could be out seeing things, meeting friends and incorporating shopping during a journey to pick up the children, or visit another place of interest. Therefore, shopping has to be convenient in another way. The daily or weekly shopping must be so supplemented by the pleasurable experience of doing it at the place of selection, that the 'chore factor' becomes a passing incursion, rather than an overriding curse. I do not believe that the average shopper wants to be stuck indoors, instead of going out and escaping the house routine. Even the disabled person wants to get out, and modern appliances on cars, disabled facilities on public transport and in buildings, rightly gives those shoppers the same opportunities available to anyone else. Shopping hours have expanded so greatly that the time to shop is now dictated by the personal schedule, not the shop schedule.

I do not believe that the inconvenience associated with shopping stems from the process of actually selecting and ordering the product. That part is the same whatever method is used. The obvious four items of inconvenience are: first getting to the shop either by public transport or car, and parking in the latter case. Second, knowing whether the shop has the type of product you are seeking. Third, the time taken to process the items selected for purchase – for example, in a supermarket with a weekly shop. Fourth, the burden of getting the items to your car and transport home. I can see that information technology will be of great help in all these areas.

Taking a short trip of imagination forward, the shopper will be able to see on screen the nearest, most convenient shopping centre, retail park, neighbourhood or district centre, or high street, by route and distance; the easiest public transport means or road travel; road conditions and a traffic report. The listing of shops will be shown; the parking facilities and availability of spaces and even which car park is best to use. Lakeside Shopping Centre on the M25 motorway at Thurrock, Essex, may have huge car parks but it cannot be much fun to queue on the M25 for ages on Saturday morning trying to get to the car park and then find a space, when you can be alerted to the problems and decide to go later, or choose a more local alternative which is free from those frustrating delays. Then you can see whether the store at the selected centre has the particular item you want in any case, before making the journey. If not, and you are pressed for time, you can go to the store which does have it, without wasting time once there, having used a kind of technological Yellow Pages, a program which, incidentally, is already available on the Internet. Once there, shops will have a system onto which you can log, so that the purchase can be made without waiting and paying at a desk. Supermarkets already have a trial barcode reader system on trolleys and this will eventually be linked to automatic confirmation and direct debit to your bank or credit card, so that arrival at checkout will not mean an interminable wait and packing but a speedy transaction. Of course, in the future, hand-held electronic notebooks may enable selection of food, etc. or bulky items which will go straight into the delivery process for home delivery the next day. This is something which is already in use in limited sites.

There has been much comment about the way one has to shop in the large superstores or supermarkets. There is a feeling that the way in which the stores are set up makes it necessary to resort to a certain amount of aggression to complete the shopping trip. Some futurists are now putting forward an idea which they think will solve the problems. It's called computer automation and looks as if it's sweeping America. On the basis that scanners are not enough to satisfy consumers' desires for convenience, fast service and few hassles, the temperamental and sometimes unpredictable nature of human beings need to be eliminated. The basic idea is that red blooded, cell-driven organisms do not fit into the 'Improved Shopping' equation. People plus people equal line ups, human error, time lost to conversation and, heaven forbid, socialising!

The best way to get rid of at least one of the 'people' in the equation is to eliminate the cashiers and let the customers do it themselves. A hand-held bar code reader, that allows customers to scan their own groceries as they pick them off the shelves, would not only speed up the checkout process, but also encourage shoppers to buy more goods. The device also enables supermarkets to target shoppers with customised advertising as they shop and provides information on their shopping habits. The Albert Heijn chain in Holland and Safeway in Britain are said to be using a system. Shoppers who have registered to use the service pass an electronic identification card through a reader and collect a scanner as they enter the store. They point the scanner at the bar code on each item they select and press a 'plus' button. If they decide not to keep the article they press a 'minus' button. To total the cost of their groceries they press the 'equal' sign and when they reach the checkout, the shopper pays and leaves without delay. The time is drastically reduced, since the goods can be placed in the shopper's bag without waiting for itemisation and bagging at checkout. Without scanning, the average shopper can wait at checkout for up to 24 minutes if they have three people in front of them with large loads. Of course, the system must have some system of control, but the risk of theft is reduced because the system is offered only to store courtesy card-holders who have generally proved their loyalty to the store.

These portable scanners allow customers to get in and out of the store as quickly as possible, since the biggest complaint from the average shopper, according to *Grocer Today Magazine*, is waiting in line at the checkout. On top of speedy scanning, labour costs for owners and managers are reduced by about 15–20 per cent.

Waitrose has followed Safeway by testing a self-scanning system for the same purpose of saving time at the checkout. Hand-held bar code scanners from Quick Check, using ICL equipment, is in operation at the Abingdon, Oxfordshire, store and allows John Lewis and Waitrose account cardholders to use it. A Waitrose spokesman said that early results have been promising, but that the trial is still in its infancy.

Imagine the scenario: the line of customers is already longer than the retailer can handle at its checkouts and the credit card transaction process is held up by an irritated customer or clogged lines to the credit card company. Efficient marketing and merchandising has encouraged customers to buy extra goods which are not essential on that trip and they are getting annoyed. Are they replacing the goods and preparing to leave the store, possibly to be lost on the next trip because they have lost confidence that they can shop without hassle? Both the queue and the slow credit processing tends to create lost business or counter-productive customer relations. There are firm possibilities that this problem can be overcome.

Systems to be standardised within shops of the future can enable customers to be reminded of items which they often buy. The system can act as a prompt – subject, of course, to an adequate data base being in place. Moreover, such a data base can be helpful by automatically advising the customer of any special features which a product has. They can be either beneficial, or a warning. For example, if a food retailer knows that a customer is allergic to an ingredient but also, at the same time suggests an alternative, it would speed up the shopping process and ensure a happy shopper who buys a suitable product, rather than one who finds that the purchase is unsuitable and tries somewhere else in the future.

Why stop there? In an unlikely place for leadership in technology, Portugal, the interbank system, with the acronym SIBS, operates a giant computer which receives information which charges the customers client account weekly. SIBS is pioneering the 'electronic purse' which is a revolutionary smart card that can be used to pay merchants, parking fees and the taxi driver. The card, known as a PMB card, after the Portuguese '*Porta Moedas Multibanco*', means that you do not have to carry around coins or small bills. 'We started this service in April 1995', explains SIBS General Manager Luis José Godinho Cid:

> Portugal's size means that our network links all the country's main banks and all the country's ATMs to our computer. Our clients are the banks, which issue the cards and provide the store owner or garage attendant with a portable terminal where the card is inserted. The terminal displays the final amount to the customer.

About one million PMB cards have been issued so far but by the end of the year he expects the banks to issue new cards combining ATM and electronic purse, with in-built security features. Although this is not much different from the use of a charge or credit card, which a retailer inserts into a swipe machine, it does show that even small countries are looking to the future in making shopping an easier experience.

In talking about the new help in deciding how to travel to a centre, there is an interesting social question. Thomas Horan, a Professor at Claremont Graduate School in California, directs the Research Institute which has a special focus on the social, political, organisational and economic impacts of advanced technology. He has referred to a case study in the area of transportation, because transportation planning is one of the more regularised forms of urban planning. The study, for the Auto Club, entitled 'Moving the Auto Club into the Information Age; Policy and Organisational Implications', looks at rights of way around the country in terms of infrastructure finance and how to share it between public and private enterprise. One of the problems is that transportation planning has usually been in the public domain, but telecommunications planning is typically not in the public sphere. That factor raises new challenges for dealing with the telecommunications structure, since this is the means of implementing many of the suggested means of future transport facilities and aids. Intelligent transportation systems foresee the application of advanced computer technology. The systems envisaged are those such as traffic control centres in cities, which can track traffic; systems at home on the television, or on your computer, so that you can look at various different video pictures of the traffic problem, as well as providing private services. Here we can see that ideas of planning the journey to the shopping centre are realistic. It also includes services like universal passes, so that people can take buses and trains without having to pay for individual tickets. In this way it cuts across modes. Somewhat controversially, it includes electronic cards that would be placed on the windscreen to allow passage directly through toll booths, emergency notification if the car breaks down with a push-button call, so that the breakdown vehicle will respond for recovery or repair. Taken to the ultimate, it might lead to automated highways, but in the shorter term it could lead to anti-collision and avoidance functions.

These potential advantages also have dangers. There is a feeling of a 'big brother' watching and tracking every move made. If passes on windscreens can be so sophisticated and register movements, they must also be capable of relaying to a central storage all the same details. For example, where a particular car is at any moment of the day? What speed it is travelling? There will possibly be beacons at the roadside – and not only instant fines for speeding (cameras will be unnecessary) but instant debit to a bank account of the fine itself. There are many socioeconomic factors which will be resisted by the public at large. Of course, if enough of the public revolt against the ideas, they may prefer to pay at each toll booth and buy individual tickets, which makes the huge cost of the infrastructure rather wasteful. This centres on the usual technological obsession with improved efficiency. Many people feel that the ability to go through a toll booth faster does not help to maintain the quality of life.

Technological advances of the sort described here must be carefully channelled, to avoid a blanket use which tends to dehumanise our everyday lives and the environment. It has the capacity of engulfing whole communities, and must be considered in the context of what benefits it can bring to those places which have indigenous and low-income populations and not just provide a greater separation of the better off, with access, and those without the means to participate.

A little earlier I mentioned new moves in Portugal. They have introduced Via Verde (literally the 'Green Lane') at a toll station on Portugal's rapidly expanding highway network. The driver of a Portuguese car, on approaching the lane, touches the brake pedal lightly and speeds through the gate at 40 mph while an antenna mounted beside the gate reads the electronic code in a tag fitted to the top of the car's windscreen. The driver is using an exit lane, and what the antenna reads is the electronic information which was written in the tag by another antenna when the car entered the highway. This includes the vehicle class, the time and date. Although it is claimed that Portugal is the only country where the system is in daily use throughout its highway network, other countries are testing the system – I have seen a system in use at New York tolls. In Europe, Britain has a DART system, France and Spain are testing similar systems, while Italy is using a system where the driver makes an initial deposit and then uses the highway until the balance expires and it is time to make another deposit. 260 000 Portuguese motorists have subscribed and the number is increasing by 600 each day.

To achieve their system, a team of Portuguese engineers inspected a system the Norwegians had installed in Oslo to reduce traffic and cut down pollution in the capital. Each driver entering Oslo ring road was automatically charged a flat fee by means of an electronic sensor. The difference between the schemes is that the Norwegians charge everyone a flat fee, whereas the Portuguese charge according to the distance travelled. Singapore has introduced a system to control entry of cars into the central core area.

Nicholas Negroponte, in his book *Being Digital*, proposes that in the forthcoming era our very beings will be transformed and become digitised.

In being digital [he says], I am me, not a statistical subset. Me includes information and events that have no demographic or statistical meaning. Where my mother-in-law lives, who I had dinner with last night, and what time my flight departs for . . .

this afternoon have absolutely no correlation or statistical basis from which to derive suitable narrow cast services.

This information is entirely personal. A major theme of Negroponte's book is the way in which old-style technology will be replaced by two styles of information – one intended for the mass market and the other tailor-made for the needs of individuals:

> But that unique information about me determines new services I might want to receive about a small obscure town, a not so famous person, and for today the weather forecast for Virginia. Classic demographics do not scale down to the digital individual. Thinking of the post information age as infinitesimal demographics or ultrafocused narrow casting is about as personalised as Burger Kings' 'Have it your way'.

'True personalisation', Negroponte says,

> is now upon us. It's not just a matter of selecting relish over mustard once. The post information age is about acquaintance over time, machines understanding individuals with the same degree of subtlety, or more, than we can expect from other human beings, including idiosyncrasies like always wearing a blue striped shirt, and totally random events good and bad in the unfolding narrative of our lives.

He then gives an example which depicts life in the future.

> For example, having heard from the liquor store's agent, a machine could call to your attention a sale on a particular chardonnay or beer that it knows the guests you have coming to dinner tomorrow night liked the last time. Or it could remind you to drop the car off at a garage near where you are going because the car told it that it needs new tyres. It could clip a review of a new restaurant because you are going to that city.

This is a machine that knows you are going to a particular city in ten days' time. And in the past you seemed to have agreed with the reviewer. All of these are based on a model of you as an individual, not as part of a group who might buy a certain brand of soap or toothpaste. That is given as one of the great promises of the information age but, as Leo Marx says, it does not have much to do with the problems of the inner city.

Data collection is at the root of this transformation. Whilst the basic infrastructure can be incorporated in design of the shopfitting specification, the retailer will need to capture data about its customer, including what they buy and when they buy it. This information will need then to be assimilated at head office to build an intelligent profile. Therefore, retailing systems will become much more interactive to assist business and improve customer service and relationships, leading to better loyalty.

IBM's World Avenue online shopping mall, which was open for trading in Autumn 1996, with claims to about twenty tenants has attracted Hudson Bay, the Canadian store group, and women's clothing retailer Express, a division of The Limited. In fact, as seen when World Avenue was visited, Hudsons Bay was not featured and in addition the twenty tenants turned out to be just six, with one duplicated. The online service was claimed to be able to record consumers' browsing habits for use in micro-merchandising campaigns.[1] This is a further confirmation that one of the main purposes, repeated elsewhere, is the gathering of personal information for added marketing uses, but it does seem rather frightening that some computers will hold the most intimate details of personal thoughts.

---

1. In Autumn 1997 IBM announced that World Avenue has officially closed.

12 Giving the Customers What They Want

You will perceive that so far I have not spoken specifically about buildings. I did say earlier that shopping centres and shopping development is all about giving the shopper what he or she wants. All developers will agree that the major ingredient, and direct driver, of the actual shops – their size, location and services – are the major retailers, and less directly, the investing institutions and their agents. In any usual circumstance, a developer cannot make any profit without a successful centre. He must attract chain stores and other major retailers and therefore anticipate their requirements. He must ask himself whether a targeted retailer will be prepared to trade out of a certain size of unit in a particular location. Most retailers have emerged from their previous tunnel vision which took account only of their own trading potential and, while still having their own interests as a priority, recognise that their neighbours and the environment play a big part in trading results. This is borne out by the first question almost every potential tenant asks: what other retailer has taken space? Letting agents, often acting for developers, are less able to hide their desire for attracting good quality names, which will be more attractive to the ultimate funding institution, but usually show a remarkable change of direction if such traders cannot be found at acceptable terms, when they suddenly recommend smaller or less well known retailers. Here, I have indirectly referred to the form of attraction through the retailer, the requirement of the developer to have such traders in a scheme to make it successful, and the service they will have to give in the future, to respond to the price, convenience and leisure requirements of the shopper. Thus, the retailer will need the right form of environment to be planned by developers within centres to do that.

Within the centre envelope, there are already tangible signs that retailers themselves are instituting designs for store formats which recognise that customers want more than static shopfronts and displays. These may be used in the proper sense of marketing, to indicate to the shopper what can be seen inside. They should invite

1. Isfahan, fabric bazaar

Bazaar – Isfahan fabric bazaar, after Coste. Isfahan was made capital of the Persian Empire under Shah Abbas I (1585–1629). The word bazaar means sale, and this word was used for the great covered streets which are filled with shops.

2. Passage de l'Opéra, Paris

Passage de l'Opéra, Paris (built 1822–25).

Demolished to make way for the extension of the Boulevard Haussmann, which was finally constructed in 1925.

The Passage de l'Opéra resurrected the Arcade fashion in the era of the Restoration.

3. A floating market, Bangkok
Courtesy Ronald A. Altoon

4. Southdale Plaza, Edina, Minnesota
Courtesy Dayton-Hudson Corporation, Minneapolis, Minnesota

5. Horton Plaza, San Diego
Courtesy The Jerde
Partnership; Photo courtesy
Ronald A. Altoon

**6. Universal City Walk,
Los Angeles**
Courtesy The Jerde
Partnership; Photo courtesy
Ronald A. Altoon

7. The Plaza at King of Prussia, Pennsylvania
Courtesy Kravco Company

Smart Shopping for Busy People

Peapod®

8. Peapod online grocery shopping and delivery service

9. Tesco product selector

Store Locations

Please click on chosen category to find the product of your choice

PlayStation
CD-ROM Software
Pre-School Toys
Construction Toys
Electronic Learning Toys
Crafts/Activities/Models
Dolls Houses/Kitchens
Dolls
Fashion Dolls
Collectable Dolls
Action Toys
Radio Control Vehicles
Train/Race Sets
Board Games
Bikes
Wheeled Goods
Battery Powered Vehicles
Outdoor Fun
Sports
Soft Toys
Money Off Coupons
About Us

RETURN TO BARCLAYSQUARE

INTERNET CATALOGUE

THE WORLD'S BIGGEST TOY MEGASTORES AND MULTIMEDIA MEGASTORES

VISA MasterCard

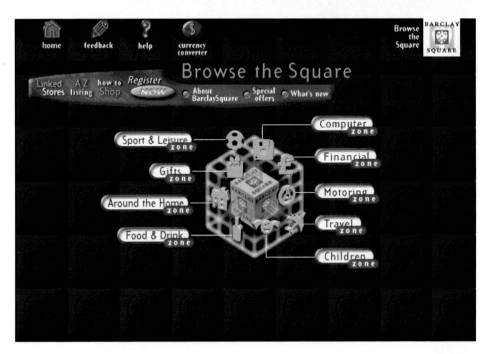

10. BarclaySquare shopping mall

11. Social use areas (Universal City Walk)
Courtesy Ronald A. Altoon

12. Canal City Hakata, Fukuoka, Kyushu, Japan
Bringing people together in the city centre. Designed by the Jerde Partnership based on its creation of Horton Plaza, San Diego, it is based
on the premise: raise the quality of human experience in places where people come together. Gross size of centre 2,400,000 sq. ft.
Open urban mall, opened 1996.
Courtesy Jon A. Jerde, The Jerde Partnership; Photo: Hiroyuki Kawano

13. Orchard Park Mall, Kelowna, BC, Canada

Computerised directories helping shoppers' way around the centre.

14. St Louis Union Station, St Louis, Missouri

Opened in 1985, incorporates retail, hotel and entertainment complex.

Courtesy The Rouse Company

and entice the window shopper to enter a world which is exciting, welcoming and likely to offer satisfaction, both in personal experience terms and also in terms of providing goods which may be purchased. The shop visit should hold out the hope of a fulfilling personal experience and service satisfaction. In such a scenario, it is extremely important that the delivery and perception meets the expectation.

As a result, retail design in some instances asks the consumer to become actively involved while viewing merchandise. Entertainment-based, interactive technologies, including high-definition television, three-dimensional headsets and customised computer kiosks, have been used by such retailers as Nike, Reebok, Warner Bros. Studio Stores and Disney Stores. The interactive technological features have also been used for information. These might give customers' guides, listings of products and general information.

One of the latest interesting concepts, which attunes to the modern environmental concerns, is the translation of the Discovery Channel from TV to the Discovery Channel Stores, which uses interactivity as a main feature of its stores. The concept of the stores is to make customers interact with a three-dimensional experience of Discovery Channel programmes. This is a completely new approach and a first in-store design, providing a fresh insight into the way retailers may be going in the future. The designer felt his task was to design a retail 'world of wonder' for science, nature and technology lovers, who also like the sensations of today's interactive media.

The design is intended to give a completely new retail experience. By extending the normal space requirements of a store, it allows Discovery Channel programmes, videotapes, interactive CD-ROM games and other activities, within an innovative but consumer-friendly environment. Some stores will have a Discovery Channel Theatre. This mini-theatre of about 500 square feet allows customers to review Discovery Channel programmes, full-length feature films and CD-ROMs. State of the art video and sound is utilised, to show what cable TV will be bringing to the home in the future.

Interactive technologies are revolutionising the retail experience. Shoppers are responding by expecting more from store designs which incorporate innovative and original technology. Customers' increasing experience and knowledge, therefore, will drive how a store's features are implemented. The 'new breed' of consumer is likely to be looking for presentation which is more attention-grabbing, and the entertainment-based retailers are turning into more than mere stockists of products in the traditional sense. Instead, they are moving to be attractive locations which, in themselves, entertain. The future should see some really exciting changes, with interactive showcasing of merchandise for the customer.

The optimism raised by these new innovations is somewhat dampened by the continuing attitudes of many old line retailers, who seem unable to change their past, well tested, formulae. The leap of imagination and drastic decisions which must urgently be addressed cannot be underestimated, but there is a fear that 'flat earth' attitudes may make such retailers fall over the edge into oblivion. One of the most important issues facing the shopping centre industry in what is always a cyclical business is the replacement of these retailers, and the form such replacements take. It is apparent to many that a lot of standard categories, such as women's ready to wear, children's wear, shoes and sporting goods are consolidating these formats, and a variety of entertainment, service and niche retailers are taking their places. Owners of shopping centres know from experience that such new substitutes are slow to become acceptable as financially sound concepts, and represent enormous front-end investment risk.

In addition, the risk is magnified because the alternative shopping centre and shopping unit choices for the retailers are also changing. Regional centres, power centres, strip centres, speciality centres, neighbourhood centres, entertainment anchored centres and others pose different sets of evaluations of tenant mix, marketing and promotion for developers and investors. This gives rise to new investment uncertainties. The industry is, fortunately, blessed with sufficient entrepreneurs and true professionals who are able to anticipate the problems and changes, and take the necessary steps to accommodate them. It is important to know that the shopping centre industry will not stand still while the rest of the world is looking a new directions. That is one of the facts which tends to be ignored, or glossed over, by the proponents of online shopping: they are not the only movers around.

I think that developers have got the form of buildings pretty near right at the present time. This is because they have finally taken careful note of what is attractive to shoppers. what draws them in large numbers, and what keeps them for the longest pleasurable length of time. The constituent parts of the centre are generally apposite to these wants. The scramble to build new shopping centres was equal only to the rush by retailers to take the space, at higher and higher rents during the late 1980s. This was based on increasing trade demand, and became a crazy and unquestioned assumption that everything would continue to boom upward. This situation tends to blur the fact that the true professionals, even at that time, were increasing their attention to market surveys, demographics and the other statistics needed prior to a development or large capital investment. This trend appears to have been adopted by more participants now that the heat has gone out of the market and the amount of market research conducted in advance of development has increased dramatically. Tenants focus the attraction, with their expert merchandising targeted to the socioeconomic profile of the shopper and the ability to alter the range and promotion reasonably quickly, for example for Easter, Christmas, Valentine's Day, etc. Regional Centres generally include much of the entertainment I referred to earlier, such as cinemas, food courts, Disney Stores and live promotion. High Streets have the streetscape of varied buildings, public areas, public buildings and the changing colour of many different people. I think that it is inevitable that the aesthetics will change, as they always do, if only to combat the criticism that all centres are clones – a point with which I agree, but which I think is more important to architects and developers than to the shopper, because the shoppers tend to only see shops in their own locality and it is only important for that centre to be attractive. Obviously, if it is attractive in a proven form elsewhere it is reasonable to replicate that form locally, so that its attraction is available to the local shoppers. If it is the same or similar to others, does the shopper care if not visiting those other places? However, shopping centres rarely change their fundamental organisational structure. Old centres may be totally rebuilt to introduce malls of different widths or directions, new services, or larger size shop units; the function of the new centre remains fundamentally the same as before. It is still a centre to house various shops and attract the public to visit and buy. For the purpose of this comparison with online shopping we should accept that a new fountain, lift, or change of flooring, is merely a cosmetic answer to the current design mode of the time, and not a wholesale change to the form.

The one major change, which I envisage as a primary requirement in the form of a sort of bolt-on, concerns signage and information. It is logical that if Information Technology is to be used before a visit, and as part of the shopping visit itself, efficient signage and information must be provided. At approaches to centres, traffic information and car park guidance should be displayed. In the centre, user-friendly touch screens should inform shoppers of the offerings, directions and all general data (see Plate 13). These units are, in a growing number of places, also being used to accept the insertion of centre loyalty or membership cards, which not only provide a good data base for the centre owners, but also offer special prizes and discounts to the shoppers. More IT infrastructure will need to be designed into centres for use by retailers and their customers.

One of the ironies of marketing, and one of the least appreciated or explained, is the way senior executives in all forms of commerce place so much importance on getting new business, and so little time in keeping it. Over the years, I can think of numerous complaints I have voiced about this to extremely intelligent businessmen; in the majority of cases the response is one of complete agreement and understanding. Regrettably, such agreement is rarely followed up by action which is effective, except in cases where it is made obvious that existing business will be taken away unless things change quickly. A typical example is when a very senior executive courts a client with invitations to lunch at a fine restaurant. At lunch the virtue of the firm, its wonderful service and great expertise, is given with expressions of having an ethos of looking after the client as a priority. Invitations to grand events usually follow. Clearly the client and his business is worth pursuing, and is seen as being a valuable addition to the fortunes of the company concerned. Often, a new friendship is forged, or an old one reinforced. In other words, a good customer relationship is established, with the first essential ingredient – trust and personal empathy between two people – in place. Thereafter, the executive disappears from the scene, either slowly or in some cases almost immediately. He is now busy looking for new clients and business and does not have time to give after-service for a client he has already secured for his firm. The client deals with the workers directly concerned with the business. This is fine, as long as the service is as good as promised. Unfortunately, there are inevitable problems and the client feels that he is either abandoned by his opposite number, or that he has to deal at a different level, often below his own. This is not an isolated example, and the amount of time and money spent on trying to find new business often results in the loss of good existing business.

That is why the current retail buzzword, being followed by an increasing number of retailers, must be viewed with at least a little scepticism. In the 1970s the word was 'location', in the 1980s it was 'design', today it is 'loyalty'. Another irony is that while loyalty schemes are springing up everywhere, online shopping is being introduced. Online is almost always remote and is a contender for the antithesis of loyal return patronage. One wonders how retailers operating both policies will reconcile the differing outlooks needed to consolidate a strategic directive. Will it be a code to give different levels or types of service to each type of customer? Of course, the retailers will say that good service, the same level of service, is given to all customers. But is this trite marketeers' answer realistic, in a world where all salesmen espouse the value of personal customer relations and the value of loyalty, as indicated by the new promotions?

Schemes are being launched every week – Safeway's ABC Card, Budgen's Visa card, Toys "Я" Us's Geoffrey Goldcard. In a recent survey of retail directors for ICL, marketing and loyalty was seen as the most important way to raise profits over the next five years.

Despite all this talk of loyalty and relationship marketing, the consumers point of view appears to have been overlooked. The Henley Centre has conducted two research programmes. 'The Loyalty Paradox' and 'Dataculture' which question a number of the existing doctrines concerning loyalty.

'The Loyalty Paradox' reaches three important conclusions. Firstly, loyalty schemes attract what they call 'the most promiscuous shoppers'– if someone belonged to one scheme, they commonly belonged to another one too. This is due to the discount nature of most schemes encouraging customers to shop. Melanie Buck, Marketing Manager for BAA/McArthur Glen, acknowledges that a privilege card is something about which the British public has become very conscious. Her further statement that 'Everyone has a wad of loyalty cards in their wallet' certainly supports the study of the Henley Centre.

Second, only a third of scheme members thought that they were more likely to buy from that company. Regardless of the discounts available, factors other than price are driving purchases.

Also, and not least in importance, only between 3 per cent and 17 per cent of participants agreed that the scheme made them think more highly of the company. Thus, loyalty cards may encourage short-term sales, but do little to achieve loyal custom once the discounts disappear. The conclusion must be that loyalty cannot be bought. Charles Dunstone, Managing Director of Carphone Warehouse, feels that some loyalty schemes have so many restrictions and conditions to their use that you feel that you have been conned.

There are now very real signs that the term 'loyalty' is becoming exhausted through over-use. It could be argued that the more loyalty schemes there are, and the more being launched, the weaker the message becomes, until eventually it will result in an even playing field. In other words, it will become a zero gain having no winner, with the possible exception of the consumer, who will be the only beneficiary from price alone. If retailers want to pursue this initiative they might need to rethink the objective of the exercise.

Customers still feel that the most important reason to visit a particular retailer is a feeling that they get value for money. You will note that I say 'value for money' and not 'the lowest price'. This is because the definition includes in its evaluation the added features of quality and service. Customers respond in a neutral and sometimes aggressive way to the terms, 'loyalty', 'relationship' and 'allegiance'. Consumers want to feel independent and not beholden. From these basic human reactions, it shows that retailers should not assume that they have some magical hold over their customers. Otherwise, the example of the business lost through projecting an attitude of customers being taken for granted, whether true or false, repeats itself.

People perceive relationships in terms of something they have with relatives or friends, and this cannot be substituted by companies and brands. People like to shop, or need to shop, but it must be seen in the context of not really being that important to them in their everyday quality of life.

One of the advantages of loyalty cards is the collection of information about the customer. Many retailers feel that this is as important as the prime purpose of the cards. By amassing this data base, retailers may be better able to understand the needs of their customers, and target future communication and promotions with greater effectiveness. In the research carried out by The Henley Centre for 'Dataculture', they found that 80 per cent of customers are pragmatic about giving personal details to companies, feeling that it is unavoidable. They know why the information is wanted with 55 per cent saying, cynically, that it is 'to sell more products and services'. Only 24 per cent think it is 'to provide a better service by knowing the individual needs of the customer'. The younger respondents (18–24) were more likely to believe the latter answer. The consumer of tomorrow, on the basis of the previous opinion that they are more discriminating, has a far more consumerist approach, seeing themselves as equal partners in a contract to buy and to sell. Each partner should expect to give and receive what is promised and as long as the deal is understood and concluded on those terms, they are happy to participate.

Fashion retailer Liz Claiborne announced (June 1996) that it is introducing its own loyalty card scheme. To be called Liz Club, it will be offered at its eighty outlets. Philippa Baker, Marketing Manager, said the scheme was implemented as a means of monitoring customers' buying patterns. This seems an endorsement of one of the most important reasons for the scheme being introduced:

> To keep customers interested and coming back to the store, [says Stephen Sinclair, Head of Marketing at Do It All] any loyalty card must offer long term benefits and this is not just about money off. Customer loyalty cards only work where the existing proposition is strong. There is a danger that the success experienced by the pioneering retailers will encourage other companies to bring out loyalty schemes. It takes time and detailed research in the initial stages of setting up a card scheme if both the customer and the company are to reap maximum benefits.

Perhaps as a result of the seemingly unending stream of market questionnaires, consumers are getting more used to them. Maybe the sheer volume is starting to wear them down and make them believe that everyone is answering the most personal details about their lives. Although I cannot fathom why a grocer needs to know the range of earning of the partner of the respondent, or whether they have a mortgage or three cars, old, new or shortly to be changed, the amount of data on shopping habits generally has helped the shopping centre industry tremendously.

The assumption that such information is helpful is, of course, based on its accuracy. In July 1996, The Georgia Institute of Technology issued its Fifth World Wide Web User Survey, conducted by Pitkow, Colleen Kehoe and other researchers at Georgia Tech's Graphics, Visualisation and Usability Center. The survey has a question which calls into doubt the validity of the information being gathered, with 26 per cent of the respondents admitting that they falsified information provided when they registered at Web sites.

Direct marketing of catalogues and credit cards has always needed customers' names and addresses to allow business to be done. Major manufacturers, on the other hand, tended to rely on advertising and aggressive sales tactics. Today, data base marketing has progressed into a marketing mainstream to compete in the fragmented market place of the era. Before, it was mainly the car industry which invested huge amounts to build data bases, which gave them the information about their potential customers and estimate what was needed to obtain their custom and loyalty. It is obvious to all that nothing is so powerful as knowledge about customers' individual preferences and lifestyles.

Powerful computers and increasingly sophisticated software have been leading us into a marketing revolution. For example, General Motors joined with MasterCard in 1992 to offer the GM Card. As a result, General Motors has a data base of 12 million cardholders and uses it to carry out regular surveys on the individuals to learn what they are driving, when they next expect to change their car and what kind of vehicle they would like. The response is directed to the appropriate division.

Blockbuster Entertainment uses its data base of 36 million households, and 2 million daily transactions, to assist them in directing customers to select films and introduce other Blockbuster subsidiaries. The company has been testing a computerised system which recommends ten movie titles based on the customer's last rentals and also offers promotions. For example, renters of children's films might get a discount at their play-centre subsidiary, Discovery Zone.

American Express has created a Decision Sciences centre in Phoenix, to process data on millions of Amex members. It examines where they shop, the places they travel, restaurants they eat in, even the economic conditions and the weather in the places they live. Amex mails precisely targeted offers, in millions of customised monthly bills, to members around the world.

This is changing the concept of 'mass markets' and customer segmentation into a few broad demographic groupings. For Amex, a customer segment might be business travellers who bought jewellery abroad in the last month. This moves us closer to true micro marketing, as some offers have gone to as few as twenty people. Of course, the real question is whether someone who has bought jewellery abroad, let us suppose for a girlfriend, wants his wife at home to see a communication which refers too that fact. There are many areas in which a shopping transaction needs to be private.

Whether it is simply the innocent wish to keep the purchase of a present secret or the price private, or the purchase of condoms by a teenager living at home, or the more selective tastes in girlie magazines, there are many instances where automatic recording of the event in some vast data base is undesirable. Let us not forget, either, that data bases are often traded widely for marketing purposes to other companies outside the one which compiles it, and can also be accessed by government and statutory agencies. Whatever the utopian dreamers may think, shoppers often want to conduct shopping expeditions as a private, personal matter, paying in cash or cheque as an anonymous member of the wide shopping public.

More people are responding, but they look for something in return. Interestingly, while 53 per cent of consumers expected discounts and promotions in exchange for their details, a much larger 66 per cent wanted better service. The fact that such a greater number preferred better service to price serves as another indication for not only retailers operating loyalty schemes, but for everyone providing online services as an alternative to traditional shopping visits.

A report (June 1996) from analyst Credit Lyonnais Laing, states that the importance of price cutting as a marketing tool is diminishing as the major food retailers concentrate on advertising and loyalty cards. The report says that marketing issues have never been so central to the fortunes of the companies in this area. Sainsbury are selected as one of the main casualties in the switch to marketing emphasis, with a marketing strategy which 'needs to demonstrate more coherence and a new central theme such as a loyalty card campaign would bring'. Sainsbury's efforts previously concentrated on price cutting, and although the company's management believes that they have a clear price advantage, it also recognises that the gap is not being fully recognised by customers.

The report suggests, moreover, that the cut of about £10 million in Sainsbury's advertising last year means losing impact within the industry. Tesco is also cutting its advertising budget by some 12 per cent, but Credit Lyonnais argues that its 'total marketing package looks destined to continue to drive superior levels of like for like sales growth'. The report also showed concern for an overly high level of advertising spending by Iceland and Argyll.

Interestingly, the report concluded that Tesco's Clubcard loyalty scheme stood out from others, because it was integrated into a wider marketing strategy and was not simply a bolt-on tool, and because good operating systems and high staff morale were in place before its launch.

Time and again we reach the same conclusion: retailers who wish to retain and reward their customers, in the widest sense, need to offer them benefits which are important to them. This could mean lower prices, but it could just as easily mean home delivery, telephone hotlines or children's crèches.

Consider the many retail functions that could benefit from being online: a shopping centre developer must consult a designer for configuring a centre's image, style and appearance; a designer must work closely with an architect in solidifying the marriage between an artistic, tasteful statement and a strong and viable structure; the centre owner must hire a leasing agent and manager who will sign retail tenants and maintain positive relations; and the tenant must construct a unique yet cost-conscious shop to draw customers in and keep them coming back.

In an article by Dan Sweeney, Vice President of IBM Consulting Group, previous electronic retailing efforts are reviewed, together with a look at where we may be going, and why. He feels that the single most powerful force propelling the electronic shopping industry is the search for incremental sales by the conventional retail industry. Traffic counts are down on malls and markets are saturated for almost all competitors. Retailers are looking for a new vehicle to provide new sales at a reasonable cost, and electronic retailing is emerging as a real possibility. The opportunity to get twenty stores' worth of volume out of one store's worth of investment is compelling. This, says Sweeney, is the most important factor in the development of the electronic retailing industry.

He asks: why have we been holding out the promise of home electronic shopping for such a long time? So far, it has not exactly revolutionised the retail business but that is not due to lack of effort, vision, capital or courage. Multi-millions of dollars have been invested by companies ranging from Warner Cable with its Cube experiment in 1973, to Sears, J. C. Penney and Dayton Hudson. In fact, according to Paul Kagan Associates, between 1986 and 1991, no fewer than twenty-seven electronic experiments were shut down. In the later 1990s, there is a new flock of participants, including retailers as well as technology and communication firms, apparently willing to invest billions more in this field.

But why is there so much eagerness to invest? It cannot be because the industry has grown to an extraordinary size and profitability over its first twenty-five years. At best, the electronic retailing industry today is still a very small part of an otherwise huge sector. Estimates put the 1992 volume at about $4 billion, about one-fifth of 1 per cent of total retail sales, and about 5 per cent of non-store retailing. Of this total about 50 per cent is accounted for by the two major home shopping networks, another 25 per cent from infomercials and 20 per cent from various online services like CompuServe and Prodigy.

After twenty years the entire industry is so small mainly because of four major factors which have accounted for the lack of success. First, the early attempts did not produce any evidence of business success, because they added little value to the shopping process. Consumers were not attracted to them for substantial purchase activity and they did not offer sufficient returns for the shoppers' investment, of time and technology, to warrant significant use. Second, with a couple of exceptions, major industry players were not attracted to the industry. The required investment was clearly not felt justified by either the profit, or the threat of competition. Thirdly, the existing technology was either too clumsy or too expensive for the average shopper. And finally, the systems were not user-friendly. They did not compare to the flexibility and choice offered to shoppers in the stores.

Sweeney believes that things are changing. He remarks on the introduction of new legitimacy and even excitement into QVC and Time/Warner Catalogue One and the fact that the high accessibility to cable will be improved by fibre-optic single lines, with ten channels of electronic information, giving over 500 channels in the home.

Based on his arguments, Sweeney thinks that the customer is now ready for electronic retailing. He says that most of today's customers are comfortable with new types of user-friendly convenience technologies such as ATMs, voice-mail and multi-media kiosks. Many customers are using home PCs, and the infamous Generation X has been honing its skills on video games and is fully trained for the rigours of electronic shopping.

The remaining hurdles are technical and economic and Sweeney feels that the next decade will see electronic ordering of most home staples, home products and apparel. But, as he says, that will be then, and this is now. While we wait to see if the promise of full interactivity is to be fulfilled, the industry will continue with a variety of tests, experiments and prototypes. Much will be dependent on the availability of PCs in the home.

So how can the Internet and World Wide Web help the retail industry?[1] Initially, the Web's advantages may be slightly masked by how it is used. Complicated URLs (Universal Resource Locators), buggy browser software, slow connection times, complicated hyperlinks and relocated home pages can give even the most knowledgeable user a migraine. However, it is not nearly as complicated as its component parts might suggest.

Only 14 per cent of companies that operate Web pages provide the option to purchase goods online. Most companies use the medium to advertise their products and services and to provide other information, such as the addresses and phone numbers of their retail stores. Several shopping centres operate informational Web pages. The World Wide Web already plays a part in the day-to-day operations of many retail companies. For example, Conshohocken, PA-based Kranzco Realty Trust Co (http://www.krt.com) is gaining additional exposure by putting all kinds of information on its Web page. Along with press releases on earnings, property openings and financial statements, Web surfers can find a full list of Kranzco properties, with every kind of statistic imaginable – shopping centre location, physical layout, square footage, tenant mix, available space, age, renovation and expansion history and contact information. There are detailed descriptions of each Kranzco-owned centre, followed by a list of tenants and their square footage.

> The primary effect on the industry with our Web site seems to be on the retail financial section [says Michael Kranzdorf, Director of Information Systems]. A year ago, our site was not known by many people. After our trip to the NAREIT[2] meeting last October, though, the majority of representatives from financial institutions had either visited our site or had at least heard of us.

In addition to the information Kranzco's Web site provides the industry, Kranzdorf sees the Web page as becoming a marketing vehicle to increase visitor traffic in the company's shopping centres. 'The Web is essentially a supplemental method of advertising that

---

1. The examples given are current and known from research carried out before the book was written. Due to the rapid rate of change and the commercial failures, and changes of direction, the cited examples may no longer be accurate.
2. National Association of Real Estate Investment Trusts.

[our shopping centres] are out there,' he says. 'Having our centres on the Web can only increase the centres and its tenants' visibility.' Kranzco offers free Internet advertising to any retailer in any of their centres that wishes to participate.

Another example of a company with a major Web presence is The Hahn Co (http://hahncompany.com), San Diego. The company's 'Shopping Universe' Web site is a way for retailers and leasing agents to come together electronically. 'The business-to-business aspect is really the most exciting part of our Web site; it helps companies communicate,' says Terese Holve, Director of Internet Business Development:

> We're streamlining the leasing process by providing all pertinent information online: shopping centre demographics, tenants, categorical listings, as well as other relevant information. Some of the most important aspects of the leasing process have taken place online.

The Hahn Company presents its information in an attractive, graphical interface, which was designed and developed for them by San Diego-based Bien Logic. 'Making a physical, visual impact on the Web should be just as important as making it in a shopping centre, which is what we're hoping to accomplish,' Holve says.

Other retail companies with a presence on the Web include, but are not limited to: The Macerich Co, Santa Monica, California (http://www.dwx.com:8181/%7Emacerich/); The Rubin Organisation, Philadelphia (http://www.rubin.com); and the Inland Group, Oakbrook, Ill (http://www.com/homes/inland.real.estate/).

Some people in the industry feel there is room for improvement in owners, managers, designers and retailers climbing on the Web bandwagon. Johnathan Westeinde, President of Detroit-based SCBB International Inc, runs the newly created Shopping Centre Bulletin Board (SCBB) (http:/www.scbb.com). Westeinde points out that more people need to populate the Web before it becomes a true marketing, promotional and business tool:

> The industry itself is slightly behind the time. [The Web], though, could play a major role in that important connection between retailer and developer [he says] The Internet offers a universal spot for industry members to connect with each other. It has great potential.

Westeinde's SCBB is not simply an electronic bulletin board, but a full-function, information-searchable Web site. Visitors to SCBB can search properties all over the world by centre name, owner–landlord, tenants and geographic location. There also is an interactive world map where surfers can click on various areas to view potential sites.

An aggressive, accessibility-minded company can provide a wealth of information and utilise graphics and photos to diversify its listing. Westeinde says that SCBB plans to list as many shopping centres in its data base as can be found. SCBB also provides Web site development services, as well as a Web Hyperlink package, where the owner pays to have their home page linked with SCBB: 'People who decide to link with us back to their home page will be able to reach that many more people,' Westeinde says.

Another industry-focused online service is Atlanta-based Internet RE•View Online, a division of Overland Park, KAN-based Intertec Publishing Corp, publisher of *Shopping Center World* magazine. Internet RE•View can be accessed in the New Media section of Intertec Corp's home page (http://intertec5.com), or through any modem communications software at (800) 647 2917.

Internet RE•View's most helpful feature for the information-hungry retail executive is its demographics data for any portion of the country, including any given population's income, median age, education, property value, employment, and work and travel habits. The service also provides all of *Shopping Center World*'s editorials dating back to 1991, including its many surveys and rankings.

'Our belief is that developing this new electronic media will allow Internet RE•View Online to most effectively enhance the information currently provided in our print publications,' says Tina D'Aversa, Marketing Director for Intertec's New Media division. She adds that having a Web presence will provide a one-stop destination for the real estate industry: 'We are developing a comprehensive real estate link on the Web with Internet RE•View for all commercial real estate organisations,' she says.

Accessorising the retail environment further, Methuen, MA-based MicroTouch Systems Inc (http:/www.microtouch.com) and Naperville, Ill-based Spyglass Inc (http://www.spyglass.com) will bring Web surfing technology (in the form of free-standing kiosks called WebStations) to the fingertips of the in-store shopper as well as the store employee. Consumers can find out more about the retailer, its special promotions, sales and complete product information; employees can learn more about company history and more effective selling methods – even take an online training course.

Annette Burak, Marketing Communications Manager for Micro-Touch, says that having in-store Web access can promote a technology-friendly retail environment as well as further justify the expense of constructing a cutting-edge Web page.

Although the Web is home to many industry companies, products and services, online shoppers also have an increasing number of choices. Some shopping centres use the Web as a marketing tool to let people know they exist; others provide store directories and online coupons; some even allow customers to shop their stores and purchase right there on the spot. And despite scattered concern of the Web's effect in replacing valuable shopping centre foot traffic with virtual patronage – and some perceived incompatibility between the Internet and the shopping centre – most people agree that the Web can only enhance a centre's accessibility and recognisability.

With regard to overall consumer Internet access, the only place to go is up. According to a joint research study conducted by Mastercard International and the National Retail Federation, 19 per cent of US consumers use the Internet. The overall signs indicate, however, that more people want to build their electronic knowledge. Another 12 per cent polled saying they plan to access the Internet for the first time during the next year.

The Plaza at King of Prussia in King of Prussia, PA (see Plate 7), offers a host of services on the Web. Introduced simultaneously with the Plaza's grand re-opening late last year. the Web site had huge online crowds and has since received electronic feedback, orders and comments from people in more than thirty countries around the world.

Begun as a 'concierge' service in the centre itself, the Plaza started its online effort by giving their Personal Shopping Service its own home page advertisement (http://www.libertynet.org/~shopfree/). That service alone receives 1000 calls a day from people who take advantage of an online directory of shops and product services, including gift ideas and a bridal registry. The page advertises the shopping service's toll-free number, which allows shoppers to buy without having to go to the centre.

Incorporated into the Plaza's page is a store directory and centre layout by section and level, a geographical map of the area, an online catalogue, a calendar of events and downloadable coupons for food and other merchandise. The page also provides links to the personal shopper page, and highlights information in conjunction with the King of Prussia Chamber of Commerce, where shoppers visiting the area can find out about hotel accommodations, car rentals, relocation services and other information about the area.

'This service is not in competition with the mall itself or with its patrons; it is a niche product aimed at Internet users,' says Hugh McGoran, Director of Interactive Design for King of Prussia-based Lorel Advertising, developers and administrators of the Plaza's Web site. 'The Plaza is now able to reach a whole new group – even the international market – people who wouldn't normally have access to or know about the centre itself,' he says. McGoran reports that the Web page eventually will be able to track how many people visit a given Plaza retailer on the Web each day which, he adds, might encourage a doubting retailer to join the Plaza's online efforts.

In another supportive argument for the continuation of the success of traditional shopping even when the centre or developer is subscribing to the Internet, Lend Lease Corporation, the Australian-owned developer of Bluewater at Dartford, Kent, has bought a 50 per cent stake in King of Prussia. Estimates of the corporation's equity participation in the centre is about $120 million. This can be seen as a further example of the conclusions stated later about experienced professional investors continuing to back shopping centres as a long-term secure medium, a scenario at odds with claims that electronic shopping will decimate traditional shopping in the near future.

CocoWalk shopping centre, a 162 000 square foot outdoor retail entertainment centre in Coconut Grove, Florida, also utilises international Web accessibility (http:/www.cocowalk.com). The centre continues to get e-mail from all over the world, including comments on and requests for directions to the centre from Hong Kong and Switzerland. Any of CocoWalk's tenants can participate in the Internet programme.

In addition to shopping centres cropping up online, there are retailers as well. To name a few: women's sportswear retailer Clothestime (http://www.clothestime.com) offers online shoppers fashion tips, a calendar of events and a guest lounge, as well as a company history, financial information, job openings and a list of store locations; shopping centre restaurant tenant Rainforest Cafe serves up its Web site (http://www.rainforestcafe.com) featuring items from its retail store, linkage to various environmental groups' home pages, and the ability to learn more about rainforests around the world; and the Athlete's Foot (http://www.theathletesfoot.com)

has its own site, which allows browsers to read about footwear trend information, learn how to start up a franchise and use an interactive map to find the chain's closest location. (Search engines such as Yahoo! are a good way to locate your favourite retailer if you don't know their URL.)

Despite an increasing amount of shopping centres appearing on-line, there are those who believe that giving the centres a Web presence is not the most appropriate way to spend time or money. Eric Dewey, Marketing Director for North Riverside Park Mall in North Riverside, IL, a property owned by Chicago-based Heitman Advisory Corp. says the Web is of limited value in broadening a centre's appeal and drawing in the masses.

As a shopping centre marketing medium, it is not a cost-effective tool [he says]. People who have jumped on the Internet bandwagon have not thought through the cost, and will, therefore, not be able to convince their retailers that they are spending their money wisely.

Dewey says he believes that the consumer Web and the consumer shopping centre markets are essentially incompatible.

The audience of the Web is world-wide whereas the shopping centre audience is regional [he explains]. Predominantly, the people surfing the 'Net' are young men who are technologically knowledgeable, which is not typical of the average mall shopper. The number of women getting online is growing, but there still is a long way to go.

But Dewey isn't totally against using the Web. 'Web pages can serve a useful purpose when done at the corporate level for leasing,' he says, adding that they also can be useful in 'gaining the economies of scale to feature and promote [a company's] portfolio'.

Stacy Armstrong, Online Program and Content Director for The Hahn Co.'s University Town Centre in San Diego, says the Web has many more possibilities than just an industry information source. 'As shopping center marketers, it is important for us to find new platforms and/or venues to reach the consumers,' she says. 'The Web is a great way to do that.'

Called 'Surfin' UTC', University Towne Centre's online counter-part (http://www.shoputc.com) is an interactive Web site with many features for online shoppers: a guest book in which surfers can sign their name; an interactive directory of stores; a section called 'Cybersavings', which is a list of coupons for various stores, printable and redeemable in the mall itself; 'Talk of the Towne', a list of special events, including fashion shows and holiday specials; an online game; and a listing of service-orientated retailers located in the centre. Armstrong acknowledges that there is progress to be made in getting a larger representation of consumers on the Web, but remains confident that its benefits will, in the end, stimulate more traffic – online and in the centres themselves:

> There is a certain scepticism out there that the Web is this small, alternative form of media [she says, adding,] I think it is extremely valuable. Consumers are time-poor, and if we can do something to assist them in their shopping needs, then our efforts are well directed. I think we're really onto something here.

Although it may take a while for the Web's small populace to grow as its usefulness catches on, many of these Web pages have become online spotlights, by automating certain retail functions and perhaps encouraging shopping centre patronage. The current examples of retail Web sites provide a foundation on which other companies can build their own Internet presence. The Web is the most convenient source of information out there. It is there, ready and willing, when needed, but quiet and unobtrusive when it is not. It will, therefore, take some computer hardware, a little initiative and an open mind to benefit from all it has to offer.

Promoters of online shopping provide articles for the trade press which try to use the Internet as a means of promoting the subject. For instance, an article in *Shopping Centre Guide* (October 1996) starts with the sentence

> In the year that European planning policies were not exactly in building large scale shopping centre schemes, there was in fact an unprecedented amount of mall development world-wide. But this development was not of the bricks and mortar type. The phenom-enal growth was in a new form of shopping centre – the Internet mall.

This is the type of comment which is leading many people into the conclusion that traditional shopping is on the wane. As will be seen from the hard evidence elsewhere in this book, the increasing amount of exposure on the Internet is not necessarily leading to increased sales of the size expounded by the promoters of the systems. The writer, Sian Harrington, goes on to say

> While the debate rages [*sic*] on as to how much of the market such forms of retailing will take, back on ground level a handful of existing UK shopping centres have been quick to see the Internet as an opportunity to exploit.

The writer gives two illustrations. The first is West Orchards shopping centre in Coventry. It is noteworthy that she reports that Jonathan Duckworth, the general manager of the Centre, believes that in the next century the Internet is the place people will turn to in order to find information. He is reported as saying 'I see it as being a cross between the Yellow Pages, public library and a glossy magazine'. West Orchards is using their site as an information provider and marketing tool rather than for electronic commerce.

The second illustration concerns Meadowhall Centre at Sheffield, one of the largest and most successful centres in Europe. They have ambitions to make their launch of a site on the Internet the best retail site on the Web. It will provide information about the retailers but will also be interactive with competitions and a virtual reality version of the centre's Oasis entertainment area. The program is intended to provide information and obtain feedback from customers. They say that the first stage is entertainment and education, but where it goes from there is 'anyone's guess'.

What is evident is that both centres see the Internet as a means of advertising and promotion, with some presently, unknown, quantity of feedback and addition to their customer data bases. To use such examples as a means of showing that there is a 'phenomenal growth of a new form of shopping centres', merely adds to the argument that many apparently well informed commentators are being swept up in the hysteria promoted by the promoters of online shopping.

We must accept that global communications are changing life dramatically, even to the extent that cyberspace is outside the control of any government. We have come a long way to reach our sophisticated shopping centres and, by comparison, the so-called shopping malls I have so far seen on the Internet are in the dark ages. By explanation, the scenario put forward today also assumes that no other competitive part of shopping will progress. There are many questions, but the biggest unanswered question for the future is whether the claims for shopping on the Net is the biggest hype of recent times.

With the advent of late night and Sunday shopping for small items at petrol stations and neighbourhood local shops, I cannot see much future for the local parades or shops in secondary positions which offer the same items as found elsewhere. Neighbourhood Centres with easy car parking for the shopper wanting a wider selection of immediate daily items, situated on main roads should prosper, and so too should the speciality centre which is something different. Unique small retailers with goods or services not to be found in a larger shopping centre are unlikely to advertise extensively, or be on the Internet. According to a report issued by Verdict Research in October 1996, there is still a huge amount of potential within the convenience store sector, contrary to the long-standing perception that neighbourhood retailing could be on the way out.

Tesco and Safeway are entering the market through petrol fore-courts, and oil company Total launched its own multi-retailer fore-court shopping outlets in October 1996 as a means of combating this trend. The first Rapide Plus outlet opened in Denham, Buckingham-shire on 12 October 1996, bringing together Blockbuster Video, Sketchley Cleaners, SupaSnaps, Thornton Chocolates, Dunkin Do-nuts and Alldays. Jim McCarthy, chief Executive of T & S Stores, said the company had short-term plans to increase its 250-plus Dillons convenience store chain by around eighty outlets. This would be achieved by extending some of its smaller Dillons stores and merging stores from the Spar, Mace and Londis groups. He believed that CTNs (Confectionery, Newspaper and Tobacco) and weaker convenience stores would come under tremendous pressure, with those at the bottom end going out of business.

Gary Croft, managing director of Spar, agreed that the conveni-ence store market, which had been controlled by 'undisciplined' retailers faced a shake up as the 'professional' retailers entered. He said that although Spar has 2000 of the best convenience stores in the country, 'a lot of work needs to be done on the remainder' which amounts to about 500 units. Clive Vaughan, retail consultant at Verdict, thinks that the independents were 'waking up and not whingeing'; they were updating their product range and increasingly opening at more convenient hours for the consumer.

Neighbourhood stores are an important amenity for local residents. The community is an important focal point for everyone. We have been imbued with the focus of the town centre, high street and civic centre throughout our history. We must have something which is a concentration of our heritage to maintain a balance to our everyday local lifestyle. Over the past few years this focal point has been attacked by a number of changes, including decentralisation of offices, movement of traditional workshops, industries and services, to outlying business parks and industrial estates, out-of-town shopping centres and more localised and easier convenience shopping parades for convenience shopping. Now the advent of electronic shopping schemes are encouraging people to become even more introspective, by staying at home.

The impact of all these changes may be seen to offer more convenience, but our lives are made up of a multiplicity of emotions and perceptions. According to our particular likes and dislikes, we tend to prefer a personal experience to one which is second-hand and remote. We may choose to actually be at Wimbledon to watch tennis at the All England Championships, instead of sitting at home watching it on television. We accept that we will see matches better on TV, with action replays and changes to other exciting matches on other courts, which we could not experience in person. However, the thrill of the occasion and the atmosphere, is more than merely a compensation for the loss of the second-hand picture. There are many examples which spring to mind, but this single one amply illustrates the general outlook of the vast majority of the population. And so, I think, we would prefer to visit the art gallery to dwell on the beauty and challenge of a fine painting at our own pace and choice, rather than watch an art programme on TV where the speed of presentation is dictated by the producer. We want to enjoy our heritage and be part of it.

Participants in electronic media can be split into many different categories, each with a particular agenda to promote. It is clear to me that many have a purely commercial objective. They are there to sell their products. The servers who want subscribers to their services, the companies who take pages to offer goods for the user to buy and the ancillary companies who see the Internet, and other technological advances, as an expansion vehicle for their own services or products all have a vested interest. There is little disguise of the motives, although many market their wares, like all good salesmen, by extolling the virtues of the product and the potential in a very beguiling way. After a while, some concerns have started to embrace the new media as a marketing tool to promote more environmental matters. This dichotomy is a further most important support for the idea I have often stated: that the computer should be the servant of the user, and not the master. It also shows that many important choices and events in our daily lives need not be destroyed; instead, they can be broadened and enhanced by letting us be more informed about those choices and opportunities available to us.

A foretaste of this sea change is shown in America by a new recognition on a page on the Internet introduced in 1995. With the header ' "In Your Neighbourhood" – The Philosophy' and a subtitle 'Welcome to America's front porch', the introduction refers to honouring the past, taking responsibility for the present and preparing our children and our country for the future and the twenty-first century. There are rousing messages of 'God, Family, Country, Neighbourhood: the cornerstones of the greatest nation in recorded history'. While many of us may feel that this is somewhat extravagant hyperbole, the opening page is rescued by the message 'Lately we've been slipping'. The message is distinct. In concise paragraphs it claims: we hardly know our neighbours; the last parade we attended was years ago; somewhere in that last move we misplaced that flag that we used to set out so proudly on the 4th of July; our cars act as shields, not transportation; our lives seem to be self-centred, exploitive, and complicated; our homes have become prisons to the very freedom this country fought to protect, namely life, liberty and the pursuit of happiness; we've simply stopped talking to each other unless we have to.

There is a clarion call with the heading 'We need to renew the spirit of the neighbourhood'. Then, we need to be accountable to one another; we need to be charitable to one another: and we need to learn to love one another: we can start right here . . . right now!!! The publishers of 'Shop-The-Net' on the Internet says it holds a 'sacred trust' to publish positive ideas, share dreams, and – above all – commit ourselves to a strong sense of community. They ask browsers to make sure that they visit 'In Your Neighbourhood' and check out . . . local movies and ratings, restaurants and menus, bookstores and guest authors, concerts and entertainment, shopping plazas, speciality shops, local merchants, special events for the kids . . . new products and services for your business and family ... discount coupons on a variety of products, services and foods ... Plus ... find out what's happening 'In Your Neighbourhood' that needs your help, your involvement, your participation, your opinion.

For each entrepreneur and business participating the publisher will set aside 2 per cent of each sponsorship towards community projects, examples of which might be graffiti removal, highway clean-ups, citizen crime watch involvement, recreational and day-care support, educational scholarships, free concerts in the park ... any project the community deems worthy.

Obviously the marketing must again be seen as a commercial operation for profit, especially by cynics. I believe that I am reasonably realistic to recognise that someone has probably seen the opportunity to find a patriotic niche message. Nevertheless, the importance of the page is that it is using the Internet as an information media to encourage users not to stay at home and shop electronically, but to go out and participate in the community life, as enjoyed through the ages.

I fully recognise that I started Chapter 5 on the premise that we could fly a 747 from home. It seems a long detour to come to the conclusion that virtual reality, and even more so, tele-shopping, is unlikely to allow us to actually experience the personal pleasure of the shopping visit as a substitute for the real thing. But I return to the example of viewing videos at home and the increasing need to go out to the cinema. The huge attendances at successful shopping centres amply illustrates their personal attraction for the shopper, despite car parking difficulties and other inconveniences. Shopping centre owners must be doing something right.

Technological progress is accelerating in leaps and bounds. This means that any perception of the market today, and any prediction of the market tomorrow, must be heavily qualified by saying that all developers, investors and retailers have to watch trends and developments with the utmost care. The scenario offers countless potential alternatives to emerge quickly in the future. For the present, I do not see a crisis for Regional Centres, High Streets, Neighbourhood Centres, Speciality Centres and, with much more circumspection, Bulk Item Retail warehouses if they offer range and service with good advice to the potential buyer. I do, however, see a demise of other types of shops, with or without the advent of computer shopping, because it is an almost universally accepted fact that we are now over-shopped.

So I leave you with this thought. The reality for today is that shopping centres are successful, but they are going to be affected by online offers. Contrary to the claims that online shopping will destroy traditional shopping, the harnessing of the Web can be beneficial, if good use is made of advertising, promotion and information.

13 Computer Literacy

The question of computer literacy is of particular importance for the future. It is undeniably clear that a reasonable degree of skill must be possessed by any user wanting to use online shopping facilities. In general, this is not perceived as a problem due to the widely held assumption that the younger generation have become so accustomed to computers in the past few years that they are all confident and facile in their use of them. I would like to look at the facts, but later also consider whether the older generation feel equally, or sufficiently, comfortable at what many find a frightening means of communication.

The *New York Times* published two features at the beginning of 1996 which are very revealing. They gave a case study to two neighbouring schools in San José, California. The first is a 'pricey and prestigious' elementary and junior high school, and the second an elementary public school attended by children of one of the region's poorest communities.

John Dixon, a fifth grader at Anderson Elementary, calls himself a computer buff. But he must make do with the school's six-year-old IBM 386 PCs, which are little more than electric typewriters compared with the multimedia machines he wishes the school could afford. He says 'so we could look up stuff on the encyclopaedias and see pictures'. As a comparison, a sixth grader at the neighbouring school uses the latest Apple MacIntosh at school to manage his own World Wide Web page. He also surfs the Web for information on research topics, such as deforestation and sends his teachers e-mails with questions about homework. He says 'I'll probably go to Stanford this summer and take a programming class.'

The digital divide between these two schools, in the heart of Silicon Valley, provides perhaps the most striking example anywhere in America, of a widening gap between children who are preparing for lives and careers in the information age, and those who may find themselves held back.

At one school, the children of the affluent are being prepared, from an early age, to take their place in the economy. At the other, children, many of them Mexican, Vietnamese, Pakistani and, most

143

recently, Bosnian immigrants, can hope for little more than a basic, traditional education. Some parents understand that computers are a way for their children to progress in the future, but technology is not the highest thing on their priority list. Some of the parents are more concerned with feeding their children, rather than knowing the latest software program release.

This typifies why computers in schools has become one of the hottest debated education topics of the 1990s. Malcolm Cohen, author of *Labour Shortages: As America Approaches the 21st Century,* puts it plainly. 'We are facing a new illiteracy – computer illiteracy. Many, many children won't be prepared for the work force because they can't use computers.' 'The way computers are used in the classroom – and the way the Internet will change their use – is really a profound commentary on education', said Michael Kirst, a Professor of Education at Stanford University:

> The Internet is a prophetic example: richer kids with access to a home computer and to the Internet can use it as a means of exploration and discovery. Poorer kids without the Internet will just use a computer, in the classroom, for drill and practice exercises.

It must be accepted that, in America at least, they are aware of the importance of computers in education. A government survey reporting early in 1996, states that half the nation's public schools have hooked up to the Internet, with bigger, richer suburban schools leading the way. Schools with many minority or low-income students are connecting, too, but at a slower pace. This would seem to indicate some support for the disparity illustrated in the San José experience; if so, the gulf between richer and poorer children will be carried through into adult life, and correspondingly their ability to use, among other things, online shopping methods. Indeed, former American Education Secretary Richard Riley noted that in some cases computers have been concentrated at so-called magnet schools, designed to attract top students. Although 50 per cent of public schools had at least some Internet access, only 9 per cent of classrooms were connected.

President Clinton announced a five-year, $2 billion programme to put computers in all American classrooms and link them to the Internet. The money for the programme, called 'Technology Literacy Challenge', is in Clinton's fiscal 1997 budget request, but it was uncertain that his proposal would be approved by the Republican-led Congress. The trend is emphasised by the statistic that, although the 50 per cent access figure has been used generally, defined low-income schools accounted for only 31 per cent, compared with 62 per cent for the more affluent schools.

While the experience to date, as shown by reports of junior schools in America, seems to indicate that many children may not be sufficiently proficient and comfortable in the use of computers in the future, the more disturbing inference is that a large proportion of all children will simply not be literate when they reach adult age, due to their financial situation. This, together with the likelihood that such disadvantages in their formative education will consign them to lower-paid employment as adults, makes them unlikely to be able to afford the capital costs of computers and associated software, phone lines, service costs and modems, presently essential to fully utilise online shopping. We must, of course, await further developments of systems before seeing whether household budgets will be able to entertain future facilities. At this time, the only real indicator must be that many lower-income households, operating on a tight shopping budget for weekly shopping essentials and a few luxuries, would be unable to contemplate such additional capital or leasing costs as would be needed to enter the online market.

Sheila Byfield, a Director of Ogilvy and Mather, thinks that of all marketing targets, children are probably the most slippery. They can be fickle, both in product and media behaviour, and targeting them 'Can be like juggling jelly'. This is becoming more of a challenge, because of the volume of new activities opening up. Researching 400 11–16 year olds recently, they found that 99 per cent played computer games and 78 per cent used computers. Among 11–14 year olds, over a quarter of screen time is spent on activities other than watching television. This is producing a generation of interacting, surfing, multi-taskers. Matching the pace of these environments and tracking trends is a core challenge, but one worth accepting. It is estimated that 7–14 year olds have over £1.5 billion at their disposal.

That is a view of an advertising and marketing agency executive, but a more practical view is put forward by Julie Forsyth, Promotions Manager of Selfridges. She says that to market successfully to children, Selfridges has found that the parents must be targeted. An offer of a 'shopping experience' packed full of entertainment and fun with the use of noise, colour and eye-catching activities, keeps the children happy while the parents are there. Regular themed promotions in Kids Universe at Selfridges, and directed communication at the parents, encourages them to bring in the family.

So far, we have spoken about younger children. We should obviously take the matter to the next stage and consider those students who progress to a higher stage of education. Despite the normal assumptions that the majority of such students will come from more affluent backgrounds, many will also overcome the disadvantages of their poorer environments and succeed against the odds because of their intelligence or determination. Whether these students generally become literate in computers because of their early education, or become informed at a later stage, is not important; what matters is that they are candidates for evaluation as potential users of a large online market.

Deakin University in Australia has carried out research that has discovered that one in ten young people suffer from computer anxiety, countering the myth that this is a condition suffered only by older users. A study into the computer habits of university students showed that, while young people were slightly less likely to be anxious when using a computer than older users, some did suffer from computer anxiety – a specific type of technophobia. Alastair Anderson, the author of the study, said 'it appears not to be as high as 25 per cent which has been reported in some of the studies overseas, but it is a significant number'. Anderson, from the Deakin University School of Management Information Systems said 'More than 50 per cent had computers at the time of the survey but there was still this 10 per cent presenting with anxiety'. The study, 'Predictors of Computer Anxiety and Performance in Information Systems', drew its definition from Howard, Murphy and Thomas who described it at a conference in Atlanta, Georgia, as a 'fear of impending interaction with a computer that is disproportionate to the actual threat presented by the computer'.

The research examined the effects of experience, perceived knowledge, programming experience and gender, on computer anxiety among first-year business graduates. Perceived knowledge, or how much students thought they knew about computers, and experience, were found to have the greatest impact on computer anxiety. As with perceived knowledge, the more experience respondents had with computers, the less likely they were to display anxiety. However, perceived knowledge was found to be a better predictor of anxiety than experience.

The two types of anxiety identified by the study were transient and persistent. Of these, users who suffered from transient computer anxiety displayed a short-term fear response, but tended to overcome their fear as they gained more knowledge and experience. Persistent anxiety tended to be more difficult to treat. This was because of their underlying personality style. However, Anderson warns against confusing the idea of frustration with a computer with anxiety. Frustration was a normal response that a user would experience from time to time, but would be able to overcome. Anxiety, on the other hand, extended over a much longer period and was usually accompanied by a cold sweat, increased heart rate and similar fear reactions. The typical behaviour of such people is said to be avoidance – even, possibly, to avoid computers completely, depending on whether this is feasible in the job being done.

We have now discussed the young and the older students, including university graduates. Having seen that the generally accepted opinion that most, if not all, young people will be able to communicate via their computers in the future, there are some questions and doubts that this assessment is as totally correct as we thought. But, for the market analysers of shopping trends, what of the mature shoppers of today?

A large number of adults are computer owners or users. A lot of this sector may be users of computers at their office rather than at home, but that would still make them part of the potential audience. Indeed, they may be even more likely to shop online because of the convenience if they are working during the day and can easily tap in to a unit on their desk. What the boss would say about the time necessary for the task during office hours might be quite another matter. Could we foresee a new directive for blocking telephone numbers above and beyond that which many offices have installed for long-distance, international and sex-line digits?

I was astonished when, some years ago, a good friend who was one of the powers that be at Lords, the headquarters of cricket in London, told me of the staggering income received from use of the dedicated telephone number for the Test Match cricket scores. But the most interesting aspect was that the revenue was reduced to a fraction of the weekday figure, on Saturday and Sunday. This was because the high cost was unacceptable to the caller from a home line, but a convenience to be used from his office line. In September 1996, a new survey of business managers reported that 59 per cent said that personal use of the Internet on company time is unacceptable. The problem is that 100 per cent of employees with Web access admit to browsing for personal use during office hours, and it seems that their bosses are doing nothing to stop them. Another survey shows that 35 per cent of City institutions are concerned about the amount of time their employees spend on the Internet for non-business searches.

Both studies support research carried out in America, with one example showing that 80 per cent of visitors to the Playboy Home Page were employees of large blue-chip companies. Steve Purdham, President of JSB surfCONTROL, who commissioned one of the surveys says that legitimate browsing can easily lead to 'involuntary' browsing. 'Most people don't intentionally waste time, but easy access to a wealth of information is highly seductive.' Involuntary browsing occurs when employees set out to find a particular piece of information and are side-tracked into related subjects, by the way the Web pages are linked to each other. They gradually lose sight of their original goal, and as a result end up wasting time without realising it, which is far more dangerous than if they are guiltily aware that they should get down to some serious work. Rather than limit access in the software, so far employers have restricted Web access to certain people in their organisations. One study showed that 78 per cent of companies gave fewer than 10 per cent of their employees access and only 8 per cent give more than 75 per cent access.

Among the adult computer users there are some dinosaurs. *The Houston Chronicle* cites an amusing story about Mr Greg Faulx. Unlike many of his suburban neighbours who have entered into the computer revolution, he refuses to take part. In answer to the question, 'What about ordering airline tickets via the computer' he says he can do it over the telephone. What about information on a new refrigerator? 'If I need one I speak to the salesman at Sears.' What about e-mail and interfacing with cyber travellers from all over the country? 'I barely speak to my own neighbours, why should I want to speak with some complete stranger from Oregon?'

But something else is stopping Faulx from plugging into the virtual world. It is as old as the dinosaur. It is fear. 'I know that if I touch the wrong button, I could erase everything', admits the financial analyst for an insurance company, who nonetheless knows that his days as a computerphobe are numbered. An impending transfer to another town means that he will no longer have a local friend to number crunch for him. But he says that he likes to get his hands on paper, to feel and read it. He says it was the way he was trained and he feels comfortable. Faulx is a dyed-in-the-wool technophobe, and he is not alone. A 1994 Dell Computer Corp survey found that 23 per cent of Americans are uneasy just thinking about computers. In fact, Faulx has a home computer, but his dislike for all things cyber means that he has not used it.

The idea of Japanese industry conjures up a vision of super efficient high tech executives using the most advanced computer technology. The story related in the *Los Angeles Times* (23rd January 1996), of an Executive Director of a major TV animation company in Tokyo, dispels this illusion. In his position, Yasumasa Fukushima commands power and prestige. But once in front of a computer, the 52-year-old manager becomes a quivering mass of nerves. 'I've never touched a mouse in my life,' he said, 'but I have no choice.' His company plans to buy him a desktop computer and has made it clear it expects him to use it. Japanese companies continue to produce high-tech innovations, but inside those firms, memos are still written by hand and calculations made using an abacus and pocket calculators. Use of a keyboard is still regarded by many male executives as women's work.

Now many Japanese companies are looking to executives to communicate via e-mail and use data bases. In an advertisement for Compaq's Presario, a young man jokes 'In our Company, the higher someone's position is, the less capable he is on computers. Isn't it funny?' The fact is that despite Japan's image, personal computer use was until recently limited to children playing computer games and young people who wanted Internet access. A lack of Japanese language software for word processing, and the difficulty in understanding terminology translated from English, also contributed to the sluggish demand for home computers.

In December 1996, the British government launched what it called an ambitious campaign to get the Nation 'wired up', as new evidence showed Britain as a country of technophobes, with millions still afraid to use computers. Many admit that they are unable to programme their video recorders, and almost one in five adults still refuse to use cash dispensing machines. As an aside, there may be an interesting reference to the need for good customer service being an essential for success in retailing in the type of personal service being experienced at banks. A cynic might even say that the cash dispenser is now about as human as anything one might expect at a high street bank! According to a survey initiated by Ian Lang, then President of the Board of Trade, women are more resistant to technology than men. Three in five are not convinced that computers have any use in society. Mr Lang had launched Information Technology For All, a £5 million drive to conquer fear of 'information technology', in partnership with leading British businesses and charities, including IBM, British Telecom, Tesco and Safeway.

Although sales are predicted to spurt nearly 60 per cent this year, according to a researcher, another recent survey of 880 companies, by Fuji Research Institute, gave a figure of only 20 per cent of executives able to use a computer. This is echoed by the Japanese government, with stories of government officials arriving at international conferences carrying bundles of documents wrapped inside the traditional furoshiki, while counterparts from other industrialised countries had lap top computers.

The price of computers has dropped dramatically in recent years, but the cost still puts buying one out of the reach of many people. That group of people risk being left behind, because they cannot afford to join the revolution, due to fear, lack of funds, or just plain reluctance. Some industry-watchers speculate that as America becomes increasingly technologically-orientated, its society will split further into two distinct groups of computer 'haves' and 'have-nots'. Demographic analysis reveals most Houston PC owners are white-collar and upscale. Other national studies have found that the division tends to be along racial and socioeconomic lines. A 1995 US Department of Commerce survey, called 'Falling Through the Net', found that poor African-Americans and Hispanics, in inner city or rural areas, are least likely to own a home computer. Again, the findings mentioned before are borne out by the fact that the less educated, the less likely a person is to have a computer.

Middle-class people who are on a tight budget, or pressed for time, might also be left out. Many feel that they could afford to buy a computer if they budgeted carefully, but buying one is a long way down on the list of good things on which to spend money.

For the moment, the person who is lagging behind is probably in the majority, but even so, probably only just. A recent *Houston Chronicle* survey found that 42 per cent of adult Houstonians owned a personal computer, equating to about four out of ten. What is significant, is that less than half are hooked up to a modem which allows computers to talk to one another and makes it possible to link up to online services. Then, only 26 per cent of that 42 per cent subscribe to an online service. This, again, raises the spectre of a split in society between those with access to the vast information available on cyberspace, and those without – the same 'haves' and 'have-nots' scenario, but with the subtle difference of having some with access to all the information, power and knowledge, and the others being kept down. David Donnelly, an Assistant Professor at Houston University, who teaches a course on the social impact of technology, thinks this vision may be an exaggeration. There are many precedents: some people have cars, others do not; some people have education, others do not; some have private health insurance, and so on. He poses the question: – 'Is technology going to close the gap, or widen it?' He points out that the hardest hit by the computer revolution are low-skilled employees who have lost their jobs to automation or to companies moving operations overseas to exploit cheaper wage costs. These groups are not being retrained with even basic computer skills, they are not in school and they have no computer in the home. A typical two-day computer training seminar can cost $600 and few minimum wage employees can afford that.

The opposite view is given strongly by Robert W Stearns, Vice-President of Technology and Corporate Development for Compaq Computer Corporation. He disagrees that computers are creating a technological underclass in America:

I'm put off by the idea that we're encouraging some elitist, stratified society [he says]. Nothing is further from the truth. On the contrary, computers have a great potential for democratisation. As they become increasingly important, everyone who needs access will have access, except perhaps in the most extreme cases of homelessness.

Those who do not own PCs, he says, will learn how to use them through public kiosks scattered in a panoply of places such as grocery stores, restaurants, post offices, libraries. In essence, they'll be forced to. In the near future, everything will be based on 'electronic commerce' – buying groceries, paying bills, banking, clothes shopping, everything. It is noteworthy that there is a suggestion that access to computers for a large section of the market will be through computers located in shops or units, often to be found in shopping centres or downtown. This is a truly revealing vision from a computer industry leader, which impacts greatly on the theory of online shopping replacing the traditional visit to the shopping centre.

Toward the end of 1995, a study identified types of interactive shoppers. This may help in considering the references to computer literacy. The new study says that it will take more than one form of interactivity to accommodate all the types of shoppers the study identified. Arbitron's New Media Pathfinder Study consisted of national telephone and mail surveys of 4199 adults, covering 612 variables, including demographics, psychographics, current media experiences and expectations. A group of 2136 was used to define segments.

Of the respondents, 14 per cent are the 'Fast laners' who are primarily teens, and what are called Generation Crossovers. They are much more open to technology and optimistic about the future, than the general population. 'Diverse Strivers', being 5 per cent of the respondents, are young and ethnically diverse. 'Savvy Sophisticates', 11 per cent, consist mainly of high-income, highly educated baby boomers. They are confident, innovative and optimistic about the future and technology. More of them than any other segment own and use personal computers. The 'Family-focused', representing 15 per cent of the respondents, are mostly price-conscious females, with average incomes and lower than average involvement with computers and technology. 'Bystanders', 16 per cent, are the least confident and innovative. They are mainly baby boomers with more than the average number of children at home. Other segments are 'Sports Fanatics' (11 per cent), 'Moral Americans' (11 per cent) and the 'Settled Set' (17 per cent).

The study concludes that home shopping channels appeal most to Fast Laners, Diverse Strivers, Family Focused and Bystanders. Savvy Sophisticates show the heaviest involvement with online and print catalogues. They do not see TV as a purchasing medium.

In another report on results, from what is claimed to be one of the largest Internet surveys to date, SRI International released data about users of the World Wide Web. This dealt with who is on it, how they use it, and why. The effort was first to augment standard demographics, including age, income and gender, with a psychographic analysis of the Web population. The survey looked at the psychology of people's choices and behaviour on the Web.

The results show two Web audiences. The first is a group that drives most of the media coverage and stereotypes of users, being the 'upstream' audience. This amounts to about 50 per cent of the current Web population, being upscale, technically-orientated academics and professionals, who proceed on a variety of institutional subsidies. However, because this group represents only some 10 per cent of the US population in the surveyed group, their behaviours and characteristics are of limited value in understanding the future of the Web.

The second audience comprises a diverse set of groups, that SRI calls the Web's 'other half'. This accounts for 90 per cent of US society and, therefore, they are where Internet growth will increasingly need to take place if the medium is to become mainstream. The findings about the 'other half' are revealing. They have a gender split of 64 per cent male and 36 per cent female, which is more balanced than the upstream split of 77 per cent and 23 per cent. Then, many information-intensive consumers in the US population are in the 'other half' rather than in the upstream population. These particular other-half consumers report the highest degree of frustration with the Web than any other population segment. As a group they have yet to find the Web particularly valuable.

But in relation to this sector of the book dealing with literacy, the 'information have-nots', who are people not on the Web at all, are excluded because of limited education and not just because of low income. Although income for the Web audience is rather upscale, with a median yearly income of $40 000, it includes a substantial number of low-income users with 28 per cent having a yearly income of less than $20 000. The same cannot be said for education, which has a high end-only distribution. 97 per cent of the upstream audience and 89 per cent of the 'other half' audience reports at least some college education. These reports confirm that education is the key to Internet participation, which, in turn, calls into question the effectiveness of proposals to empower information 'have-nots' with income-targeted subsidies for Internet access.

In the upstream audience, accounting for 50 per cent of the current Web population but only 10 per cent of the US population as a whole, members of the segment are highly educated and work in academic or technical areas, such as technical professionals, scientists and professors, which were the three top job categories. Their primary motivation for using the Web, especially in terms of initial usage, appears to be work-related. But the separation between work and play on the Web is obscure. 70 per cent of mainstream users regularly use the Web for recreational purposes, with 44 per cent reporting occasional conflicts with work in this regard.

SRI believe that if the Web is to become a truly mass medium, it must expand beyond this segment and include more of the remaining 90 per cent of US society. They look to responses from the Web's 'other half' for clues about how this expansion may take place.

Currently most of the Web's 'other half' are students or recent graduates working in technical, managerial or professional fields. The population is overwhelmingly a Generation X crowd, with some 70 per cent of 'other half' respondents having ages under 30 years. This population is represented by two different segments, which are similar demographically, but different psychographically. The group referred to as 'Strivers' are more technically sophisticated and notably more pro-Web than the other group, called 'Experiencers'. Strivers report spending most time on the Web and disagree that the Internet is less useful than claimed by the media. Their engagement with the Web is something of a surprise because, as consumers, they typically represent followers rather than leaders. In this regard SRI thinks that it could point to a faddishness in the current excitement surrounding the Web.

In the other main group for 20-something Web users, Experiencers seem more easily bored by the Web than Strivers. Experiencers think that the Internet makes them less productive, which is a significant deviation from the overall pro-productivity view of the sample. As consumers, this group are innovative, stimulation-seeking and fashionable. Their relative coolness to the Web suggests that its content and form are not meeting their expectations. For recreation, this group tends toward action, either physically, or vicariously through video games and action movies. The click and wait procedures of the Web, and its amount of text, probably causes much of this group's dissatisfaction.

Researchers at Rochester Institute of Technology, Rochester, New York, add that Internet shoppers are pioneers more in the way that they shop than in what they actually buy. 'They're not risk takers. You can tell by their purchases', said Eugene Fram, the J. Warren McClure Research Professor of Marketing. Fram and Dale Grady, RIT software specialist and assistant professor, used the World Wide Web Directory services to see attitudes and compile a composite of the electronic shopper. This indicated a median age of 32, predominately male (only 21 per cent of respondents were female) and well educated. More than two-thirds hold a four-year college degree. 82 per cent of the 461 respondents purchased something electronically during the preceding three months. The researchers did not ask browsers to respond, but said that their participation indicates high interest in interactive shopping.

A contrary view emerges from a survey by GVU of over 23 000 users, in late 1995. In answer to the question on why people use their browsers, it found that the most common use was simply for browsing (79 per cent). This was followed by 63.6 per cent for entertainment and 51.8 per cent for work. The Seventh Survey, conducted in April 1997, changed some categories but provided a valuable update on the primary uses of browser. The most common Web activity was to gather information (86.03%), followed by searching (63.01%), browsing (61.29%), work (54.05%), education (52.21%), communication (47.02%) and entertainment (45.48%). Shopping remained stable at 18.65% following 18.83% in the Sixth and 14.9% in the Fifth. In the Fourth Survey it was a lowly 11.1% and the lack of use of the Web for shopping was also found in their other surveys, where the previous one showed only 10%, and the one before that 8%. Hence, although they said, while the Web is being used for academic and business purposes, the main uses were still recreational, the US now reports one in five users shopping on the Web. This trend is expected to continue.

Further data from the American Internet Survey by Find/SVP shows that 31 per cent of the estimated 8.4 million adult users of the Internet are ages 18–29, while 'baby boomers' between the ages of 29 and 50 account for 53 per cent. Users under the age of 18 add another 1.1 million to the Internet population, making a total of 9.9 million. As we have seen, the World Wide Web is the primary sub-component of the Internet for shoppers, because of its graphics and point and click features. The number of adult users of the Internet trebled from 2.2 million in 1994 to 6.6 million in 1995.

A Global Concepts Inc. study, sponsored by MasterCard International, found that although 62 per cent of the US population have a personal computer, only 31 per cent have Internet access capabilities, and only 19 per cent have accessed it. 12 per cent have accessed the World Wide Web and only 1 per cent have actually purchased anything on it. A *Business Week*/Harris Poll of 1186 people in June 1996 found that 19 per cent had accessed the Internet or the Web during the past year, which corresponds to the Global Concepts Study.

At the moment, users of the Internet are primarily those with higher levels of education and income, who tend to be people who adopt new technologies. It is therefore difficult for retailers to target specific demographic and psychological customers, because its user profile is changing as it gains wider acceptance. In addition, major changes in the Internet itself are forseen. These changes may drastically affect the user population if, for example, higher fees are introduced to pay for required Internet capacity upgrades. This may cause users to reduce their frequency of use or to lose interest.

The extent of a consumer's use of the Internet is a strong determinant of whether goods will be purchased online. As an example, 44 per cent of users who access the Internet for 30 hours or more each month have purchased goods online, compared to only 5 per cent of those who spend less than 10 hours per month using it.

With another reference to earlier remarks about the telephone, no one argues with the fact that machines have streamlined the business world, but sceptics point to the puffery which accompanied the arrival of the telephone. Proponents claimed it would erase all social barriers, defend morality, bring peace on earth and save the family farm. Likewise the advent of the microwave oven, which was supposed to transform the way everyone cooks, in retrospect, has merely changed the way most people heat instant food, bearing in mind that much of that food is 'oven ready' and therefore has already been prepared and cooked by someone else. 'Historically, there has been this idea that the new technology is going to save us', says Michael W. Apple, John Bascom Distinguished Professor of Education at University of Wisconsin. 'But we need to ask ourselves: Are we being sold a bill of goods?' He does not want to be misunderstood and says computers definitely have their place. But he feels that Americans are being misled by self-serving technocrats who want to convince us of a wealth of high-tech jobs that we could get if we learned the manual. Professor Apple says that is not true, because job growth these days tends to cluster in the low-end service sector, such as maintenance, health care, fast food, and not in highly paid techno jobs. And how much technological skill do you have to know to push a button for a Big Mac? He discounts some of the more zealous claims being made about the benefits of being online. Donnelly says 'I think what the have nots are missing out on is overstated. There are people who are perfectly happy and content not logging on.'

Obviously, we all know that five-year-old Johnny can play games on the screen better than I can, even if he can't do simple addition or spell his name. I think Johnny will be able to use the system in the future much better than we can now, but still doubt the attraction other than as a means of advertising and pricing. And I will venture an opinion why. We have to remember that computers are tools, and not the master of what we do. They, like all means of implementation, are to help us to carry out what are generally normal functions faster and to achieve our wishes. Therefore, we need the intellectual ability to know what we seek, what we want to do, and when we are satisfied with the result. If we do not exercise intellectual ability and personal choice through our own power of thought we become robots, merely responding to the enticement of a message, order, or direction beamed at us. We don't need computers for that; we already have TV commercials with their seductive sales campaigns.

Since the mid-1960s, everyone has been talking about computers and the information revolution. About 25 years ago there were books describing almost everything about life in this context, apart from the details. We have been living through this. Alvin Toffler's *Future Shock*, Drucker's *The Age of Discontinuities* and Bell's *Beyond Post-Industrial Society*, illustrated the possibilities. Since we were given this information and its potential, and seeing that it is intellectually so obvious, why have we been so slow and reticent to embrace the Third Wave?

The first reason may have been given by C. P. Snow in his BBC Lectures, as long ago as 1959. Snow argued that during the last century, and particularly during the preceding sixty years, Western civilisation had split into two cultures: a scientific engineering culture that mainly dealt with the language of mathematics, and an arts and literary culture which spoke the language of literary allusion. These two cultures had grown further apart, with the result that in modern times many of those who have knowledge are inarticulate and a lot of those who are articulate have little knowledge. In essence, he said that even if you do not know what you are talking about you might still make it sound interesting and plausible, but if you are really brilliant it is difficult to explain the details in words which are understandable or interesting. Every day, we see politicians and newspaper reporters giving opinions on matters on which they have little expert knowledge, while people who do have the expertise either cannot express themselves in a common language which we can understand, or are not given the opportunity to do so. Perhaps I should take a clue from this criticism!

The problem is compounded by the fact that most entrepreneurs who make breakthroughs are almost, by definition, psychologically uninterested in working in dull, slow processes in which one has to listen to people who often do not know as much as they do. In addition, the science and engineering sector is generally set against being active in a political sense. Thus we end up without entrepreneurs and scientists involved with governing, and with a society in which regulators dominate.

Part IV

The Future of Electronic Shopping

14 Power Centres, Online, TV and Catalogues

As I said before, staple purchases may be bought by tele- or computer shopping. As we know, shopping has been in effect for some years through such systems as Prestel and QVC in Britain and America, Minitel in France, as well as the Home Shopping Channel in the States. These offer a wide range, including DIY, cooking utensils, fashion and jewellery. We can obviously relate this to the large market of mail order. For many items, however, the better reference may be to such bulk trading units as Costco. These offer bulk purchases of cases of baked beans, cartons of toilet rolls but also televisions, car tyres, and so on. Will the housewife really want twelve bottles of Fairy Liquid with the upfront cost on the weekly budget, or simply one bottle? Does a store want to deliver one bottle of Fairy Liquid? How will a careful shopper, watching the budget, compare weekly offers and loss leaders without comparison shopping personally? How can the consumer see the special offers and loss leaders of the moment?

I am sure that these questions must have been considered by the promoters of all home shopping and bulk systems. Nevertheless, there is an unavoidable cost factor to be inbuilt into home deliveries of all, and particularly small-item, orders. Therefore, even staple goods purchases by home shopping are not as clear-cut as would first be supposed. Indeed, it may be just as convenient to buy all staples at the same time as the fruit purchase, apart from the burden of transporting them. One might ask whether shoppers will go to a supermarket for just one item, in any event. Since supermarkets or convenience stores are often located within shopping centres or high streets, it is quite convenient for a shopper to combine the purchase of that item at the same time as others. Clearly, the shopper will approach home shopping of this type with the same scepticism that they have for all new things. Grocery delivery services are not new, as we have seen. Many previous companies have tried it and failed, with for example, Safeway's Shoppers' Express and several others, going under before 1993. The experience of many consumers, expecting delivery on a promised day, of say their furniture from even the most prestigious and expensive supplier, does not encourage great confidence that orders will be correct, or will arrive at the time expected. Or even at the time indicated as convenient. There has been little response to the question of what the consumer does if the food for that evening's dinner party does not arrive, or is delivered to the wrong address? As stated at the beginning, systems tend to depend on the human factor, no matter how good the software program.

Richard Adams, the founder of eco-friendly Out of This World, which claims to be the first green supermarket chain in the United Kingdom, hopes to set up a national mail order service with 1000 products on offer. He makes the statement which supports some of my arguments about the problems of delivery of food by saying: 'The plan is to focus on ambient foods, because perishables are too difficult to deliver in prime condition.'

The convenience of shopping for routine items, and the additional costs associated with that luxury, is well illustrated by Peapod Interactive, which is an online grocery shopping and delivery service mainly trading in Chicago and San Francisco (see Plate 8). Peapod Online Services and Shoppers' Express, the largest players in online grocery shopping are in stiff competition. Shoppers' Express has now entered Atlanta, which will become the second city where the two will compete directly, having already done so in Dallas.

The battle comes as more players enter the online grocery market, which some expect to grow to $60 billion in the next ten years. Anderson Consulting predicts that in the next 7–10 years, alternative grocery channels will represent from 8 to 10 per cent of the consumer package-goods channel and that between 15 and 20 million households will shop via alternative methods. Until now, Peapod and Shoppers' Express have enjoyed relative success by being the major operators in the market. Currently in a quiet period before it makes a public offering, Peapod markets its services to 50 000 subscribers in Chicago, Boston, San Francisco, Houston, Dallas, Atlanta and Columbus, Ohio. Shoppers' Express claim that their subscriber base is in 'tens of thousands', in Los Angeles, Phoenix, Atlanta and Dallas.

Fred Schneider, world-wide director of electronic commerce programs at Anderson, said: 'Clearly, Peapod has proven that there is a significant demand for this type of service. But Peapod has yet to demonstrate they can do that profitably.' For 1996, Peapod reported a net loss of $9.5 million on revenues of $29.2 million. Getting to profitability increasingly requires a mix of grocery alliances and partnerships with local online services. The big difference between Peapod and Shoppers' Express is that the latter offers its' services on NetChannel, a competitor of WebTV Networks.

Women currently make only a fraction of online purchases, although some 80 per cent of Peapod's 10 000 clients in Chicago and San Francisco are women. Peapod was founded in 1989 and went online in 1990. However, it was a proprietary dial-up service and clients had to have Peapod's software to use the service. Tim Dorgan, President of Peapod said

> I don't know how many of our members truly cruise the Internet. Basically our members are people who would rather not be in the grocery store or are too busy to be in the grocery store.

Peapod gains new members through word of mouth, advertisements in grocery stores and radio ads during drive time. Busy Americans lacking time for grocery shopping 'was clearly a problem in search for technology rather than the other way around', Dorgan says, 'Often people create technology and then it's "Let's find a problem for it to solve"'. He thinks that this is a long-time problem because people do not have the time or the interest to be in the grocery store. Technology was applied to solve the problem. Peapod's members use their computers at work or at home, to order groceries. There is access to about 20 000 items in a traditional retail store, and they can be seen on screen. Current pricing and current promotions are displayed. The goods are ordered and then delivered to the members door. He says: 'If you say, I want eight bananas, and I want four of them to be green and four of them to be ripe, that's what you'll get.'

Dorgan gives no details of how the deliveries are guaranteed. What he does give is information on added costs of the service, on top of the access costs. Goods are sold at retail prices, but additionally there is a membership fee of $4.95 per month and each order carries a delivery charge of $6.95, plus a 5 per cent charge on the value of the order. On the basis of a $100 order the added cost is about $12. Dorgan accepts that the value depends on how busy the member may be. It could be a good deal or pricey.

In 1996, Peapod launched its service for the Columbus, Ohio, area in cooperation with The Kroger Co. The new service allows Columbus residents and businesses to pick out and deliver any item from the Kroger stores via modem-equipped computers, phone or fax. The charges are similar to those described later in this section. The interesting thing is that at about the same time, Kroger Food Stores announced its newest location in downtown Atlanta. According to Brent Scott, Kroger Vice President of Marketing, the basic services needed for a residential community, such as a grocery store, were missing from the downtown district. He added

> Kroger has a long history of supporting metro Atlanta communities. When we learned about the City Plaza project, we didn't even hesitate on making the decision to open the first downtown grocery store to help revitalise what was once the heart and soul of Atlanta.

The new store will offer 18 000 items, including gourmet foods prepared by chef Roger Jennings, who operates the newly renovated cafe in Kroger's Ponce de Leon store. This features fresh pastries, sandwiches, pizzas and main courses, and is seen to be particularly popular with the large downtown business community. Other amenities include a pharmacy with an over-the-counter selection and an automated bank teller machine. My comment about the way retailers are viewing online shopping as a direct threat to their traditional selling methods is best typified by this concurrent investment in a new property, staff, merchandising and promotion, at the same time as the Peapod initiative elsewhere. The big question remains: Why does a group such as Kroger invest in a longish-term massive capital project while taking advantage of online services? Perhaps the comments on this question, which I give later, provide the most likely answer.

Another local supermarket chain in Baltimore is taking their services online. They will be distributing a CD-ROM disc which houses their 'virtual shopping programme' monthly. When a customer wants to go shopping, they boot up the program which dials into the company's computer and downloads the latest price list. At that point, it is claimed, the customer can browse the aisles, put the items in the cart, and even virtually weigh their produce. When they are finished, the order is transmitted to the closest store to be filled by an employee. The customer can then either arrange to come by and pick up the order, or can have it delivered for an additional cost of between $8 and $15.

The programme is also split screen, with a coupon or other advertisement in one of the two screens. Frequent purchases can be placed on a special list, so that the basic weekly shopping can, in a sense, become automatic. The company says it is expecting a favourable response for two-career households wanting a collection with no waiting, or home delivery.

Although this is not marketing on the Web, it shows how retailers are trying to embrace electronic commerce on a wider scale. It is a comparatively simple way for small local businesses to add to their customer service. This example, though, shows how faltering is the start of such new techniques. It will be interesting to see if it is successful, when compared to the full online offers which are becoming more frequent on the Net. The disadvantages of a project of this magnitude, with such a large number of standard items on offer, is the speed at which transmission is used. It might fail simply because ISDN needs to be used to avoid the frustration of customers who are becoming more accustomed to the speed of the Net or cable. In addition, the usual extra cost of delivery makes the service of value only to those who require convenience above budget considerations. It depends heavily on very high efficiency by the supermarket in filling the order correctly, giving the required quality of produce second-hand, and in ensuring that the goods are quickly available for collection or delivery, on time. It may be a brave attempt by the supermarket chain, but they will almost certainly need to consider whether the increased sales generated by the initiative justify the comparable increases in labour.

In 1991, the former marketing director for Winn-Dixie Stores in America predicted that, by now, remote shopping would account for about 20 per cent of the chain's business. In fact, last year Winn-Dixie decided to terminate its trial in computerised shopping through America Online. The group continued to take orders through a toll-free telephone line, but they say that it is a tiny part of their business. However, Winn-Dixie intends to continue through a link up with ShoppingLink, which is already online handling deliveries from Pavillions stores in Southern California and Kroger in Dallas. A spokesman for Winn-Dixie said: 'This is a future proposition for us. We don't expect it to be a huge percentage of sales, but we want to be out ahead of the trend.' We reviewed an access to ShoppingLink on the Internet and found some interesting facts. For example, under the sub-heading 'prices' it states that ShoppingLink prices are updated weekly, so a few prices may change at the supermarket serving you in between updates. Because of these changes, the order total displayed on screen is an estimated total and does not include any applicable sales taxes. But the message offers the following doubtful comfort:

> After your order is shopped, we scan all your items through the store's checkout system, so you are guaranteed the same price you would have paid had you gone to the store and shopped yourself. Your register receipt will be attached to your order and will show the exact price you were charged.

In other words, whereas comparison shopping for best value leads to a decision on whether to buy because the price is known, this type of shopping is based on displayed prices which, one is warned, may not be the price finally charged. However, the amount charged will be that which is the updated price after your choice is made, and the shopper is assured that they need have no worry because it is the correct price, as updated by the store, after the shopper has made the value decision to buy. This seems to be an extraordinary marketing method, not without risks to customer satisfaction.

Alison Bergland, director of marketing at Hannaford HomeRuns, says that although establishing a brand is important, the biggest hurdle is educating the customer:

> Our biggest competitor now isn't an online service but the grocery retailers in the area. We need to change consumer behaviour and convince them to shop online instead of at the store.

This is echoed by Smart Shopper CEO, Jeff Feenstra. He said:

> This business is a no-brainer for grocery stores and manufacturers. The trick will be breaking consumer habits and helping them realise that it's OK to have other people do their grocery shopping for them.

The question of deliveries on a commercially viable scale for small items to consumers who are geographically spread, compared to bulk deliveries, is something which is exercising the minds of logistics managers. It can be seen that customers are being charged at rates of between £5 and £10 for the delivery itself, plus membership–order charges which together amount, on average, to about 10–12 per cent in addition to the order. Apart from the customer response to the additional charge, the question is whether this type of sum will be sufficient to support an efficient delivery system. Perhaps we might obtain some guide from the report that Sainsbury's distributor, Applied Distribution, issued its second profits warning in three months in November 1996, sending its shares crashing by 30p to 32p. They warned that they would only break even during the second half, and blamed demands for enhanced services from customers, without additional income. It is clear that the problems of this company cannot be directly associated with Sainsbury, or may even be totally unrelated. However, the indicators are that distribution of bulk food is getting tougher for the experts and it would not seem unreasonable, therefore, to question whether small-item delivery services will be profitable. It may be viewed as an additional service to customers and, therefore, may not be expected to show a profit. But, as we all know, supermarkets are not in the habit of absorbing loss leaders, without review at some time. This would usually mean that charges are increased, or that other charges, or costs of goods, are uplifted to compensate. In online shopping, the problem is that ordering does not always follow comparison of competitive prices, and particularly in food ordering, it tends to be dictated by the degree of convenience seen to be worthwhile by time-poor customers. That the present system requires upgrading beyond a basic scheme, which is little changed from the one in which I was a panting delivery cyclist during the 1950s, is also recognised by Sainsbury themselves. In March 1996, they announced that they are exploring the possible launch of further home services.

There has already been reference to Sainsbury using a specialised service through Flanagans. This is a dedicated service using telephone ordering, and conforms to what is a rather basic way of seeking real convenience compared to the Net. Flanagans have said that they expect to join the Web shortly; this confirms that the shopping services is to run alongside the Supermarket Direct initiative, which is run by Flanagans, using Sainsbury products. But Sainsbury said it will not compete with Flanagans, which itself intends to expand beyond its current South London area.

The uncertainty which is being faced by many retailers is epitomised by the statement made in October 1996 by Martin Wright, IS infrastructure manager at Sainsbury: 'The Internet is viable for information provision, but for selling we are not so certain. Its viability for food retailing is getting there, but it is not there yet.'

Having issued that statement, Sainsbury announced at the end of 1996 that it planned to launch a computer supermarket on the Internet in 1997 with a full range of goods. But Sainsbury says its Internet supermarket, developed in association with Hewlett Packard, will offer consumers an enhanced shopping experience with product images and links to a dedicated recipe site. Sainsbury expected to launch its supermarket in March 1997, but it was thought that access will first be restricted to about 200 shoppers who are presently carrying out home shopping trials in Watford and Bracknell. In the second half of the year they intended to test the programme on between 500 000 and 1 million customers in the catchment areas of five–ten stores. Customers are likely to be charged about £5 for home delivery and £2 for self-collection from the store.

Tesco seems to be getting there by a series of steps which, if not trial and error, are at least confusing. Having established the Tesco Wine Selector, a sales sector in common with other groups, the Tesco Product Selector (TPS) builds on the abilities of the wine selector (see Plate 9). TPS is a Windows application, presenting information from a host of data bases published by Tesco and available for downloading. Whereas the Wine Selector can only ever search through the weekly downloadable wine data base, TPS can search through any quantity of TPOS-compatable data bases that will be published on Tesco's Internet pages. Products from different data bases can be mixed together in Personal Lists, so that complete shopping lists can be compiled, which have their availability and prices updated as the updates are downloaded. TPS can create an order via e-mail which can be sent to Tesco for process and delivery. The Tesco information page says: 'The important thing is that TPS is used offline – you browse at your leisure without hogging your telephone line'. What it does not say is that you need to subscribe to CompuServe, which is the only way you can actually see the range of products promoted. That service costs both the subscription, plus an hourly rate charge while logged on.

The description of how downloading can be achieved and particularly the TPS Support Page, answering what are assumed to be simple posed questions, are clearly too technical for the average shopper who is not reasonably well versed in computer operations. This would tend to drive the user toward CompuServe, with its icons and simplified use. From these facts, it would seem that Tesco have been directing their promotions toward computer literate markets, which is not likely to be the majority of supermarket food shoppers.

The Tesco offer of about 20 000 product lines is said to be an electronic shopping pilot. It is also said to be a trial offer to a limited number of customers through CompuServe. Paul Arnold, business consultant with Tesco Direct, said this latest trial is an extension of its home delivery system which is running in Ealing, West London, and which uses a paper-based catalogue and telephone ordering system. Both trials deliver goods the next day, from Tesco's Osterly store for a £5 charge per order, using Tesco vans. However, the WWW site will continue to sell gift items, wine, beer and flowers using a third party service for national delivery.

In the 25 July 1997 edition of *Retail Week*, it was reported that Tesco confirmed it was talking to a number of computer companies about supplying PCs to its customers. Commentators suggested that the deal being considered could involve as many as 1 million customers being provided with computers enabling them to place orders with Tesco Direct over the telephone. Tesco Direct business consultant Paul Arnold is quoted as saying that the company 'is very interested in talking to all suppliers as clearly they are facilitators for home shopping operations'. It was noted, however, that Tesco Direct operated through only five stores in London and one in Leeds. The most significant pointer to emerge in the report, as relevant to this debate, is Arnold's confirmation that the division's growth would be pegged back by Tesco's desire to maintain its existing supermarket trade. The vital comment was: 'We are certainly not in the business of taking customers out of the shop.'

The reported moves by the largest food supermarket group in Britain, and, more specifically, the over-riding wish to maintain visits to the shop by customers is consistent with the general trend which can be seen from other major retailers. There is a comment later about the defensive approach by retailers, which indicates uncertainty about the future success rate. Some of the moves shown here indicate such an attitude of testing plans on a step-by-step basis before a full launch. In August 1996, rather late in comparison to the development of many systems, it was announced that Budgen's supermarket chain was to expand its trial of home delivery service to other stores. The chain had been testing the service at its Chorleywood store for several months. It said it was close to introducing the new format to its Haslemere store, and possibly two more units, for further evaluation. This cautious trial, apparently on a most careful 'suck it and see' basis, which does not indicate a seriously considered marketing policy, is operated using vehicles owned by staff, who arrange delivery times between Mondays and Thursdays to suit customers. The company said that if the system proved viable a more detailed analysis of the vehicles and logistic systems needed would take place. Orders can be telephoned or made at the store and deliveries are free within a radius of five miles. It is said to be aimed at elderly and disabled people.

The decision by Budgen's comes at the same time as Marks & Spencer extended its home delivery trial at its Oxford Circus branch, with a business ordering service being planned for its Moorgate, City of London store later in the year. In October 1996, it was reported that Marks & Spencer was considering expanding its home delivery service after doubling of business, in both its 'Homechoice' catalogue and food delivery services, during the previous year. A spokeswomen said 'Home delivery has been growing significantly'. M & S's food delivery business 'has grown rapidly' over the two and a half years since its launch at London's Kensington and Marble Arch stores, and a Sunday delivery had recently been introduced. They said that a roll-out to other stores was being considered, particularly where there were car parking difficulties.

M & S's 'Homechoice' catalogue is also being expanded, with a larger range of specialist home furnishings and gift items. It was also confirmed that software developments were being considered to expand the M & S site on the Internet on a 'big scale', with a view to selling electronically.

Again we turn to the American experience, as the most advanced. In October 1995, a study by Carol Wright Promotions found that consumers had reservations about grocery shopping online. While 49 per cent of the consumers surveyed were aware that shop-at-home grocery services were available to them, 23 per cent showed some interest in using them but only 4 per cent agreed strongly with the statement 'I would be interested in shopping from home electronically through a personal computer service, fax and/or telephone hook-up'. Overwhelmingly, survey respondents expressed a desire to see food products before purchasing them.

One product category that is an obvious candidate for retailing on the Internet appears to be making progress. Wine is a high-value, high-interest item that people dislike carrying home, and has a user profile which closely matches that of the Internet user. Especially in high-price areas among discerning buyers, in which wine lovers certainly fall, the number of actual transactions which has taken place has been limited, because of security worries about credit card numbers. Sainsbury's Wine Direct is a fairly recent arrival, which illustrates the early method. The site contains a facility to browse the Sainsbury direct wine catalogue, with detailed descriptions of varieties and vineyards, to enable intelligent decisions about the cases to be made up for home delivery. However, to complete the transaction it is necessary to telephone the order using a Freephone number.

A more advanced approach is taken by Virtual Vineyards from California. They have gone much further down the line by offering secure purchasing environment, by avoiding the need for a salesman, with payment direct on the Net. Of course, delivery charges would be prohibitive from America to Britain, but it is likely that Sainsbury will offer the same type of deal in the future. Wine is subject to national, state and local laws, and some American offers cannot be supplied outside state boundaries. A supplier will also want to take care that they are not subject to legal prosecution if orders are accepted from under-age customers, and this obviously provides great regulation difficulties. The shopper might waste a great deal of time, compared to the traditional way of buying from the local off-licence, supermarket or wine merchant. In the latter instance, delivery is usual, as it is with many discount wine warehouses such as Majestic. The personal advice and tasting usually available at such specialised suppliers may be more dependable to a real wine connoisseur than the rather more simple descriptions fit for a mass market of varying knowledge.

Although the number of outlets on the Web is very substantially less than can be found in the local Regional Mall, there is actually no shortage of what are sometimes referred to as cyberstores on the Web. In America, these include Nordstrom, Foot Locker, Office-Max, Omaha Steaks, Borders Books & Music and Harley Davidson. But the question is: is anyone buying anything?

15 Shopping on the Net and Security

According to a study released in February 1996, from MasterCard International and the National Retail Federation, if consumers have not taken to cybershopping yet, they will do so. The report found that 84 per cent of current Net users said they would buy something from the Net that year. The more time they spend on the Net, the more likely they are to buy. This seems to be a logical assumption, based on the normal thought that the more one is exposed to the message, the more likely it is that an opportunity will arise to respond. The study concludes that real-life retailers are going to lose customers in droves to their cyberequivalents. This is a message which has been often repeated, but is yet to be proven.

A separate study released at the same time predicts that by the year 2000, 1.8 million Internet users in Europe alone will be shopping from their home computers. However, information technology consultancy, Datamonitor, says that insurance and vacations will be the most popular items to haggle over online.

But some other observers say that online services have a long way to go before they pose a threat to suburban malls and mail order catalogues. Maxwell Sroge, President of Catalogue consulting firm Maxwell Sroge Company, says online shopping will be 'an explosive opportunity' for retailers once they learn to replace the visceral enjoyment of walking into stores, or buying something over the phone. I would find this grouping rather strange if it was not for the obvious interest Mr Sroge has in the Catalogue market:

People enjoy thumbing through a catalogue with a cup of coffee. You see something you like and you call the 800[1] number. It's a very simple, relaxing process, [said Mr Sroge]. The way that it's being done on the Net right now is almost like a storm trooper

---

1. The use of Freephone numbers, usually denoted by the 800 prefix, is widely adopted in America and now in many other countries.

approach to things, you push a button, and it will take you there and that's it. I think it's a horrible way to buy things.

Sroge also says that most current online shopping services are being designed by male engineers, and this may result in sites that are unappealing to female consumers:

I think there are more men on the Net than women, and 85 per cent of the shopping is done by women. Online shopping will only take off when women are welcomed into the store and given a pleasant overview of what's there.

In a commentary on the Internet which was directed at the change of men-to-women ratio using the Net, there were a number of quotes from prominent women users and reporters. Marleen McDaniel, Chief Executive Officer of Women's Wire, said:

We've done four surveys now of women online and what they want to see, and we find their main interest areas are careers – career is huge – finance, health, fitness, fashion, relationships, parenting . . . actually shopping right now ranks last.

This statement, which is clearly opposite to the promotional hype given by online shopping promoters, is echoed by many other female commentators. Beverly Brown, Career Forum Host, Women's Wire, says 'When you ask women why do you come online, why are you here, what's in it for you – it's the connections'. This may be consistent with the message being advanced by Mr Sroge, or a present factor of women interested in the Internet being career-, rather than housewife-orientated?

Research specialist Mintel produced a report into the impact of IT on UK retailing, called 'Retail Intelligence', in October 1996. It points out that electronic media cannot yet match the attractions of catalogues:

A catalogue is portable, colourful, entices browsing and has friendly staff at the end of a telephone. Delivery in 48 hours is becoming standard and out-of-stocks are fewer. The system works.

Mintel feel that predictions that mail order catalogues will soon be supplanted by electronic shopping methods over-estimate the acceptability of technology among UK consumers. They said that the greatest fans of home shopping are C1, C2 and D women, many of whom are unfamiliar with computer technology, or lack home-based equipment. Home shopping amounts to only 3 per cent of retail turnover in the UK

Mintel say ' Shopping over the Internet is still slow, unappealing to all except those very familiar with computer technology and poses payment difficulties'. Penetration of PCs capable of connection to online services in UK homes is expected to reach between 10 and 15 per cent by the year 2000:

> IT will play a greater role in home shopping, particularly for wealthier, time-poor shoppers, but there will be a continuing role for printed catalogues. Home shopping of all types is unlikely to account for more than 5 per cent of retail turnover at the start of the new millennium.

The figures given by Sroge are not wildly different from Master-Card/NFRs study, which found that 75 per cent of Net users were male with a median age of 34. Sroge also refutes the idea, put forward by the MasterCard/NFR study, that online shopping will take off after consumers are persuaded that that online transactions are secure:

> I don't think the guys talking about the so called safety issue are shoppers. I think it's all a bunch of hype. You give your credit card number to a company over the phone, so why wouldn't you give it to a company over the Internet? [he said]. Safety isn't the problem; companies haven't realised what consumers want.

Starting with the earliest free-standing electronic cash registers, up to today's automatic scanners connected to a central computer unit, the use of technology by retailers has been expanding rapidly. This has now become what is termed 'electronic commerce' which, of course, involves personal computers, cable television and other electronic devices. In 1995 it was estimated that more than 19 million modem-equipped computer users entered cyberspace daily in America. Fans of multimedia shopping predicted that within ten years this would amount to sales of as much as $300 billion per year, representing about 15 per cent of total sales of $2.2 trillion (based on the publication of 'The Future of Shopping' in 1992).

In April 1995, there were 27000 Web sites and, according to Sun Microsystems Inc., the population was doubling every 53 days. But consumers often get lost in the Internet and are frustrated with its lack of central authority and cohesiveness. Software developers have, therefore, been rushing to create the software which will simplify users' access to cyberspace, making it easier for technophobes to cope.

The actual purchase of goods on the Internet includes the discomfort of buying from unknown suppliers who are remote. The product cannot be tested or actually seen prior to purchase, and no face-to-face assessment or opinion of the vendor can be made. Security is a big issue, because the Internet is an open network and can be subject to abuse. No central authority regulates this global network. Also all transactions on the Internet tend to leave a 'trail' which can be uncovered by hackers, used by aggressive marketing firms or made available to government agencies.

If payment is being made online it is necessary to 'think security'. This starts with the connection, which is the way the computer connects through telephone wires to contact the Internet and the browser, the software that acts like a telephone to receive information on the Internet. Unsecured information sent over the Internet can be intercepted. A secure browser encrypts or scrambles purchase information and such a browser should comply with industry standards, such as Secure Sockets Layer (SSL) or Secure Hypertext Protocol (S-HTTP); these are often included with Internet connection services. In the meantime, the credit and charge card industry is continuing to work on an enhanced security using Secured Electronic Transactions (SET), which provides a highly encrypted communication between card companies, merchants and card members. However, if encryption software is used to secure the transaction, it is recommended that the order be faxed, or paid by cheque or money order.

The steps being taken are encouraging. However, they do highlight the dangers of fraud, hacking and other violations of privacy, otherwise they would not be necessary, or seen as so important. The added cost of incorporating security is a factor in the online purchase cost. Anyway, it seems that the convenience of online purchases is somewhat spoilt by having to use the telephone and fax to make payment, or the delay in sending a money order before the delivery time lapse commences. There is no current recognition of the problems of money order or cheque payment when using a non-domestic supplier, such as the case when ordering from America and paying in sterling drawn on a British bank.

There are some other recommendations which have been offered as a means in order to protect the user, when buying online. Firstly, it is prudent to shop with companies one knows. This, of course, may limit the attraction of the large variety of goods on offer, especially when many merchants are small specialist firms in foreign countries. If a new merchant is chosen, it is an idea to ask for a catalogue or brochure, to obtain a better idea of that company's status. This again means time and delay, and may contradict the main purpose of speed and convenience associated with the medium. Satisfaction about the merchant's refund and return policies should be obtained before an order is placed. The fact that a merchant is on the Internet does not signify that it is an old-established company. This is supported by the promises of a North Carolina company in the States, which says that, with its $795 software package, 'a novice user can set up an online mall in minutes and start leasing space to local merchants, manufacturers and distributors'.

The shopper should never give out the Internet password which should, ideally, be original when created. A combination of numbers, letters and symbols, or a phrase, could be used, but birthdays, addresses or Social Security numbers are reasonably easy to discover. It is another set of numbers to remember, in addition to the many PINs[1] and another complication for what is supposed to be a more convenient means of shopping. You do not simply choose and pay as in a shop, but go through a process while strictly observing a security protocol.

When the shopper goes into a shop and holds the chosen article, pays and walks out, she or he has it in their hand. The Internet provides an information communication for shoppers, but the shopper sees a picture or details only. Some confidence tricksters who have used telemarketing, newspapers, magazines and the mail, to attract customers, are turning to the Internet to promote their frauds.

The requirement for consumers to make a phone call or send a cheque to make a purchase on the Internet is a situation similar to the Yankelovich study noted on p. 12, which showed that they were likely to leave a store because they did not get immediate service. If it is too much of an effort to make the phone call, especially if they are

---

1. PINs are Personal Identification Numbers and are recommended to be kept secure to avoid misuse by unauthorised persons.

using a modem to browse catalogues, the consumer may well reconsider the purchase, or simply forget about it.

Consumers gave this as one of their main objections influencing their decision to shop online. According to the Hermes Survey 4 results, 62 per cent of respondents think it unwise to give credit card information online, and 60 per cent say that security concerns are a primary reason that they would not buy anything online. The strongest feelings were displayed by women, who make up the majority of consumer purchases. 75 per cent felt that providing credit card information online was not clever, and 71 per cent of women said that security of financial information was a reason not to buy. It should be noted that this survey was done online by a self-selected group of people and the results may not be representative of the whole population.

Particular attention is needed when making an order. For example, one inadvertent stroke can order ten shirts instead of one. It is necessary to check the delivery charges and that all charges are correctly calculated. Note the shipping time to ensure that it is acceptable. There may be an extra charge for express delivery. In general orders should be sent – not received – within 30 days, but where no shipping time is specified, in America at least, the company has up to 50 days after receiving the order, to ship. If something is needed by a certain date, or the shopper is excited at the prospect of having it in their hands, this could mean over two months. Let us hope that a new model or fashion, or even a better price, has not been announced by then!

Even then, shoppers and retailers hoping to do business on the Internet have been frustrated by banks' refusal to sanction credit cards on the system. This has nothing to do with the security systems mentioned, but the fear of banks that criminal computer operators will see the credit card numbers and use them to make fraudulent purchases, leaving the banks to bear the costs. As already stated, each transaction on the Net leaves a trail which could be hacked. The banks have therefore decided to refuse authorisation to small firms for credit card orders. The firms are left with no alternative but to request payment by cheque, which will delay purchases, or use the facilities of a larger merchant on payment of some kind of commission for the facility.

It is the small companies that have the problem of getting authorisation from the banks. They need a proven track record and must provide a Bond. There is nothing special about giving your card details over the Net. It is no different from phoning them to arrange a holiday or book a theatre ticket. People expect to be able to buy Internet services with their credit cards and when we tell them we don't take cards, most of them go elsewhere [says Tim James of the Impossibly Small Print Shop]. If you use good security, there is no risk of interception. But banks hear the word Internet and run away as fast as they can.

However, Barclaycard believes that the security measures are vulnerable and have become increasingly cautious as a result of fraudsters activities on its own BarclaySquare online mall. It is concerned that information travelling through the Internet is routed through a series of computers on its journey. In theory, any one of these computers can keep a record of the card number and other personal details. Under UK law, if a number is used fraudulently to buy goods, the retailer has to refund the credit card company until an investigation is undertaken. If that shows the retailer was not to blame, the credit card company must reimburse the customer.

The whole question of security can be highlighted by the US government's increasingly untenable policy over encryption, which classifies certain software as munitions in order to prevent it from being exported. This policy means that American companies, who build products incorporating industrial-strength encryption, can sell those products only in America, and must produce a watered down version for export. The idea is to stop people deemed 'unsuitable' by Washington from getting hold of uncrackable codes. This class includes drug dealers, terrorists and hostile regimes. But the result also means that e-mail and Web server software sold in Europe is less secure than that sold in America.

With the ban in place, people outside the United States, in theory at least, only have access to encryption technology which the FBI can decode reasonably easily. The latest news that Japanese chips being developed will be available legally in Britain and other countries for the first time now makes the ban ineffective, and in reality, if it is continued, will only serve to make Americans less able to commute internationally. As we have noted, the Internet, by its free global interchange of information, is presently beyond the control of any authority and the efforts of the American government have shown that they are trying to exercise some control in the interests of law enforcement and national security. Whatever the response to this in the sense of freedom of communication, it shows that there still exists a threat to security. If such a threat exists at the high powered level of nations, can we be really secure about an individual PIN or personal financial and social details given over the same medium? In January 1997 it was announced that America Online has shut down its dial-up service in Russia after widespread fraud. This is the first time it has had to close off access to an entire country, but is was reported that Russian computer users were found to be accessing American Online using stolen credit card numbers.

Personal experiences often show that there is no such thing as a totally secure situation. Even in cases when the system is considered reasonably fail-safe, human apathy or carelessness takes a hand to help someone overcome the measures designed for a good purpose. The careless glance at a password, or the helpful hints at what a forgotten password may be, are all too commonplace. We all have conversations with banks where account details are unfortunately given to unauthorised third parties. If this is an example of the general standard, why should we be certain that any system will protect us? In fact I read of a wonderful example of how even the most sophisticated security system is being overcome by a simple ruse by relatively simple and uneducated people.

In the South African Province of Kangwane, an unmarked van escorted by armed guards visits the rural areas to deliver pensions to around 400 000 people. On the back of the truck is one of the most sophisticated cash dispensing machines in the world. Because of the high level of illiteracy in the region, each pensioner is required to swipe a card and roll a thumb across a biometric sensor to authenticate their identity. Their pension is then issued. Many believe that biometrics is becoming the only really secure means of activating a secure transaction. Biometrics include fingerprints, voice coding, image digitising and retina scanning. But the point is again proven that where there is a system, there is a way to bypass it. The people of Kangwane are collecting their grandparents' pensions after their death by removing thumbs, pickling them and using them to carry on receiving the cash. As a corollary to the way retailers, such as the major supermarkets, have ATMs to provide cash for their customers, in Kangwane, hordes of merchants follow the cash dispensing pension truck wherever it goes, tempting the pensioners, now with ready cash, to buy their wares.

I suppose we could say that the security system in Kangwane depended on having a card and a thumbprint, obviously a simple matter to circumvent for a simplistic mind. Equally obvious, then, is that such systems are set up by very clever-minded people who cover all the clever ways their system can be thwarted, but not the easy ways. Without a card provided by the security system it would be much more difficult, if not impossible. The very entertaining movies about teenager hackers getting into government systems and playing war games which the experts think are real because there is no way the system could have been triggered, are merely good entertainment. However, much to the consternation of the security companies concerned, it has been announced that a team of Cambridge and German researchers has used ordinary hacking methods and £150 worth of electronic equipment, to crack the 'world's most secure computer chip' used in ATMs world-wide. They say that the technique could be used to reprogram a wide variety of supposedly secure smartcard applications including bank cards, GSM phones and satellite TV scramblers.

Graphics, Visualisation & Usability Centre's (GVU) fourth user survey, which was run as a Public Service in October and November 1995, and collected over 23 000 unique responses, provided further information on users' attitudes towards security. The results indicated that users did not spend much time on shopping, but rather preferred to use the Web for entertainment and work, or research. This supported the notion that this resulted from a perceived weakness in Web security, people agreed fairly strongly that having to provide credit card information over the Web was the main reason for not buying. On a scale of 5 this represented 3.6. This dropped to 3.4 in the Sixth Survey and 3.2 in the most recent Seventh Survey in April 1997.

As reported on *CNET: The Computer Network* of 23 August 1996 a survey by O'Reilly & Associates determined that 33 per cent of US Internet users and 36 per cent of commercial online service users are women. But the Editor of *Interactive Publishing Alert* says that only 10–15 per cent of online users shop. While 85 per cent of television shoppers are women, 90 per cent of online shoppers are men. The conclusion is that, unless women can be convinced to participate, online commerce is doomed to failure. For men travelling the Internet, the process is still the attraction. Women, however, cannot be bothered. They want to go to the online destination without going through the process, and use the time instead by doing other important things in their lives. Even on CompuServe, the percentage of female users is estimated at between 25 and 30 per cent. When asked what keeps them from going online, 55 per cent of women blamed the lack of discretionary time. Another 14 per cent said that they worked with computers all day and were reluctant to use them in their own leisure time. Of those surveyed who do use the computer, they said that they had an average of 8.77 hours of discretionary time each week and spend four hours of that time on their computer.

According to a report from KPMG, reported in *Computing* of November 1996, UK retailers have to provide something new and exciting if they expect to win customers on the Internet: 'If a surfer finds nothing but boring corporate news and uninspiring visuals, they will never return to the site' said Jonathan Reynolds from the Oxford Institute of Retail Studies which carried out the research with KPMG:

> Many retailers are responding defensively to the challenges posed by the Internet [he said]. The limited investment that such sites sometimes represent may do conventional retailers more harm than good. While some organisations are spending up to £300 000, boasting of spending as little as £50 000 on a Web site is hardly a vote of confidence in the strategic importance of this channel.

The report, which studied the European development of the Internet rather than the more advanced American situation, showed that the United Kingdom and Germany dominates, with almost 1 million hosts between them. Scandinavia, and particularly Finland, have relatively high levels of *per capita* Web involvement, but not much offered in retail.

The Future of Electronic Shopping

GVU's WWW User Surveys

PRIMARY USE OF BROWSER SPLIT BY LOCATION

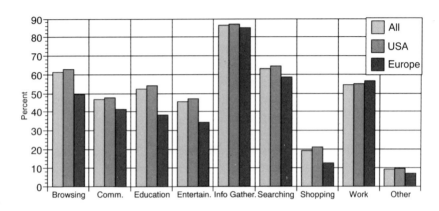

	Browsing	Comm.	Education	Entertain.	Info Gather.	Searching	Shopping	Work	Other
All	61.29	47.02	52.21	45.48	86.03	63.01	18.65	50.91	9.29
USA	62.71	47.46	53.97	46.69	86.66	64.19	20.32	54.72	9.76
Europe	49.63	41.62	38.08	34.08	84.92	58.29	11.92	56.05	6.61

Source: GYU's Seventh WWW User Survey™ (Conducted April 1997)
< URL:http://www.gvu.gatech.edu/user_surveys/ >
Copyright 1997 GTRC – ALL RIGHTS RESERVED
Contact: www-survey @cc.gatech.edu

Figure 15.1 Primary Use of WWW Browser Split by Location

PRIMARY USE OF BROWSER SPLIT BY GENDER

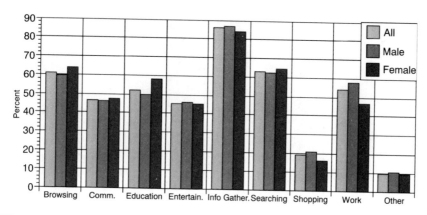

	Browsing	Comm.	Education	Entertain.	Info Gather.	Searching	Shopping	Work	Other
All	61.29	47.02	52.21	45.48	86.03	63.01	18.65	54.05	9.29
Male	59.98	46.67	49.38	45.88	86.9	62.43	20.16	57.46	9.61
Female	64.27	47.82	58.36	45.07	84.2	64.27	15.65	46.65	8.43

Source: GYU's Seventh WWW User Survey™ (Conducted April 1997)
< URL:http://www.gvu.gatech.edu/user_surveys/ >
Copyright 1997 GTRC – ALL RIGHTS RESERVED
Contact: www-survey @cc.gatech.edu

Figure 15.2   Primary Use of WWW Browser Split by Gender

PRIMARY USE OF BROWSER SPLIT BY AGE

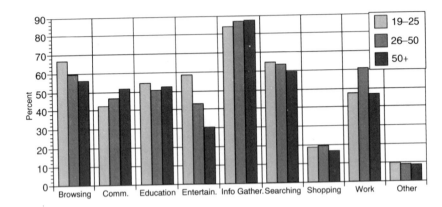

	Browsing	Comm.	Education	Entertain.	Info Gather.	Searching	Shopping	Work	Other
19–25	67.01	42.83	54.85	58.65	84.18	64.53	18.54	47.16	9.27
26–50	59.6	46.7	51.03	43.27	87.29	63.44	19.9	60.52	8.62
50+	56.53	51.92	52.64	30.33	87.48	59.21	16.27	46.4	8.35

Source: GYU's Seventh WWW User Survey[TM] (Conducted April 1997)
<URL:http://www.gvu.gatech.edu/user_surveys/>
Copyright 1997 GTRC – ALL RIGHTS RESERVED
Contact: www-survey @cc.gatech.edu

Figure 15.3   Primary Use of WWW Browser Split by Age

FREQUENCY OF ONLINE SHOPPING SPLIT BY LOCATION

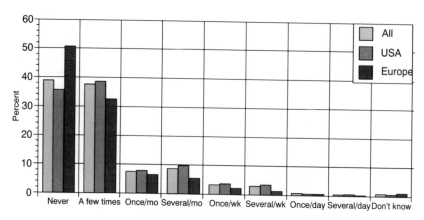

	Never	A few times	Once/mo	Several/mo	Once/wk	Several/wk	Once/day	Several/day	Don't know
All	38.53	37.43	7.42	8.73	3.19	2.9	0.58	0.45	0.77
USA	35.38	38.71	7.73	9.72	3.42	3.27	0.56	0.5	0.71
Europe	50.47	32.68	6.42	5.31	2.14	1.21	0.56	0.19	1.02

Source: GYU's Seventh WWW User Survey™ (Conducted April 1997)
< URL:http://www.gvu.gatech.edu/user_surveys/ >
Copyright 1997 GTRC – ALL RIGHTS RESERVED
Contact: www-survey @cc.gatech.edu

Figure 15.4   Frequency of Online Shopping Split by Location

The Future of Electronic Shopping

FREQUENCY OF ONLINE SHOPPING SPLIT BY GENDER

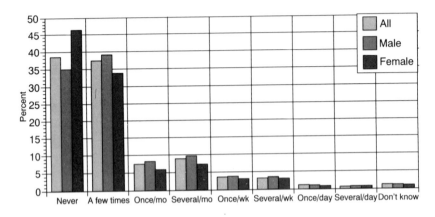

	Never	A few times	Once/mo	Several/mo	Once/wk	Several/wk	Once/day	Several/day	Don't know
All	38.53	37.43	7.42	8.73	3.19	2.9	0.58	0.45	0.77
Male	34.92	39.12	8.15	9.6	3.4	3.01	0.57	0.48	0.76
Female	46.34	33.89	5.76	2.73	2.73	2.65	0.51	0.39	0.74

Source: GYU's Seventh WWW User Survey™ (Conducted April 1997)
< URL:http://www.gvu.gatech.edu/user_surveys/ >
Copyright 1997 GTRC – ALL RIGHTS RESERVED
Contact: www-survey @cc.gatech.edu

Figure 15.5   Frequency of Online Shopping Split by Gender

FREQUENCY OF ONLINE SHOPPING SPLIT BY AGE

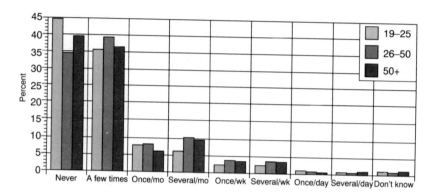

	Never	A few times	Once/mo	Several/mo	Once/wk	Several/wk	Once/day	Several/day	Don't know
19–25	44.41	35.54	7.69	6.11	2.25	2.05	0.71	0.44	0.81
26–50	34.45	39.13	8.06	10.08	3.52	3.23	0.51	0.41	0.61
50+	39.54	36.42	5.95	9.45	3.45	3.21	0.34	0.72	0.91

Source: GYU's Seventh WWW User Survey™ (Conducted April 1997)
< URL:http://www.gvu.gatech.edu/user_surveys/ >
Copyright 1997 GTRC – ALL RIGHTS RESERVED
Contact: www-survey @cc.gatech.edu

Figure 15.6   Frequency of Online Shopping Split by Age

16 Convenience, Comparison and the Retail Results

For those involved in the retail and merchandising industries, it is sometimes more difficult to perceive the broad changes reshaping the environment than for onlookers on the outside. We may also forget how vital the retail function is to the economy and to society as a whole. If we can view the basic fundamentals which help make retailing such an important industry, we can begin to understand the changes taking place and think of responses to the challenges.

In what I think may be stretching the search for verisimilitude rather far in making connections to aid the hype, there is a belief, among some, that the daily experience of retailing allows individuals in society to experience the productivity, creativity, values and results of the economy at large. There is an argument that it is in the retail and merchandising function that one gains an understanding of society as a whole. Examples are cited of open air markets, or lines of people waiting for food at shops in the old Soviet Union, the corner grocery store of the 1930s, or the mega malls of today. Inherent in the location, organisation and variety of goods being offered, is a fundamental statement about the society. What is reshaping the retail environment today is nothing less than a set of fundamental changes in the overall economy and society. The impact of technological change and the demographic change is altering the behaviour of people in the market place. People will behave differently as they are influenced by rapid changes in society, standards of conduct, acceptable morals, work practice and ethos. The fact that consumers do not behave the way they did in the past must be recognised in how approaches are made to access, position, distribute, market and service the products. The consumers are smarter, more demanding, more diverse and less wealthy. They now expect better quality of goods and service, at lower cost and better value.

Taking account of the present state of technology, it is inconvenient at best, and impossible at worst, to comparison shop. Television shows only one product at the time, and usually does not stock more than two products which compete. Online and traditional catalogues usually feature only one vendor with non-competitive items. On the other hand, with traditional shopping, in the mall or high street, the consumer has the opportunity to comparison shop at the large department stores, standard shops and speciality retailers. In that way, the shopper can browse visually through a large number of items very quickly in reality, which obviously cannot be done with television home shopping or online. Of course, shoppers cannot compare by browsing in a New York shop when they are physically in London, but the universality of merchandising and products now apparent helps to overcome a large part of that problem. International marketing has progressed so far that, unlike the past, when certain retailers and goods were available only in a small locality, today most well known brands, retailers and products are easily purchased from high streets around the world. Not only can Gucci, Ralph Lauren, Bennetton, The Gap or the other retailers be found with ease, but products which once were found only in specific areas are widely marketed almost everywhere. Sometimes it can be annoying, as I found in Tokyo. Seeking a gift to take home, it seemed easier to find items from Burberry, Gucci or Yves St Laurent, than anything truly Japanese in the department stores on the Ginza.

There are many illustrations of the convenience of the Internet or other electronic means of home shopping, but these are mainly shown to be cases where the shopper is looking for a definite item, or a reasonably defined classification, and has a degree of skill in computer use. Those who shop on the Internet and like it seem to do so because it is quick if they know what they are doing, and because it is new. A typical response is 'I can log on to get my e-mail and check my stock quotes, and I can buy a pair of shoes too'. Mind you, the thought of buying a pair of such personal items as shoes, which one normally wants to try for fit and comfort, is something which is most surprising. My son tells me that he sometimes buys shoes from the Next Directory and has had no trouble with fit. I recently went to the same shop in which I have bought shoes for the past six years, and tried on the same make and style I had bought during that period, and which I was wearing at that visit. I tried the same size and width. The left shoe was perfect but the right was too tight. I tried four pairs, before taking the last as a very comfortable fit. That had never happened to me before, but I was able to deal with it personally. My son would have returned the shoes and obtained a new pair or a refund. It does depend on the shopper's outlook, because that risk and process does not bother my son, but would be intensely annoying to me.

For every online shopping enthusiast, there is another one who dislikes the idea. Partly for the reason that many think the experience is a pale imitation of printed catalogues, online shoppers continue to be a very small minority. A random walk through the Internet involves a lot of pointing, clicking, searching, and, most of all, waiting for something to happen. The slower the computer and modem, the longer the wait. Basically, it is not easy for the average person to log on looking for a particular item, find examples of it and then find which are the best deals in that commodity.

Random walks can have unexpected surprises, though. It is possible to stumble into an Internet shop with interesting products, such as A World of Tea with a vast offering of exotic teas by mail, or coffee from Harvard Espresso Co. But when we went shopping, the everyday selection of items available to choose was disappointing. There were many repetitions of some articles such as flowers, jewellery, cosmetics, sunglasses, books, compact discs, magazine subscriptions, electronics, and loads of computer equipment and software. Within those categories, there was not nearly as much choice as can be found in a typical suburban shopping mall.

The best selection available is on the commercial online services that operate their own online shopping services. CompuServe, for instance, includes such upscale retailers as Brooks Brothers clothing and the Metropolitan Museum of Art reproductions. America Online has a lot of lesser known businesses, including offbeat shops such as the World Wrestling Federation souvenir store. The Internet Mall, one of the largest, is actually a free listing of some 4500 businesses on the Web. The companion Internet Mall Listings, gives a number of mall sites.

To test this I relate an article I read where the writer put together a list of items and then set out to see how easy it would be to get them via mouse and modem. Looking up 'fly fishing' under Prodigy's hobby listings, she found several retailers on the Web, including The Fly Shop and the Virtual Flyshop Mall. Also, she found needlepoint supplies at Exclamation Point, using the word needlepoint in the Yahoo search engine. Children's pullovers were quite hard to find, but turned up Irish handknitted sweaters at $107 and more. Because of the high price she looked elsewhere. J. C. Penney, in CompuServe, showed one cotton sweater for boys at $18, but none for girls. The full Penney catalogue gives many more sweaters, and this catalogue can be ordered online, although it is of no use for online shoppers until it arrives.

It is probably true that many obscure items can be found on the Internet which are not readily available in your average shop. This may mean a lengthy search and considerable time, but will allow shoppers to locate that very unusual item. Typical is the newspaper report with the lead 'just when you thought shopping on the Internet couldn't get any stranger, it does'. This gives details of products from the Wall o' Fun, said to be much more than yet another online mall; it is an advertisement-free consumer service, geared toward women. The Disturbing Product of the Month item includes designer water for cats and dogs, with a selection from tangy fish or crispy beef flavours.

A search for vitamin tablets provided what seemed to be a good price, until realising that the dollars quoted were Canadian, which is something which must be looked at very carefully, especially by consumers who are not fully versed in exchange rates. Nevertheless, most of the items were found online. But the search was not much fun, because Web shopping has to be conducted at the Internet's pace, or not at all, whereas traditional shopping is conducted at the shopper's own pace. The Internet pace means a lot of waiting, and when the screen does scroll you are likely to see pictures that are like a TV test pattern, or no pictures at all. Some Internet malls have a search function, but if the enquiry is not specific, they give a list of unrelated items whose descriptions include the word asked for, or a partial word. A search for 'range', for example, provided 'chocolate dipped reception sticks' which had a 'range' of flavours, one of which was orange. Agents can now provide offline searching to a known profile and then update online. This is much quicker. Bargains are unlikely on the Internet at this point of time. Even the discount service Shoppers Advantage did not necessarily undercut deep discount newspaper advertisements checked.

An account of an online shopping experience supports the view that prices should not be assumed to be cheaper if on the Net. PC Flowers and Gifts offered a browser a dozen long stemmed red roses as a gift for a loved one at $59.95 plus 4.5 per cent state tax and $6.95 handling charge. A phone call to the local florist gave a price of $24 with 25 minutes' availability, and no tax or other charge.

Retailing grew in an environment where the idea was to merchandise, to sell and to convince someone to buy. The advertising, promotion, point-of-sale design, store layout and mall development was geared toward shopping being fun, enjoyable and an experience. Consumers were measured through the volume of sales they generated. This has been referred to as 'Talking' to the customer. Recently, there is a growing opinion that consumers themselves are considering shopping as a task, rather than as entertainment. The many mentions of shopping becoming a chore reflects this. Therefore, to succeed with the consumer today it is necessary to intensely listen to them and watch to see how to make their shopping easier. This can be termed 'Listening' rather than 'Talking', and there are examples of how it has led to startling success.

For example, Wal-Mart, a company which is serious, dedicated and enthusiastically serving 'the rest of us'. There is nothing fancy, but the company evinces its deep commitment to customers and employees. Similarly, the Body Shop has produced goods after listening to what women have shown they want – natural ingredients, no animal testing, no fancy packaging, no paid advertising, and environmentally responsible commitment. This has resulted in a dramatic success in one of the most competitive industries. There is a feeling that the customer matters. IKEA sells basic furniture and household items as simple, well designed, but flat pack items; IKEA followed their belief that if the designs and values were perceived as good enough, the customer would do their own searching, collection and assembly.

If retailers are now starting to listen to their customers and producing some good returns as a result, what do they think their customers feel about online shopping? In theory, if not in practice, retailers with their huge research departments of strategic analysts, marketing and promotions specialists, should be able to interpret the responses from their own shoppers. The added information given from the data bases from account systems and loyalty cards, allow more direct marketing responses than ever before. Yet, retailers who were questioned gave a message of uncertainty. One respondent was quoted as saying 'None of us want to be left behind just in case the whole thing unexpectedly goes up like a rocket'. Researchers found it difficult to classify retailers' activity online, because of the lack of comprehensive listings of sites, whereas signage is far better in the United States. The report also warns: 'Links expire, sites change name and new links emerge, on a daily basis.' Careful consideration is needed for the confusion that this produces for potential customers.

Larger UK retailers are not encouraging with their news of their Internet experience to date. After one year of trading, Sainsbury reports that its online chocolates, flowers and wine are not selling like hot cakes, and Argos says that after nine months of trading from its site, the biggest selling item, which is a wine rack, was only bought three times. They also admit that after one year of trading they have actually sold only 22 items in total. This early assessment by Argos was further reinforced in September 1996, when they announced their interim profits. Their pre-tax interim profits were up an impressive 45 per cent, on sales up by more than 18 per cent to £561 million. Mike Smith, the Chief Executive, suggested that future growth is likely to come from further store openings and planned expansion overseas, rather than from electronic shopping. He said 'we're cynical about the speed of growth of electronic shopping'. A factor in this opinion was the disappointingly low sales over the Internet. By this time, only 40 products had been sold in over a year. He says 'our development is focused on using telephony to sell rather than technology'. Tesco says it is not expecting a major shift to home shopping on the Internet. Much of the uncertainty appears to arise because retailers cannot decide whether to pursue a policy of information or selling.

Coca Cola Retailing Research Group have issued a report, as reported in 'FX' of July 1996, which says we will still be doing 95 per cent of our food shopping face to face with the goods in ten years time, despite the growth of the Internet. This is a surprising conflict with the statements of many who forsee food as being one of the leading consumer shopping items to be affected electronically. For an organisation such as Coca Cola to take this view supports many who claim that electronic shopping is not as clear-cut as promoted by those who have a vested interest in the medium. Furthermore, Coca Cola say that supermarkets will not have become so large that there will be just three shops selling everything we need. Although super-stores will continue to grow, 'The Future of the Foodstore' says that other formats, such as discounters and specialists, will still be around in the year 2005.

The report adds 'no single new megatrend will dictate structural shifts as was arguably the case with, say superstores and hypermar-kets'. Also, while today's market would already account for £22 billion of trade compared to 2005 values, only 5 per cent of shopping will be made by computer by that year. By the year 2020 it is likely to make up 15 per cent of our purchasing.

Further research issued at the beginning of October 1996 by KPMG, and based on a survey of 100 major UK companies, reveals that the retail and consumer industry is generally more pessimistic about the growth of sales from the Internet than the rest of industry. By the year 2000, sales attributed to Internet are expected to grow from 3 per cent now to around 20 per cent, but for consumer-based companies this is expected to be only 7 per cent. Company budgets for marketing their Internet activity are also surprisingly low, with 31 per cent spending less than £10 000 per year. However, this is anticipated to increase to an average spend for each company of nearer £120 000 per company. These figures reveal that the promotion of the advantages of Internet using a spend of around 15 per cent of the market may be right as an overall average, but do not necessarily apply to retail consumer spending. The dangers are apparent, and seem to have been recognised by retailers. This may be supported by research, which also showed that most companies are presently testing by 'toe in the water' approaches.

The KPMG report says we are now more likely than ever to accept new technology. It took the telephone thirty-eight years to achieve 10 per cent of the market; it took the video recorder nine, and now the Nintendo generation, for whom the screen is natural, is growing into consumers. Yet in November 1996, they also reported that, although sales from Net commerce were expected to reach £170 million that year, more than 80 per cent of companies surveyed by KPMG cannot attribute any sales to the Internet at present.

Once again, we hear the same arguments. The factor holding back new technology in food shopping includes the usual preference of consumers to see, touch and smell fresh produce.

However, computer shopping will have a vital role to play as supermarkets differentiate themselves in what is likely to become an even more cut-throat market in 2005. The report thinks it will be as much about 'differentiate or die', in the chase for a unique consumer proposition, as about 'imitate or die', in pursuit of operational best practice.

Sarah Charles, Head of European retail at KPMG, says:

> Any new channel to market has to be examined thoroughly. However, a profitable, transactional presence on the Internet is somewhat more problematical than retailers have been led to believe. They need to be aware of the different characteristics of the electronic channel, the range of experience of similar retailers and the positioning opportunities available to them. Only then can they make informed decisions about the potential of the Internet.

The overall message to retailers was 'handle with care'.

17 Price, Convenience, Electronic Retailing and the Internet Store

I referred to the American, but now international, bulk discounter, Costco earlier, in commenting on the probable budgetary and delivery problems associated with small purchases. So far Costco are operating in Britain with a traditional club membership, permitting personal visits for bulk purchases. I imagined the scenario if the system allowed shoppers to be selective on individual items, rather than bulk. I have no reason to think that the system is likely to change, at least in the short term, but it was a useful hypothesis.

In November 1995, however, Price Quest, a subsidiary of Price Enterprises Inc. and Price/Costco Inc., announced that it will begin offering over 9000 brand name items online through America OnLine Place. With Price Online, members will be able to browse through 30 departments, which encompass 280 categories of products including jewellery, cameras, sporting goods and homewares, at the same discount levels found in the discount centres. There is no mention of whether the prices, and the discounts, will assume that purchases are bulk, i.e. cases of product rather than single items, but there seems to be no reason to suppose that the sales policy will differ from the store format. For individual items, such as those mentioned in consumer durables, the prices are often very competitive. The disadvantage is that the choice is also often more limited than in a full-line store.

Purchases can be made by using major credit cards. Orders are placed directly through American Online (AOL) and are delivered anywhere in the continental United States, generally within ten working days. Ted Leonsis, President of AOL Services Company, added 'through shopping online, AOL Members will find a hassle free alternative to crowded malls without forfeiting quality and selection'. Let us consider these words. Firstly it is surprising that a major power retailer is suggesting that the offer of his store, with price to the forefront is not, in itself, the alternative to the mall as a draw for shoppers. Presumably, he is seeking the proportion of shoppers who visit the mall rather than Costco stores, as an added shopper influx to his business. But if the offer is so attractive, why not present the store as the alternative directly, without referring to the malls?

Secondly, it must be a stretch of the imagination to suggest that neither choice of selection nor quality, as available in a major shopping mall, will be prejudiced. For example the offer online by Price/Costco amounts to some 9000 items. A single standard supermarket offers in excess of 20 000 items, to which can be added the huge selection in a mall of individual shop units, department stores and service trades.

As price advantage is so obviously questionable, because of the upfront cost of equipment, delivery and bulk purchase, the other advantage is convenience. Have you used the Internet? If so, you will know how long it takes to surf the system, especially if one is not computer literate. Bearing in mind how many product lines a normal supermarket carries, once you have found the entry after the repeated steps, you will have to look at the thousands of items offered. All this time your modem line is open. How many pence are you saving on the item? How long will it take you before you have made your selection and confirmed your order?

It may be helpful to firstly understand the key aspects of electronic retailing. What is meant by 'electronic retail media'? There are three main methods of shopping from home. Mail order, or catalogue shopping, has been around since at least the last century. The Sears Roebuck catalogue was widely seen as a means of purchasing goods in remote or under-developed areas, such as the wild west, where cowboys and ranchers ordered clothes and home improvement products which were not available locally. Mail order has therefore established not only a long history, but a system of marketing and efficient delivery with which its customers have become accustomed and confident in using. The standards of marketing have improved over the years and modern catalogues are costly to produce, containing very high-quality photography and presentation. The data base of the mail order companies is extensive, and with the advantage of direct mail they are able to target their sales efforts directly without unnecessary waste. Catalogues clearly have an advantage of quality, but another disadvantage of presentation. They reproduce static two-dimensional representations, based on photographs and illustrations, which rely heavily on the degree of reality to the actual product, in texture, quality and colour. The expert presentation and merchandising must inevitably be as attractive as possible, without misrepresentation, in order to encourage a positive response and increased sales. When the customer receives the actual goods the degree of satisfaction can be expressed only by acceptance, or return as a result if disappointment. Even if a customer keeps the goods, it may not signify satisfaction and may be only a reluctant frustration at avoiding further delay and effort, which might have been avoided by a personal visit, trying on for fit and handling at a shop. Nevertheless, other than the fact that catalogue photography follows the established pattern of showing the most attractive shot, as we should expect, and that it is two-dimensional, the representations are a much better quality than can be obtained on a monitor using the Internet graphics. Immediacy of use is obviously another hurdle to overcome. With the advances of computer technology it is a logical step for catalogues, produced via graphic transfer of images and text, to move directly into direct use of interactive computer discs such as CD-ROM. This will allow prospective shoppers to view articles of interest from various angles and perhaps see a video advertisement for the product.

The way in which almost everyone is attempting to use some form of technology to sell is shown by another pilot scheme which is an adoption of the inflight catalogue. British Airways expected to offer an inflight interactive mail order shopping mall in July 1996, with over 200 products from leading retailers being offered to passengers. For three months, as a pilot scheme (no pun intended), twenty major retailers including Disney, Harrods, Mulberry, Liberty and Interflora will be offering their products on a single BA service. Passengers will be able to view the selection on a screen on seat backs and order using a hand set which acts as a card reader for swiping credit cards. The mall is to be divided into ten sections, for toys, accessories, and the gold and silver counter. Within each department are the individual stores, which have the 'look and feel' of the real outlets, using the same colours, styles and logos. The original idea is said to have been for a virtual shopping mall, but technological limitations has made it 'very much a slide show'. This may not impact on shopping as a major change to the way passengers buy duty free inflight, but it does show that technology is creeping in, even if in a very basic way.

The television has become a big part of almost everyone's lives. The dedicated TV shopping channels present a mix of hard sell and 'infomercials'. The manager of one of the largest channels, QVC (UK), has said that they do not expect to be in business in five years time doing what they do today. By this, he means that they expect to be selling exclusively through interactive television. QVC was founded in June 1986 by Franklin Mint founder, Joseph Segel, and began operations in November 1986. In the United States, QVC operates two cable shopping services – the original QVC which broadcasts from West Chester, PA and Q2, which also broadcasts from the same place. QVC broadcasts live 24 hours a day, 364 days a year and introduces 250 new products every week, to viewers in over 54 million homes across the United States. In addition, there are another 4 million households, through a joint venture with BSkyB in the United Kingdom.

Today, QVC is the leader in electronic retailing. It reaches over 80 per cent of all US cable homes, as well as 3 million satellite homes. Since April 1996, Q2 has been transmitting up to 12 hours a day, 7 days a week to 11 million cable households. London-based QVC's The Shopping Channel, reaches approximately 4 million homes in the United Kingdom. In 1995, QVC received over 70 million phone calls and shipped over 46 million packages. They claim to add over 150 000 new customers each month and 60 per cent purchase again with the year.

QVC is one of the world's largest purveyors of 14 carat gold jewellery and its lines account for 35 per cent of QVC programming. It averages 113 000 orders each day, with 35 000 through automated Voice Response Units. In February 1995, QVC was bought by cable operators Tele-Communications Inc. and Comcast. With $1.2 billion of revenue in 1995, QVC is the owner of America's largest electronic shopping channel. Douglas Briggs, who has filled the top position after the departure of the former CEO of Paramount Pictures and Fox, Barry Diller, was interviewed by Becky Beyer of *USA Today*. Observing that Diller's background was in entertainment and Briggs' is in retailing, Beyer asked, 'Is QVC going to focus more on selling and less on keeping viewers entertained?', to which Briggs responded that they had been pushed toward giving viewers more information about products. They were going to continue working on providing as much information as they can: 'Our business is electronic retailing, which really is about a third retailing, a third direct marketing and a third entertainment. Technology is changing that, but it's still primarily a business of selling products.' He sees the target as expanding all the basic businesses, with the overall goal of making QVC synonymous with shopping from the home. They have been concentrating on England and expected to see a profit in 1996. They intended to have an online service, but recognised that it is unlikely to be a big business right away. There are several interesting and conflicting understandings of the offer. For example, Briggs sees the ability to demonstrate items on QVC as a great advantage over stores, because he feels that it is not economically viable for a traditional retailer to do this. Yet, one of the main arguments against home shopping is that the customer cannot try out the product. This seems to point to each side holding a contrasting opinion and effect derived from the same question; in other words the same answer means the same thing, but with very different effects, to each of two totally different merchandising offers.

Briggs also answers the question about some retailers suffering from price-conscious consumers, by explaining that QVC raises prices more than they lower them. When an item is introduced it will be a special offer for a short time, then the price is raised to the regular cost. And returned products may also be a problem at QVC. They wish returns were lower, but is conveniently explained as being an asset, because it tends to show that as customers become more comfortable shopping from TV, they have learned to trust that they can send things back. Finally, it is noted that something like forty companies have either launched, or thought about launching TV shopping networks, so it is not an easy business.

Television home shopping channels may be perceived as selling tacky jewellery and dubious hair products, but many feel that these channels are the tip of the iceberg of future versions of interactive home shopping. By the year 2020, ordinary shoppers will almost certainly be able to buy any product at its cheapest price through the information infrastructure. Even today, QVC can buy in such bulk from wholesalers that it can mark up its items by 100 per cent and still undercut retail stores that have higher overhead costs. In reality, anyone who wants to trawl the market can already find the cheapest bargains, subject to some of the cautions which have been stated. One of the concerns of retailers offering good service are the customers who takes an assistant's time, get special expertise and advice to select the best product, then go elsewhere to buy it cheaper. The shop selling at the lower price can do so because of its lower standard of service and consequently with a lower overhead. A typical example can be found at computer software shops. Many customers are unsure of the best product for their needs and ask searching questions about the features contained in a package. Specialist retailers, who care and have the necessary expertise, often open a piece of software to demonstrate it. This specialist advice is valuable and clearly adds to the customer service and satisfaction element. However, many other retailers refuse to open the shrink wrapping on the package, with the result that the customer has to try it after purchase. It has become a common trend for shoppers to avail themselves of the advice, see the product demonstrated and then go to the other retailer to purchase at a cheaper cost, knowing what he wants to buy. The second retailer can afford to sell cheaper because it does not have the extra service costs associated with the time and detailed knowledge of the product.

The consumers will have the advantage of having more diversity of products to choose from because of the economies of scale. Local stores cannot stock many specialised products, because they tend to cater for the average taste. Therefore, online shopping of the future will be able to service shoppers of the arcane. Future shoppers may be faced with a proliferation of niche products far beyond today's levels, but the average American city already has access to about 1 million products. How many more does the consumer want? In fact, it could be argued that the stock carried by retailers meets the needs of the shopper, and items which are not stocked by any accessible shop are likely to be limited in their market and are therefore unlikely to be of much attraction, commercially, to an online provider.

Presently, advertising repeatedly targets a mass audience with sales pitches that many want to ignore. As much as 18 per cent of American TV time is given up to commercials. It is said that under the new system, advertising will evolve from its hit or miss quality to precision targeting, that future advertising will be directed to consumers who actually ask for the information about a particular product and do not have to be seduced. I find that premise rather bizarre. I thought that the basis of much advertising is that many consumers are unaware of the product and/or did not know what they wanted until seduced. That certainly is the basis of the success of the catalogue business, and of retailers relying on impulse purchases. In my opinion, the advocacy being used to sell and promote online shopping in this way greatly tests its credibility. These arguments, put forward by promoters of online shopping, do not really stand up to even the initial questions. Why, for example, does an electronic retailer on the Net have a Home Page? The answer is this is to attract the customer by a general seductive presentation and lead the browser onto more selective and detailed messages.

The argument that individual needs will be met by the future systems, is further advanced by reference to 'mass customisation', where computer technology will be used to modify a product to fit an individual's need. Again, there seems to be a contradiction in terms, in using 'mass' and 'customisation' together. I cannot quite reconcile how anyone can be treated as an individual, if it is the same for the mass. Oh Well!

As an example, Levi Strauss & Co introduced 'Personal Pair' jeans, which they have made available in a few test stores. A woman's exact measurements are entered into the store's computer to form a digital blueprint that is sent, with choice of colour, material and style, over a computer network to the factory. A computerised machine cuts cloth to the precise specifications and tags it, before it sends it to the standard manufacturing process. At the end of the line, the tagged pair is retrieved and sent back to the store, or directly to the customer via Federal Express. The total price difference, compared to off the shelf, is an extra $10. Although one must allow for the fact that this is a test exercise, I see a similarity to the additional charges by grocery stores for ordering and delivery. We should question the economic logic of the supporting argument that this type of customisation would save the clothing industry an estimated £25 billion each year, which is the value of stock which fails to sell, or only if marked down. In other words, on the basis of computer ordered customised clothing, all items would be pre-sold before manufacture, with the added benefit of cash flow to the store. On that basis, why is there a higher cost to the consumer? Surely the cost should be less. In the same way, groceries should be less because the cost of delivery is likely to be less than the savings in staff and overheads at a store. Overall, the statement that economies of scale will allow online to provide the cheapest prices becomes confused when customisation is introduced. Methinks some promotional people are trying to show that everyone can get anything at the best value; by making the pitch so overwhelmingly universal, the message is bound to get blurred and attack confidence in what is a future unproven system.

An interesting example was recently related to me by a colleague. He uses the Internet for holiday bookings and decided to book a car. He logged on to the Home Page of one of the biggest, best known, car rental companies and obtained the rental figures for the car he chose. He was asked to enter the place from which the enquiry was being made, which in this case was London. He then decided that he would enter a different, overseas, source. The result was that the rental quotation was substantially cheaper, for the same car and the same period.

The PC is, by its nature, interactive and, in theory, responds only to the user's requests or directions. The PC needs a modem as the basic tool for online communication. Compared to other systems, online is very new, having grown from, principally, a limited data exchange medium to the friendly graphics for information and entertainment of the World Wide Web. The Community is now estimated at over 40 million and is growing by some 10 per cent per month.

It would be very foolish to simply dismiss the question of online shopping by assuming that the present methods will be adhered to, willy nilly. As in all matters pertaining to shopping centres, one must consider the alternatives carefully. This means that we should examine the way in which a typical shopper presently conducts a shopping visit, and compare the alternative advantages, and disadvantages, offered by the new and emerging technology.

Today, the focus is on the retail store. For simplicity, and for the purpose of this basic example, I will take a shop in a shopping centre, rather than a large discount unit which is free standing, or part of a retail park. The steps taken generally follow the pattern of the shopper allocating time to carry out essential shopping requirements. This time has to be found regardless of other commitments, because certain items, such as food purchases, toiletries, medicine, or even dry cleaning, are basic needs for a family. For other less essential items such as fashion, time can be found when it is more convenient, or when leisure time is available. It is often stated that much of the essential shopping needs have to be undertaken when it is inconvenient in terms of other commitments, and that they concern staple items which could be bought more conveniently without the need to actually inspect the goods. The housewife knows what brand of baked beans she usually buys. However, many shoppers are still selective and not totally wedded to a particular brand loyalty. Therefore, the opportunity of comparing prices, size/price value and special offers of loss leaders, has to be considered.

Having found the time, the shopper travels to the centre either by private or public transport. If by car, she finds a parking space which is hopefully close to her final exit point, for ease of carrying the purchased goods to the car. She then looks for the shop which may carry the product(s) on her shopping list. She walks round the shop seeking the items and also considering other items as alternatives, comparing prices and other information, such as ingredients. While doing this, the shopper has to pass other products which the retailer has merchandised to attract additional sales, often as impulse decisions. The shopper then pays for the purchases, with the disadvantage of a delay in being served if the shop is busy. The goods are then carried to the car and taken home. They will have to be unloaded, but that would have to be done if they were delivered.

On the other hand, we should think of the way in which a shopper might use an online store. This is held out to be a similar concept, but through a different medium. I fear that I do not personally agree with such a simplistic viewpoint. It seems to me that there is a world of difference between a personal real experience, whatever the convenience factor, and an artificial experience with a computer in two dimensions. Nevertheless, we can use the example of using Internet to access BarclaySquare, one of the new kind of 'virtual' shopping malls featuring a number of high street retailers, and backed by Barclays Bank. It seems important that we note, at this point, that the expression 'virtual' cannot be associated with the usual impression of virtual reality. When in Chapter 5 I raised the possibility of echoing the flying of a 747 from an armchair, or wearing a virtual reality headset, it gave a vision of really being there, of doing and carrying out the functions, with a real feeling and experience. Virtual Malls are graphic layouts with merchants' logos, directories and home pages leading to product and corporate information. There is no sensation of walking through the mall, window shopping and entering the store with a feeling of expectation, as would be the case in actual reality.

The user goes to the store. There is no journey and no parking. The shopper looks for the product, asks for information, seeks out alternatives and compares prices. In doing this, other products were passed and some could have been selected on impulse, or when memory is jogged. The amount due is paid and that's it. The goods will be delivered by a third party and there is no carrying or transport home. That is the simple way in which shopping online is illustrated but there are, unfortunately, a number of things which advertisers of the simplicity and merits fail to explain.

First, let us look at BarclaySquare (see Plate 10). Let us think about the 'journey' to get there and what is actually on offer at this 'virtual' shopping centre. Although there are a great number of 'virtual' malls on the Internet, BarclaySquare is one of the most written and talked about UK sites, considered to give an excellent taste of things to come. Laid out like a new town shopping arcade, it has two streets and virtual shopping malls occupied by individual companies. *Business Age* magazine showed it as one of its Online Winners in 1996. It said that BarclaySquare is confident of attracting many more vendors to the site 'in the coming months'. It also reported that

> The number of shops on the Net and on BarclaySquare will increase significantly with the number of users; but the biggest breakthrough will come when people overcome their fear of tapping credit card numbers into their computers.

The page on the Net shows the following offering their products (Plate 10): Argos, Campus Travel, Innovations, Toys "Я" Us, Sainsbury's, BT, Airline Network, Eurostar, World of Scotch Whisky, Interflora, Victoria Wine, Barclays, Sun Alliance, Blackwell, Thrust, Barclay's Merchant Services and Car Shop. This is hardly a good comparison with the alternative large selection found in most shopping centres or high streets. Not only is the choice of trades very limited, but the element of choice within any trade is almost non-existent. In reality, there are so few retailers that the equivalent would be a very small local shopping parade. It is, therefore, somewhat of a stretch of the imagination to use this as a comparison with the type of shopping facility the normal shopper has come to expect and demand.

In the August 1996 edition of *Shopping Centres Today*, the highly informative and specialised journal of the International Council of Shopping Centres, New York, there is a leading editorial about IBM's venture which 'aims to revolutionise online retailing'. According to the article, company executives were already counting on about twenty retailers to be paying rent when the virtual mall opened for business by the autumn. In fact we accessed the new mall Web site, called 'World Avenue', on 5 August 1996.

To show that the hype and expectations may often exceed the reality, I will firstly repeat much of the promotional verbiage of the article, and then describe the actual experience of a visit to the site.

The mall had among its tenants, Express, a division of The Limited Inc., and Hudsons Bay, one of Canada's largest department store groups. At presstime, IBM declined to identify other retailers setting up shop. Soon you will see why this may have been so. Experts said that, with the entry of IBM into the electronic market place, World Avenue may have become the catalyst that the mostly stagnant

Internet mall sector had needed. IBM promised shoppers and retailers everything that they would expect at a regular mall, and more. Nonetheless, IBM did not believe that it was about to drive the conventional mall into extinction. 'We believe that this environment will not replace stores' said Jason Morsink, IBM's North American solutions manager for electronic retailing. 'Our view is that the stores are still very important'.

It was stated that IBM's relationship with its retailers would be similar to that of a normal mall owner. The company would provide the space and guide retailers as they used its software to set up their stores. A typical mall merchant marketing 300 items would pay $30 000 to sign up for the service, plus a monthly 'rent' of $2500 and a percentage rent of 5 per cent of sales. The economics of this deal, compared to a normal shop large enough to sell only 300 items, is an interesting exercise for shop letting agents and retailers.

So, albeit much earlier than advertised, we found World Avenue on the Internet. Was it the all-dancing, all-singing offer we expected? The Home page showed the following 'retailers'. 1996 Olympic Games Merchandise: Exclusive Venue Collection, Express, 1996 Official Olympic Catalog, Robert Waxman's Worldwide Camera and Video, Shows and Events, and Wimbledon. No Hudsons Bay or the other fifteen retailers promised, although IBM still had until the autumn to meet their advertised offering. We visited the Olympic Games site and found offers of T-shirts, baseball caps and other items celebrating the Games. Of course, when we viewed this page the Games had closed three days previously, but the page ended with the message 'See you in Atlanta'. We considered the Olympic Water Polo T-shirts at $22 each. Then, we visited Express and clicked on 'outfits'. This showed small pictures of five outfits. Generally the presentation of the Home page, and the individual retailers' pages, were unimaginative and drab and could not start to compare with the standard of merchandising and window dressing of a normal store. There is no way of telling whether the prices quoted were good or high, since there were no comparisons with other comparable merchandise.[1]

This experience is not uncommon. Last year MCI Communications Corporations, introduced its electronic mall called 'Marketplace MCI', with 27 stores, including Nordstrom, Hammacher Schlemmer

---

1. IBM World Avenue officially closed in Autumn 1997.

and Borders Books and Music. The amount of merchandise available, however, varies considerably. In the Borders online music section only eight CDs were available, and only two non-fiction books. Nordstrom invited e-mail enquiries and showed no merchandise. Browsers entering Hammercher Schlemmer pages, on the other hand, could choose from 124 products.

Time Warner's Dream Shop listed 15 retailers, including Williams-Sonoma and Eddie Bauer, but only a sampling of their products was shown. Even then, none of them could be ordered over the Internet, and shoppers were invited to phone an 800 number instead. Therefore, the comments of Les Duncan of Express may be a very good guide to the thinking of retailers who are taking the decision to be present on the Net. He said 'We aren't sure how much volume we'll do on the Internet'. He predicted that the IBM mall site would appeal most to people in rural areas or overseas, who do not live within easy reach of an Express store. This indicates that most retailers are looking to the Internet as a promotion and marketing tool to advertise products which they are selling by visits to the actual store, in a real mall or high street.

Retailers like to see sales and hard cash: shoppers like to buy merchandise which is attractive, convenient and value-related. Therefore, all the indications and opinions will ultimately be of little importance in comparison to the actual experience of those using the Internet, or other online services. I have already referred to the experience of Argos and Sainsbury on BarclaySquare. More information became available at the end of October 1996, which was more surprising than had been thought. The most revealing figure was that BarclaySquare mall had takings of less than £10 000 since it opened 18 months earlier. That is a staggeringly low amount. Sainsbury's said that it had taken only 1000 orders for flowers, chocolate and wine over the Web in nine months. Argos, in another revealed fact, abandoned the sales of sofas over the Internet and offered a selection of low-cost gifts, including an alarm clock at £18.95 named after Wallace and Gromit. Argos has sold only thirty of its low-cost items.

Based on these figures, there would seem to be even more support for my contention that the Internet will not replace traditional shopping for some time, if ever. The facts reported are a stark contrast to the many claims made by the promoters of the systems, and probably a similar shock to those major retailers who have participated on expectations and promises of marketing men.

Part V
Future Trends

18 The US Shopping Centre Experience and UK Trends

We have seen that the experience of developing shopping centres in America has led the way for the rest of the world. Even the adverse effects of out-of-town regional and strip malls on the American city centres, and the more recent attempts at regeneration, carry lessons for us all. The market-led economy of the United States is in many ways quite different from other countries. There, the consumer demand and commercial drive means that there is a vitality and volatility which is missing in Europe, or which is controlled by more central or local regulations. It is not uncommon, in America, to see a huge regional mall on highway intersections being challenged by one or more additional malls, in close proximity. It becomes survival of the fittest, with service, attraction and sheer commercial promotion and drive directing development. In Britain and France, for instance, such a scenario is hardly able to happen, due to the planning infrastructure, which dictates to the consumer what may be offered, rather than the customer directing what and where they find most desirable.

Because the past history of UK shopping has followed the American experience so closely, albeit with a time delay in the past, it must continue to be useful to look at that history and glean indications of what the future may hold in store. It is interesting, therefore, to note that the International Council of Shopping Centres (ICSC)[1] published its *Research Quarterly for Summer 1996*, with a lead feature of 'The Shopping Centre Industry: A Look at the Last 10 Years'. This examines ten years of Scope data. Its main findings refer to the economic impacts, geographic distribution, development trends, and types of centres being built. Shopping centres have gained increasing importance to the economy, accounting for $914.2 billion in retail sales in 1995, or 58 per cent of all non-auto retail sales, compared

---

1. The ICSC, which was established in New York forty years ago, now has over 35 000 shopping professionals as members world-wide. It is considered the largest and most authorative body on shopping centre matters and produces a large amount of statistical data.

with $512.2 billion in 1986. When we see the predictions of sales volume potential on electronic sales, we should remember that auto sales in the United States is a big player. A number of large automobile traders are showing huge sales through the Internet. With this in mind, a useful statistic is that auto sales in 1995 amounted to $561 billion, or 24 per cent of the total retail sales in the United States. An estimated 10.9 million workers were employed in shopping centres in 1995, about 9 per cent of the total non-agricultural workforce. This does not include the people employed on construction, shopfitting, consulting and other ancillary employment arising or connected with shopping centres. At the end of 1995, there were 41 235 shopping centres, containing 4.97 billion square feet of gross leaseable area (GLA). The volume of space, the sales generated and the numbers of people employed has to impact on the question of the economic benefits of direct and indirect taxation.

The data on geographic distribution of the shopping centres is of little interest to European developers. But there is one interesting feature which reflects on the introduction and use of technology for shopping. California, the recognised technological home of the computer and chip, has more shopping centres than any other state. Indeed, California, Florida and Texas, the three primary areas for computer technology, contain together 27 per cent of the total GLA.

The level of population is a commonly used indicator of the likely demand for retail space. Growth in the number of shopping centres, as well as growth of total shopping centre GLA, has been slowing, aligning more closely with the level of the US population. However, *per capita* GLA of US shopping centres continues to rise, albeit at a decreasing rate, from 15.2 square feet per person in 1986, to 18.9 square feet per person in 1995. These figures relate only to shopping centre space and not to all retail space. Of the 239 million square feet of retail space on which construction began in 1995, only about 27 per cent of the total was in shopping centres. The balance was either in downtowns or free standing units. The report says that several industry analysts are concerned that retail space is currently being over-built, and they attribute much of that activity to the construction of big box stores, driven by retailers who are seeking to boost market share, but are not necessarily concerned with the profitability of individual stores. Other analysts attribute much of that construction to retailers' needs for bigger stores than those currently existing. In either case, the predicted result is the same. Excess space will affect the neighbourhood and community sector of the shopping centre industry.

The pace of shopping centre openings during 1995 might suggest the potential for added sales growth. However, while developers held back their production of space during the first half of the 1990s, retailers did not. This is supported by construction data which shows that new shopping centres slowed down, but that large retail stores of between 50 000 and 200 000 square feet more than doubled. The annual increase in shopping centre space added, reduced from 143 million square feet in the period 1980–90, to 115 million square feet in 1990–5, whereas free standing large stores increased from 34 million to 79 million in the same period. These are annual figures, and thus it can be deduced that large stores represented 19 per cent of retail activity to 1990 and 41 per cent during 1991–5.

Of course, the retail recessions have also given us bankruptcies and store closings. Recently announced retail store closings have been estimated to be about 4800 units.

The fact that women's ready-to-wear store sales have remained steady, at $30 billion a year, has contributed to at least 3000 store closings or bankruptcies, but they are not alone, as can be seen from the above indications. Women's ready-to-wear has maintained sales around $30 billion per year since 1990. The figure reflects the competition which has come from other retail formats, such as discount stores and the promotional, family apparel stores, from The Gap, Eddie Bauer to Filenes Basement, T J Maxx and others. The fact, though, is that the demographic tide has simply been going out of women's clothing stores. This has much to do with the change in the annual population growth in women aged 14 to 34 years, which showed a decline which should continue to the year 2000, when it will reverse and start to grow again. The growth prospects in the first decade of the next century are substantial. However, the report issued by the ICSC, New York, projected shopping centre-inclined store sales of $1.555 trillion for the year 2000, using an annual growth rate of 4.7 per cent over 1995 sales, and partial data for 1996 suggests that such growth is, in fact, occurring. It is felt that underlying consumer demand will change the market's space needs, altering the distribution of demand across store types and will reward those shopping centres that are able to respond accordingly.

So, what are the thoughts of ICSC on the outlook for shopping centre performance over the next few years? There will be more space, driven by retailers' desires or needs. Retailers will generate more space as they try to present themselves to customers as favourably as possible. Against this bad news are the facts that sales should increase in the future, based on present projections. Regional mall openings will average about nine a year for 1996–9, equalling less than 1 per cent of existing supply per year. Retailers looking for the most attractive and efficient formats, in the best locations, continue to create attractive new investment opportunities, although those same retailers will be leaving older property as a result.

If, as expected, the competition and suicidal price-cutting sales inducements of the big box and category killers leads to contraction and vacancies, landlords may look for replacement tenants from the regional malls. However, most regional malls have already felt the impact of competition from this sector.

The continuing amount of space and the saturation in evidence means that competition to attract tenants will continue, and the availability of offers will direct tenants toward the best stores, making those less attractive struggle to survive. For retailers, there is a great opportunity to expand relatively cheaply by taking space vacated by bankruptcies.

The winners among shopping centres will be those which are well anchored, which are in a fairly sole attraction market and which have withstood the big box discounters: open-air speciality centres, particularly when fashion-led, in affluent areas being five miles or more from the nearest regional mall; strongly anchored community centres in strategic locations, which are difficult to copy. Also, neighbourhood centres with leading grocery store anchors and a selection of small stores, in solid trade areas in good locations.

Of course, the really interesting feature which emerges from these details, is not whether the United States will be over-shopped, nor even the form and content of the new shopping centres. What must be the most important thing is that developers, retailers, bankers, insurance and pension fund actuaries, and the host of other advisers, are proceeding with more and new shopping developments, despite the warnings that online shopping will replace them. Can so many people be squandering so much money on pure trust that the future will continue to provide the prosperity it has done in the past? We should bear in mind that these 'risk takers' carry out detailed and substantial demographic and socioeconomic studies before embarking on a scheme. Even if we consider the investment as a short-term anomaly of being caught up in the race, think of the huge investment by the major department stores and chain stores. It is difficult to surmise that they would continue to invest appreciably more than they have to date, if they think they can reach the same market on the Internet. One could understand a policy of standing still while the future potential was uncertain, but active expansion and investment clearly indicates that those who effectively contribute the major ingredient in the future of online shopping also suspect that they control the outcome. They will ensure that the outcome fits with their own plans and future economic prosperity. Since shopping is being served by the major retail names, if they want to safeguard their massive existing investments in property and people, and their added ongoing investments, the retailers will have a strong incentive in making sure that online shopping, as presently promoted, does not succeed in that precise form. As an added tool for promotion and advertising it will be a fabulous medium; as a direct selling method replacing the visit to the store, on the predications I have put forward, it is unlikely to be supported sufficiently to succeed in a really massive way.

On p. 203, I gave an example of how prices differed for car rental. In a recent discussion with leading retailers they responded to this story by voicing great concerns about pricing generally. For instance, would a shopper be able to see a television set offered by a US retailer online at a fraction of the cost from a local retailer and order it from the United States? On the basis of the Internet having no geographical boundaries, such a scenario is certainly possible. But a further question was raised. Why shouldn't manufacturers offer products direct, thereby cutting out the retailer completely? The only apparent safeguard against this likelihood is the historical inability of most manufacturers to operate efficiently in the marketing, sales and delivery of single items to consumers. Nevertheless, the offer of compact discs by record producers may be an example which induces great concern for retailers.

Traditional retailing must ensure that the high street or shopping centre attractions continue to be of sufficient standard to bring the shopper to their stores. We all accept that America has a very volatile economy and can change direction very quickly according to latest market demands. Nevertheless, the amount of investment seen in the past, which would need to be written down massively, together with the added capital investment being undertaken now, must be of a scale which over-rides any quick fix change of marketing promotion in the foreseeable future. But, if this argument is not, in itself, sufficient evidence of the attitudes of retailers, developers and investors, the news from the United Kingdom is. Comparatively, the United Kingdom does not respond to market pressures as quickly as the United States. Therefore, the path of capital investment is more of a long-term nature and unlikely to be embarked upon just for a short while, especially if online shopping is at all likely to completely undermine the stability and prosperity of the retail scene.

It seems that many assumptions about retail trends which are taken for granted are susceptible to being undermined. There are various examples of the ways in which the shoppers' preferences, or assumed preferences, that promoters of electronic shopping believe will lead to success for their new methods can be shown to be different to the common perception. Even the perceived trend assessed by retailers themselves may be wide of the mark.

In the August 1997 edition of *Shopping Centers Today*, conclusions drawn from the fourth annual survey of ICSC/Gallup of consumer spending habits illustrated this surprising fact. Each year Gallup questions 1000 people about their store preferences and spending. Among its findings, the survey found that 60 per cent of respondents in the 18–34 age group shopped mainly at discount department stores. The propensity to do this declined as age increased, with 44 per cent of the age group 35–54 and 29 per cent of over 55s saying they sought out discount department stores. Similar results were reported for off-price stores. While 27 per cent of the 18–34 age group said they shopped at such stores, 20 per cent between 35 and 54 are off-price customers and only 10 per cent over 55 frequent those stores.

A continuous emphasis on value was shown among those with higher incomes. Of those with an annual income over $35 000, 22 per cent said they shopped more at off-price stores compared with about 15 per cent with incomes under $35 000. Similarly the tendency to spend more was greatest among the younger age groups, inversely decreasing with age. As baby-boomers grow older many question whether they will follow this pattern of reduced spending with age, or will remain strong spenders. Nevertheless, the reasons given by those spending less was generally either 'I can't afford it' or 'I don't need it'. Another response was 'I don't get out as much/shop as much' The survey indicated that 90 per cent of those who gave this explanation were over 55 years old. Research officials speculated that this may account for a substantial drop in respondents who said they were spending less to save money.

When asked to name their favourite place to shop during the holiday season, 40 per cent chose traditional enclosed shopping malls, making them the clear favourite. These American survey results will be of interest to all retailers but they also provide some further thought-provoking data for the promoters of online shopping. The trends among defined age groups who may desire or be capable of using computer shopping media, together with the reinforcement of the preferred traditional shopping venue, raises more doubts about the scenario of online dramatically replacing the form of shopping we have come to know.

If the American survey gives such indications, the signs of shopping centre activity in Britain are therefore of great interest. Some of the recent announcements should be considered, and, although they are not being detailed here, they do give a flavour of the thinking of the movers and shapers of the industry. The Healey & Baker *Quarterly Report* for July 1996 said that shopping centres remained in demand although they are increasingly hard to find. This was for investments, and it would be hard to think that the expert analysts and actuaries of the major insurance companies and pension funds would be advocating further investment on a long-term basis with yields appearing to be reducing from 6.75 per cent to 6.5 per cent as an indicator of continuing demand and security in the future of that investment medium. A number of shopping centres were acquired by new owners, including The Arcades, Ashton-under-Lyne; Victoria Place, London; Selbourne Walk, London; Elmsleigh Centre, Staines; Fort Retail Park, Birmingham; The Maltings, Salisbury; Princess Square, Bracknell; and Charles Darwin Centre, Shrewsbury. In addition to these, Prudential purchased a 999-year lease for 15 per cent of the income from Bluewater, which is not due to open until 1999. Analysts' estimated expectations of rising consumer demand, over the three months to June 1996, and this is supported by prime rents, which increased by 2.1 per cent, the best quarterly figure for seven years.

The Richard Ellis *Retail Market Bulletin* for Autumn 1996, issued in December 1996, gave details of a survey carried out jointly with the University of Salford, of thirty-one retail property investors, and where whole cumulative commitment to retail property was approximately £10 billion. 87 per cent said that they intended to commit further funds to the retail–leisure sector. Asked to specify which sectors of the retail property market were most attractive, 40 per cent of respondents said leisure–retail parks, 35 per cent retail warehouses and 19 per cent shopping centres. Richard Ellis said that, since the survey, in-town retail has proved to be increasingly popular and that their assessment of investment yields for prime property had decreased from 5 per cent in July 1996, to 4.5 per cent in November.

Elsewhere, I used the increase in profits of Argos and its plans to increase its stores in number from the present 390 to 600, for the purposes of showing a comparison with their poor online sales. But in the food sector, which many feel should lead the online convenience onslaught on traditional shopping, German retailers Netto, Lidl and Aldi reported a combined increase of 50 per cent to £2.1 billion in their UK sales. The three have a total of over 360 stores in the United Kingdom.

The Dixon Group reported underlying profits up 35 per cent to £135 million in the year to April 1996 and over £190 million in 1997. This is a retailer in the very forefront of electronics and appliances, and must therefore be considering the impact of online shopping as seriously as anyone. The Group says that it plans to add ten Curry's superstores, ten PC Worlds and revamp 100 Dixons' stores, creating 2500 jobs.

Retailer Property Intentions were analysed in a recent report by the British Retail Consortium and Jones Lang Wootton. The report noted that an increasing number of retailers are unable to satisfy their space requirements in town centres; this is particularly noticeable amongst retailers seeking stores of over 10 000 square feet.

In July 1996, Boots said they planned to spend more than £300 million on its core chemist chain over the next four years. In 1997 it planned to spend £70 million on stores, including forty new outlets and upgrades of eighteen Central London sites. John Hoerner, Chief Executive of the Burton Group, announced a 31 per cent increase in profits resulting from better performance from its chain, which includes Top Shop, Burton Menswear and Dorothy Perkins. He said that he planned to grow the Group by adding more stores to the Debenham's Department Store portfolio, with a further four stores to open in the next two years, increasing floor area by 20 per cent by the year 2000. Debenham's is to be found at BarclaySquare on the Internet.

The acquisition by Burton Group of Racing Green, announced in October 1996, for £19 million is not an item which might seem very significant for a group with annual sales of almost £2 billion. However, it is a continuation of a trend which follows its acquisition earlier in the year of the Innovations mail order business. Racing Green is a specialist, which has succeeded by having a number of new ideas in the mail order business. The successful formula was based on the offer of quality casual clothing at reasonable prices, and probably has as its closest comparison retailer, Next. Next has used its catalogue business partly as a means to test its designs on the market. By the responses to its catalogue, Next is better able to judge which items are likely to sell well in its stores by the time they are stocked there. If the supposition is correct that this well tested method, which has had a lot to do with the tremendous success of Next, may be deployed by Burton through Racing Green and Innovations, it points toward an optimism in the future of the mail order market, added to the probable introduction of the ranges into Debenham's or Principles' stores. Burtons announced (6 November 1996) that it would launch home shopping catalogues within the next two years for all its high street shops, including Debenhams, Evans, Principles and Top Shop. This follows the two acquisitions made during the year. John Hoerner said that Burton now had the skills to handle mail order. He also said

> I can imagine a customer who enjoys a shopping experience at Dorothy Perkins but also likes the ability to flick through a Dorothy Perkins catalogue at midnight, order a bra over the telephone and have it delivered the next day.

The announcement carries several surprises. Firstly the specific reference to mail order and catalogues, rather than the Internet. It is clear that a customer will be seen as using a printed catalogue and a telephone ordering system. Mr Hoerner probably does not think of one of his customers browsing the Internet at midnight, but rather reading a glossy brochure or catalogue in bed. Reference to next-day delivery also indicates that the delivery system envisaged by Mr Hoerner may be via an established courier such as DHL or UPS. But how can an order be taken, processed, filled, packed, and dispatched in time to actually be delivered the next day? I may be too cynical, but it seems that either Burtons still do not understand the logistics (unlikely) or, more likely, that this is more hype in promotions of a new venture. But the most revealing part of the statement is the decision to go down the mail order–printed catalogue route, after Burtons have been featured on the BarclaySquare shopping mall since its start.

I have mentioned the moves by Marks & Spencer in offering a home shopping service at its mainline stores and their interest in the

Internet. The retail market closely watches M&S, who have an enviable success record based on a large dedicated shopping attraction. Therefore, the announcement in the *Financial Times* of 2 April 1997 that they are planning to expand into the mail order clothing business, intending to introduce a catalogue in Spring 1998, adds weight to the conclusions drawn from the Burton moves. It is yet another sign that major retailers have not reached a conclusive policy on the merits of the Internet as the alternative to traditional shopping methods which have been accepted by consumers and proven over a long period.

So we are left to think that perhaps it is during the leisure periods that potential shoppers will be able and willing to use their computers to shop. The latest Healey & Baker survey on Sunday Trading shows that consumers want to see more large stores open. Marks & Spencer and Boots were the two names most frequently mentioned by consumers, when asked where they would like to shop on Sundays. Since the previous year, according to the Healey & Baker Report, there was a significant increase in the number of shops open in Central London, Bristol, Birmingham, Nottingham, Canterbury and Bath. The large regional shopping centres such as Lakeside, Meadowhall and the MetroCentre, together with shops in the major cities such as Manchester, Birmingham, Bristol and the West End of London are those which are mainly open.

Are my doubts well founded? I can find little better evidence of the future part to be played by electronic shopping than that provided by those whose participation, and wholehearted support, must be needed for a big retail draw to the online. Clearly, the retailers are unconvinced, otherwise they would not be investing so heavily in traditional shopping areas. Without the full offer of the high street, I do not think the average consumer will support the electronic substitute in a significant manner.

KPMG issued a report in June 1996, on 'The Internet: Its Potential and Use by European Retailers', which concludes that a truly profitable, transactional presence on the Internet appears more problematical than many of its proponents would have retailers believe. Also, Verdict, the retail consultants, warn that 'Electronic Shopping will have no impact in the next five years and minimal impact over the next ten years' in their 1996 report. Perhaps the most disturbing and damning quotation to emerge during 1996 was from George Colony, Chairman of Forrester Research, who said: 'Clients say we've spent all this money on the Web – we want to start making money now. Well, you can't. The Web is dead technology.' This seems logically to have some support, in terms of electronic commerce, from Netscape, who have abandoned the consumer browser sector. Instead they are positioning their system, Navigator, as part of a product suite for the Intranet[1] business-computing market.

---

1. Intranet is any network that provides similar services within an organisation to those provided by the Internet outside it, but which is not necessarily connected to the Internet.

19   A View of the Future?

Douglas Rushkoff, author of *Cyberia*, *Media Virus* and *Playing the Future*, looks at technologies and the cultures they spawn as expressions of nature and the benevolent force of chaos. He has published an opinion which ideally leads me into this conclusion. He said:

> With each successive development in communications technology comes a corresponding leap in the number of ideas with which it requires us to cope. As we incorporate each new invention into our daily life, we must accelerate our ability to process new thoughts and ideas.
>
> What we need to adapt to, more than any particular change, is the fact that we are changing so rapidly. We must learn to accept change as a constant. Novelty is the new status quo.

It would be utterly stupid to conclude that the advances in technology and the progress in electronic commerce will have no effect on retailing as we have come to know it in the past. As with all changes in the market, we must form our opinions based on current moves and trends and try to reach a conclusion based on facts as they exist, rather than how we would like them to be. However much we wish the world to stay the same, resting in the comfort of the situation which is known and which has worked well for a long time, we must face reality. The two big questions are, firstly, how much of an effect technology will have and, secondly, whether shopping will finally continue in much the same form as the past. These are questions which will undoubtedly generate many answers, depending on the opinions of those closely involved in traditional shopping methods, mail order, catalogue shopping and the electronic media, influenced not only by their general knowledge of the overall situation, but also by their perception of the advances and responses they are seeing in their own specialised sectors. The upbeat statements made by promoters of electronic shopping, once examined in detail, have tended to be based on an acceptance and assimilation of rapid technological advances which improve the service and response of information, but which also tend to be founded on the assumption that the consumer is both enthusiastic and able to use the medium with ease. They also appear to assume that the rest of the world is standing still, with the effect that their technological progress will outstrip the present situation, which will remain static and consequently become more and more outdated. We should accept that the existing system of shopping, with architecture based on buildings and comparatively set methods of technology, is bound to move at a slower pace of change than the advances in high technology, but we also know that the world simply does not stand still and that for every advance announced there is more than likely to be another on its way. That is illustrated by the doubts already raised about the capacity of the Internet to continue to provide real and worthwhile information freely to users who pay a modest subscription. Even if it will be available, there are many frustrations being voiced, such as the service slowing down dramatically in afternoons, when US users enter the system. There have been suggestions that the Internet, as we now know it, will take another form in the future. I have no expertise in such academic conjecture, but it serves the purpose to indicate that things continue to develop instead of standing still. There is also the suggestion by Forrester Research made above that the Web is dead technology, which implies that other methods may soon supersede it.

During the research which has been conducted, without special attention to the advanced technological detail, but rather toward the applications and likely effects, many important points have been stated and other trends and possibilities have become apparent. These are included in the preceding discussion, but I have tried to think of those factors which probably have the greatest impact on the estimation of the future use of electronic shopping as it may affect traditional shopping to which we have become accustomed. Without any order of priority I will summarise my 'bullet points', which should influence a viewpoint for the future of shopping, if we want to crystal ball gaze at the present time.

It is my opinion that there is rarely little new in the world but merely a different, updated or technologically superior way of presentation or production. It may be faster, more efficient or have greater convenience, but the advantages need to be judged by consumers and retailers as alternatives to what has gone before, *to which they have become accustomed and comfortable.*

As I explained early in the book concerning my college days' holiday work, remote shopping ordering and home delivery is not a new phenomenon and has a long history. In the meantime, traditional shopping has continued and retail development has grown and prospered.

No matter how sophisticated the management system, the most important thing remains the need, expectations and human desires of the consumer. Acceptance by the consumer of the method of buying the goods is a priority requirement for any retailer and must include choice, comparison of price–value, service, delivery, security of payment and quality assurance, together with convenience and a pleasurable experience for the customer, with the opportunity of added-value sales for the retailer.

Human behaviour relies on the senses, and consumers are used to the see–feel–smell factor in making decisions based on their own psychological reactions to the inherent feelings generated by these experiences. The impulses which these senses give to the brain, leading to decisions and actions to accept or decline the offer to buy a product, makes it essential that any alternative must adequately compensate for absence of a sensual stimulus by offering other advantages.

Personal security has become a very important feature in public places. Shoppers need to be reassured that they will be safe when shopping personally in the traditional way. However, in view of the vast parade of financial pitfalls awaiting a relatively unsophisticated shopper, used as they are to having the product as seen as exposed in hand and paying for it on the spot, they must also have security if they choose electronic ordering and payment methods.

In stores, good quality service is essential. Quality of personal service is often criticised. Retailers need to improve their customer service training programmes so that the shopper feels an important customer – an individual, valued, advised and attended. Transactions have to be as convenient and speedy as possible.

Price alone is unlikely to be a sufficient reason to make shopping an enjoyable experience for shoppers. To make it an enjoyable experience shopping should also include convenience and entertainment in all its forms.

The growth of computer use is undeniable. As users become more accustomed to using their computers they will undoubtably look for more useful and rewarding programs to justify the capital investment in the hardware and software and to overcome the boredom of leisure or simple tasks. There are presently about 40 million Internet users and more are joining at a startling rate.

Many commentators think that home shopping is not a threat to retailers and can run alongside their existing businesses. Significant costs are associated with building up a presence and retailers should be aware of the many disadvantages as well as the advantages. Without a powerful retailing brand name people are less willing to pay upfront for goods, and the costs arising from returns have been high.

The reference to personal sensation also seems to be pertinent to a comparison of remote and personal participation in events. Although such media as television and radio allow immediate communication of a current event, many people would choose to attend the event itself to become involved in the personal experience, the atmosphere or the self gratification of simply 'being there'. The growth of video rentals and sales has seen a comparative increase in the attendance at the cinema. Televising live sports has indicated a comparative increase in the demand to attend live sports events. The conclusion is that a home experience may act as an advertisement which increases the awareness, whetting appetites for personal experience. The obvious question is whether the Internet will fulfill the same function in relation to shopping.

For technology to be used to a sufficient degree to replace shopping in its traditional form it clearly must be used by technically proficient consumers. Surveys indicate that 75 per cent of British respondents do not know how to get onto the Internet and 43 per cent of the population do not use mobile phones, computers, electronic organisers or pagers. This factor has clearly been recognised by many appliance manufacturers who are in a race to produce information appliances, directed at bringing the unwired masses into the Information Age. Differing views are held by experts about the form future devices will take, adding doubt about the continued growth of the systems presently being promoted as the answer to electronic commerce.

The importance of the consumer's ability to use technology is shown in a poll by MIT which asked people what invention they could not live without. It gave a top answer of the automobile with 63 per cent, and only 8 per cent for the PC, which tied with the hair dryer and was less than the microwave oven.

The ability to use computers is of crucial importance for the future success of online shopping. Computer literacy is now being addressed by governments using concerted efforts to get the population wired for the future. This is a recognition of the many surveys which show a lack of literacy and general fear of the medium. Among the young at school, where the general opinion has been that they are comfortable with computers, there is a gulf between poorly funded and expensive schools and between poor and better-off children. This is likely to limit the roles poorer children will be able to play in economic society in adult life. More mature students also show a surprisingly high degree of anxiety in using computers. Of adults, a survey by Dell in 1994 showed that 23 per cent of Americans are uneasy just thinking about computers. The British government survey indicates that three out of five women are not convinced that computers have any use in society, millions of people are still afraid to use them and many admit they are unable to programme their video recorders. Only about 20 per cent of Japanese executives are able to use a computer.

Computer literacy is of particular importance. The common feeling that the young are best able to use computers because of their familiarity from such an early age may be a misconception. Education has so far failed to ensure that schoolchildren are having a fair share of facilities to enable their future full sociological use of technology. There is some evidence that College students suffer computer anxieties and adults show a low degree of knowledge and comfort as users. The present system is perpetuating the gulf between the better-off with access to education with proper facilities and the have-nots with poor facilities.

Surveys show two types of Web audiences. The one that drives most of the media coverage in USA is 'upstream' and amounts to about 50 per cent of the current Web population. These are upscale, technically orientated academics and professionals but represent only 10 per cent of the US population. The other 90 per cent of US society is where the growth of the Internet will have to occur. This is roughly split 64 per cent male and 36 per cent female and represents the bulk of consumers. This group report the highest degree of frustration with the Web and have yet to find it particularly valuable. 97 per cent of the upstream audience and 89 per cent of the 'other half' have some college education which confirms that education is the key to Internet participation.

Internet shoppers are pioneers in the way they shop, rather than in what they buy. They are not risk takers. A major survey found that the most common use was simply for browsing. In Europe over 34 per cent used it for entertainment and 58 per cent for work. Only 11 per cent was for shopping, showing that the main uses were still recreational.

Users of the Internet are primarily those with higher levels of education and income, who tend to be people who adopt new technologies. As a result, retailers will find it difficult to target specific demographic and psychological customers.

Tele-shopping, such as QVC, will probably reinforce its position as an alternative method of remote shopping. Catalogue and mail order shopping will similarly continue to produce superior graphic illustration of products which can be considered at leisure by consumers, with added electronic applications to make ordering easier. Retailers such as Burtons look likely to expand catalogue shopping to supplement their stores, following the acquisitions of specialist companies.

Retailers have a defensive approach, which indicates uncertainty about future success rates for online shopping. They continue to expand their home shopping and delivery programmes, but these are exceeded by a continual expansion of their traditional shop openings and growth of floor areas.

Payment security remains a big conceptual problem with customers, especially when buying from a trader which does not have a brand image. Buying from a shop where payment is made personally and the goods, which are personally seen and selected, are in hand, will remain the most secure method for the large majority of shoppers. While cash remains the preferred option, online shopping offers no alternative to personal visits. This is an important consideration in economies where cash payments for work done are given, or where 'black economies' are operated.

The majority of shoppers expect to be able to compare prices and styles before making a decision to part with their money. Comparison shopping on the Net is, at best, inconvenient due to the limited competition offered on most shopping channels. Bargain shopping on the Internet is unlikely at the present time with specialised discount services not undercutting discount newspaper advertisements. Cheaper prices on the Internet are often negated by delivery charges and fees.

Online shopping needs basic computer and modem investments which may be considered an unacceptable up front cost to the average shopper.

Retailers' sales results to date with their participation online has been disappointingly low. They will continue to be featured but are likely to view the medium as a cheap alternative means of providing promotions and advertising informationals giving a listing of products and other corporate and store location data.

Many shoppers regard shopping as a chore. Shopping centres have been changing their attitudes to offer more convenience and entertainment to make a visit more pleasurable. Retailers have been introducing better design and merchandising to attract custom, which itself reinforces the greater attention and priority they are giving to traditional sales methods over online methods at this time. In the future, technology will be more attuned to shoppers' needs so that they will be better advised about travel conditions, parking availability, product location and stocks. Shopping centres and individual stores are likely to be provided with better infrastructures which will enable them to offer more convenient service to customers.

Data collection on customers is seen by retailers as an essential element in future marketing. Potential customer data bases are being compiled through the use of loyalty card systems, Internet browsing and store EPOS systems, to which customers are contributing on a widespread scale. The trend of indiscriminate membership of loyalty schemes is increasing the danger of such schemes becoming self-defeating and many consumers are aware of the real reason for them with only short-term sales being helped and little encouragement for the longer-term loyalty once discounts disappear. There is a general feeling that loyalty cannot be bought, but has to be earned through service and value.

Shopping centre owners are using the Internet to promote their centres with details of retailers and the products available, together with other corporate and marketing information. The aim is to encourage shoppers to visit the centre rather than for them to purchase online. Neighbourhood and convenience centres are continuing to provide important shopping facilities and new initiatives are continuing for the expansion of retail growth at petrol stations and other places with big passing trade for convenience goods.

Despite the threat from the Internet, retailers are continuing to provide improved sales and profits results, and many are announcing large expansion plans for the future. The increases are in terms of both new stores and added floor areas to existing stores. This is while the stores are proceeding with tentative participation with online shopping.

At the start of this book, I said that I remain interested by the way matters evolve and revolve. The simple example of the way collections of small shops located together in the early arcades became the forerunners of the department stores, the growth of small grocery shops into larger supermarkets which were located in town centres, then superstores out of town, now expanding their supermarket presence as 'metro stores' in town centres, shows how things change – but not out of recognition. The original traders on medieval crossroads became stalls, then what we came to recognise as shops. As shops became more commonplace the introduction of mail order by, among others, Sears Roebuck, provided goods to consumers who were unable to buy them locally, or were in remote locations prior to the improvements in travel and communications. Mail order and catalogue shopping became an alternative and ancillary shopping means, but did not destroy traditional shopping used by those consumers who were reasonably able to use personal shopping visits. This has continued for more than 100 years, and as communications have improved dramatically and personal travel has become so easy, there has been no evidence to suggest that traditional shopping will cease, or even be greatly impaired. The introduction of the telephone may have made personal conversation possible with someone far away, but has not made personal social meeting and the need to mix with other people less desirable to the human psychological want.

The inevitable conclusion is that established norms become part of the human scene, and may be changed without losing their essential basic purpose. They may be improved and become more convenient, but the service they offer keeps pace with modern life's expectations; the shopper has become accustomed to the way in which everyday shopping is conducted and has an innate dislike, or even mistrust, of change. In this context, to be compared to other new innovations such as mail order in the past, it is difficult to believe that the basic ingredient of shopping – the shop and its retailer occupier – will be so affected that it will be replaced. We are asked to accept that new technology, in the form of the Internet or some other sub-set of the World Wide Web, will so drastically alter our habits of centuries that shops and shopping centres will no longer be the place consumers will visit. Convenience is claimed to be so important to some shoppers that everyone will undertake a completely new way of fulfilling their shopping needs.

Throughout history, there have been opinions expressed, often by extremely intelligent and powerful figures, which have scared populations into thinking that the existing situation will change dramatically. One of the most recent examples was generated by the Arab oil embargo in the early 1970s. As a result of predictions that the world's energy supply was finite, petrol rationing was introduced in many countries. America, the home of the gas-guzzler car, had lines of motorists at petrol stations with alternate day rationing. People were shot and killed as fights erupted over queue-jumping allegations. Energy management became one of the most important new technologies, the demise of the internal combustion car was predicted, and everyone thought that unless stringent government measures were introduced we would run out of fossil fuel by the turn of the century. The example may be far from the subject of shopping, but it shows how reactions to new situations spark a typical human psychological response of doom for what has become an accepted lifestyle. The reality is that we have adapted and advanced in a way which has protected the features we wish to continue. We still have fuel and cars, our homes are heated and lighted.

So we can see that current claims about the Internet replacing usual shopping methods are far from likely reality. A large proportion of the shopping community is unable to afford the technology required. A large number are not sufficiently computer literate to be able to use the present technology, are afraid of it, or simply do not want to use it. Problems of comparative choice, value and price, delivery, security and not least, the human factor of the sensibilities when making the purchase decision, remain matters which raise major questions about future service and customer satisfaction.

As we look at the present situation, technology advances at an amazing rate. It is possible that many of the drawbacks now perceived may be overcome through new methods, greater capacity or response, or more developed logistics. But shopping centres, shops and retailers will undoubtedly realign their services, designs, merchandise and competitive offers at the same time. So shopping will continue to evolve and revolve to meet the customers' demand, as it has done since the earliest days. Who will be brave enough to say what the form of shopping will take in the year 2020? In 1997, the signs are that the shopping centre industry will proceed as a strong and vibrant developer of a recognisable form of traditional shopping. The most important clue today is that the major retailers appear to be placing their strength behind expansion of new branches and extra floor areas at the same time as they are tentatively participating in informational pages on the Internet. Without the merchants, online shopping cannot succeed, so they are effectively the controllers of the future of online shopping, which presently appears to viewed by them to be a promotional medium to support their shops and sales rather than to supplant them. I think the most likely scenario is that online shopping will take a part of sales from mail order and catalogue shopping and a minor part from traditional shopping. The percentage of online shopping predicted by the promoters of the medium, if proved correct with time, still leaves a huge volume of traditional sales so that major shopping centres, town centres and convenience shops will continue to succeed. However, many shops in secondary locations, offering poorer choice and service, are likely to fail, as the main shopping centres consolidate their attraction to shoppers. That attraction will almost certainly include greater leisure and entertainment to keep and amuse visitors wanting a personal experience of purchase, browsing, discovery, eating and entertainment. The problem of personal travel by car will have to be addressed by local and central governments and will be an urgent requirement, which will not be able to be ignored whatever the cost to society. In the next twenty years or so, advances generally may make these predictions seem naive, but we cannot do more than use the present facts and guess at trends. That, I believe, is the definition of a true professional in shopping centre development. I remain confident that there is a future and that I, for one, will not have the sole choice of sitting at home at my personal computer, rather than speaking and meeting other human beings and promoting, managing and building shopping centres.

Leaving this opinion with my own views alone seems to invite the comment of the reader 'he would say that, wouldn't he?' I therefore end with an extract of the speech given by no less than Robert J. Herbold, executive vice-president and Chief Operating Oficer of Microsoft. Speaking to the Annual Convention of the International Council of Shopping Centres' Spring Convention in Las Vegas in May 1997, he told the 4000 plus audience at lunch, that delegates have nothing to fear from the Internet. He maintains that the experience of shopping can never be replicated by the computer. He added

The thing that you folks have going for you is the psychological needs of shoppers. People really do like a stimulating break in the daily routine . . . and that's not going to change.

Bibliography and Acknowledgements

As I have said in the Preface of this book, I have used material from many sources, for some of which it is difficult to attribute to other authors directly. However material has been gleaned from the following and grateful acknowledgement is made by the author and publishers. If any copyright-holders have been inadvertently omitted, the publisher will be pleased to make the necessary arrangement at the earliest opportunity.

- Alfred Chandler, *The Invisible Hands*.
- Alison Clements, 'Green Superstores in Mail Order Foray', *Retail Week*, 13 December 1996.
- Alistair Anderson, *Predictors in Computer Anxiety*, Deakin University School of Management Systems.
- Amanda Seidl, 'End of the Road', *Estates Gazette*, Issue 9635, 31 August 1996.
- BCSC Staff, *Town Centre Futures: The Long Term Impact of New Developments*, The British Council of Shopping Centres, Report, November 1996.
- Betty Luman, 'Peapod Grows with Female Clients', *Houston Chronicle*, 1996.
- Bill Gorman, *New Product News*, New Product Introductions.
- Bill O'Brien, 'Technically Inclined: A Tale of Two Strategies: TV or PC?', *Computer Life*, 15 July 1996.
- Boston Associates, 1913.
- British Broadcasting Corporation, *BBC Lectures 1959*, C. P. Snow.
- British Retail Consortium and Jones Lang Wooton, *Retailer Property Intentions July 1996*, Checkout Newsletter, The British Council of Shopping Centres.
- Capital Shopping Centres, *Traffic Impact Report on MetroCentre*.
- Dale Grady, Rochester Institute of Technology, Software Specialist and Assistant Professor.
- Dataquest, 'December 1996 Report', *The Daily Telegraph*, Connect, News, 24 December 1996.
- David Donnelly, Houston University, Assistant Professor, Social Impact of Technology.
- David Nye, *Electrifying America*.

- Douglas Rushkoff, *Cyberia*; *Media Virus*; *Playing the Future*.
- Edmund Mander, *Grocers Test Self-Serve Scanning Device*, ICSC, *Shopping Centers Today*, September 1996.
- Eugene Fram, Rochester Institute of Technology, J. Warren McClure, Research Professor of Marketing.
- G. Howard, C. Murphy and G. Thomas, 'Predictors of Computer Anxiety', *Educational Research Quarterly*, 1987.
- Glynn Davis, 'C-Stores Feel Pinch from Food Giants', *Retail Week*, 18 October 1997.
- Glynn Davis, 'M & S Set to Build on Home Delivery', *Retail Week*, 18 October 1996.
- Harris International Marketing, *Report*, June 1996.
- Healey & Baker, *Quarterly Market Report July 1996*, Checkout Newsletter, The British Council of Shopping Centres.
- Healey & Baker, *Sunday Trading – The Implications*, Checkout Newsletter, The British Council of Shopping Centres.
- Howard Segal, *Technological Utopianism in American Culture*; *Future Imperfect: The Mixed Blessings of Technology in America*, University of Maine, Professor of History.
- Ian Cundell and David Thame, 'Labour Stands Firm on PPG6', *Property Week*, 6 June 1997.
- ICEP Staff, 'Green Lanes and Coinless Consumers/The "Multibank Electronic Purse"', *Investmentos*, Comercio e Turismo de Portugal, Special Advertising Section.
- Intelliquest, *November & December 1996 Survey*.
- James Young, *The Information Age and the Potential Effects on the Commercial Real Estate Market, 1995*.
- Janice McGinn, 'Net Commerce Fails to Make any Impact', *Computing*, 14 November 1996.
- Jim McCartney, 'Mall of America May Grow Even Bigger', *Shopping Centers Today*, December 1996.
- Jo Bacon, 'Property Investors Back Retail ...', *UK Retail Market Bulletin*, Richard Ellis Research Consultancy, Autumn 1996.
- John Lewis, 'Labour Policy Flip on Retail Planning', *Property Week*, 8 November 1996.
- John Lewis, 'Lib Dems take Tory Side on Town Plans', *Property Week*, 27 September 1997.
- John Lewis, 'Meacher Retreats from Out-of-Town Relaxation', *Property Week*, News – Labour Party Conference, 4 October 1996.
- John Naisbitt, *Megatrends*.
- John Stewart Mill, English Philosopher and Economist (1806–73).
- John Toon, *GVU's 7th WWW User Survey April 1997*, Georgia Institute of Technology, Graphic, Visualization, and Usability Centre (GVU).

- John Toon, *Politicking Goes Electronic: Web Offers Fertile Ground for Candidates' Messages, Research Suggests*, Georgia Institute of Technology, July 1996.
- Jon Jerde, Architect, Horton Plaza, San Diego, California, USA.
- Jonathan Tucker, 'How We will be Shopping in 2005', FX, ETP Ltd, *Business Retail Trends*, August 1996.
- Kate Lowe, 'Traffic Probe Runs Down PPG Dogma', *Property Week*, 4 October 1996.
- Kate Oppenheim (ed.), 'Working for a Common Goal', *Retail Week*, 6 June 1997.
- Kevin Kenyon, 'Microsoft Exec: Net No Threat to Malls', ISCS, *Shopping Centers Today*, July 1997.
- Kim Cleland, 'Peapod: Shoppers Express Vie for On-Line Grocery Business', *Advertising Age*, 14 June 1997.
- KPMG, *The Internet: Its Potential and Use by European Retailers – June 1996*, Checkout Newsletter, The British Council of Shopping Centres.
- Leo Marx, *The Critical and Historical Perspective and Other Sources*, MIT.
- Lisa O'Carroll, 'Blockbuster Summer at the Cinema', © *Evening Standard*, Associated Newspapers Ltd, 13 December 1996.
- Los Angeles Times Staff, 'Japanese Executives being Told to Get in Line Online Technology', *Los Angeles Times*, 23 January 1996.
- Malcolm Cohen, *Labor Shortages: As America Approaches the 21st Century*, Ann Arbor: The University of Michigan Press, 1995.
- Mastercard International, *Why Consumers are Deciding to Shop from Home*, Yankelovich Partners, Consumer Survey.
- McKinsey & Co, *Estimate of Warehouse/Discount Store Penetration*.
- Michael Kirst, *The Way Computers are Used in the Classroom*, Stanford University, School of Education, Professor of Education.
- Michael W. Apple, University of Wisconsin-Madison, John Bascom Distinguished Professor of Education.
- MIT, *Colloquium on Advanced Information Technology, Low Income Communities, and the City Department of Urban Studies and Planning*.
- MIT, *What Invention People Couldn't Live Without*.
- Mitchell Kapor, *The Problems of Closing the Gaps between the 'Haves' and the 'Have Nots'*. Founder of Lotus Development Corp., and co-Founder of Electronic Frontier Foundation.
- MORI, *Use/Knowledge of Net Survey October 1996*.
- NewsPage, *Bringing Neighborhood Necessities to Downtown*, Individual Inc., Business Wire, *US Retail Distribution Review*.
- NewsPage, *Peapod Online Grocery Shopping and Delivery Service Launches in Columbus with Kroger*, Individual Inc., Business Wire, Internet Commerce.
- Nicholas Negroponte, *Being Digital*.

- Nils Pratley, 'Burton to Challenge the Mail-Order Giants', *The Daily Telegraph*.
- Nils Pratley, *The Daily Telegraph*, Questor column, 22 October 1996.
- NOP, *1996 Internet User Study*, NOP Business, NOP Research Group Limited.
- *Pathfinder Internet Study 1995*, The Arbitron Company, Arbitron New-Media.
- Peter Cochrane, BT Labs, 'Beggars at the Information Feast', *The Daily Telegraph*, 13 August 1996.
- Peter Cochrane, BT Labs, 'Instant Access', *Estates Times Review*, 8 March 1996.
- Peter Leyden, Staff Writer, 'Techno-Utopia We Seek May be Mere Illusion', *Star Tribune*, Reality Check, 6 November 1995.
- Peter Leyden, Staff Writer, 'To See Future of Shopping, Turn on the TV', *Star Tribune*, Everyday Living, 6 November 1995.
- PPG6 Revised July 1996 (contributed by Healey & Baker), Checkout Newsletter, The British Council of Shopping Centres.
- Professor Philip L. Bereano, University of Washington, Professor of Technical Communication.
- 'Report of Expenditure of Top 200 Brands', *Advertising Age*.
- Ric Manning, 'Push your Grocery Cart on the Web', *The Courier Journal*, Gizmo Page, 9 July 1996.
- Richard Riley, *Comment*, Former American Education Secretary.
- RIPE European Host Count, *Statistics for European Region*, RIPE, Amsterdam.
- Robert J. Herbold, Excerpt from Speech at Annual Convention of ICSC, Microsoft Corp., Executive Vice-President and Chief Operating Officer.
- Rose Aguilar, *Online Shopping: Future or Flop?* Cnet: The Computer Network, Cnet News, 22 February 1996.
- Sawgrass Mills, Northern Florida, USA.
- Sian Harrington, 'Better Web than Dead', *Retail Week*, Shopping Centre Guide 1996.
- Southdale Plaza, Edina, Minnesota, Dayton Hudson Corporation.
- SRI International Staff, *Exploring the Worldwide Web Population's Other Half*, SRI International, Internet Study.
- Staff Writer, *Burton Chief Would Like Long-Term Co-operation with Developers*, Shopping Centre, BCSC in Edinburgh, December 1996.
- Staff Writer, 'Carol Wright Promotions Study October 1995', *ICSC Research Quarterly*, Fall 1996 (originally in 'The Big Squeeze', *Chain Store Age*, 29 May 1996).
- Staff Writer, 'Continuing Need for Mail Order Catalogues', *Retail Week*, Internet, 18 October 1996.
- Staff Writer, Discovery Communications Inc., Discovery Channel Online, CyberRumble Panel – Future.

- Staff Writer, *Financial Times*, 3 and 11 July 1996; 12 and 20 August 1996, Checkout Newsletter, The British Council of Shopping Centres.
- Staff Writer, *Grocer Today*, 'Biggest Complaint from the Average Shopper is Waiting in Line at the Checkout', Canada Wide Magazines & Communications Ltd.
- Staff Writer, 'Home Shopping "No Threat"', *Retail Week*, 4 October 1996.
- Staff Writer, 'How Do You Successfully Market to Children?', *Retail Week*, 14 June 1996.
- Staff Writer, 'In Brief – Best Month for Videos Since 1989', *Retail Week*, 25 October 1996.
- Staff Writer, *Independent*, 17 May 1996; 16 August 1996, Checkout Newsletter, The British Council of Shopping Centres.
- Staff Writer, 'Misplaced Loyalty', *Retail Week*, 29 March 1996.
- Staff Writer, 'Nonstore Retailing: Implications of the Internet', *ICSC Research Quarterly*, Fall 1996.
- Staff Writer, 'On the Edge', *Retail Week*, 29 March 1996.
- Staff Writer, 'Retail Futures: A Review of Innovation and Creativity in the Retail Environment 4.4', e-Media LLC.
- Staff Writer, 'Retail Giants Struggle as Web Shoppers Leave Surfers Cold', VNU Publications, *Computing*, 14 November 1996.
- Staff Writer, 'Special Report on Value Retailing', *Shopping Centers Today*.
- Staff Writer, 'The Shopping Center Tenant Report – "The Electronic Landlord"', *SCT Retailing Today*, August 1996.
- Sunil Gupta, *Obstacles to Overcome (Hermes Survey 4)*, University of Michigan, Director – Hermes Project, School of Business Administration.
- Susan Stellin, *Closing the Gap: The Net goes CoEd*, Cnet: The Computer Network, Features: Now on the Net, 23 August 1996.
- The Henley Centre, *The Loyalty Paradox*; *Dataculture*.
- Thomas Horan, *The Urban Planning Implications of Advanced Information Technology*, The Claremont Graduate School, Director – Research Institute, California, USA.
- Tim Miller, *How Many People on the Net? 1st Quarter [1996] Estimates*, I/PRO Cyber Atlas, Find/SVP Emerging Technology Research Group.
- Tony Parker, Assistant Director of Architecture and Engineering, various comments, Maidstone District Council.
- Verdict Research, *Report*, October 1996.
- Victor Gruen, Architect, Southdale Plaza, Edina, Massachusetts.